Selected Chaff

MORE
OR LESS
PERSONAL
CHAFF

AL McINTOSH

Selected Chaff

★ ★ ★

THE WARTIME COLUMNS OF
Al McIntosh

1941 – 1945

ZENITH PRESS

First published in 2007 by Zenith Press, an imprint of
MBI Publishing Company, Galtier Plaza, Suite 200,
380 Jackson Street, St. Paul, MN 55101 USA

Zenith Press titles are also available at discounts in bulk quantity for
industrial or sales-promotional use. For details write to Special Sales
Manager at MBI Publishing Company, Galtier Plaza, Suite 200,
380 Jackson Street, St. Paul, MN 55101 USA.

To find out more about our books, join us online at
www.zenithpress.com.

Editor: Steve Gansen
Designer: Tom Heffron

Library of Congress Cataloging-in-Publication Data

McIntosh, Al.
    Selected chaff : the wartime columns of Al Mcintosh, 1941-1945 /
by Al McIntosh.
        p. cm.
    ISBN-13: 978-0-7603-3355-6
    ISBN-13: 978-0-7603-3303-7 (softbound)
1. World War, 1939-1945--Minnesota--Rock County--Anecdotes.
2. World War, 1939-1945--Social aspects--Minnesota--Rock
County--Anecdotes. 3. Rock County (Minn.)--History--20th
century--Anecdotes. 4. Rock County (Minn.)--History, Military--
20th century--Anecdotes. 5. Rock County (Minn.)--Social
conditions--20th century--Anecdotes. 6. Rock County (Minn.)--
Biography--Anecdotes. I. Title.
D769.85.M61R636 2007
940.53'77625--dc22
                                                    2007019730

The Rock County Star-Herald

VICTORY
IN
EUROPE
••• EDITION ▬

Dedicated to the Men and Women of Rock County who made
Victory in Europe a Reality Today

Contents

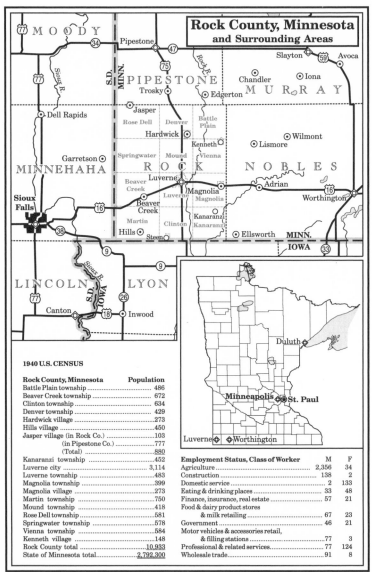

Rock County, Minnesota
and Surrounding Areas

MOODY · Pipestone · Slayton · Avoca

PIPESTONE · Chandler · Iona · MURRAY

Trosky · Edgerton

Jasper

Dell Rapids · Rose Dell · Denver · Battle Plain · Wilmont

Hardwick · Lismore

Kenneth

Garretson · Springwater · Mound · Vienna · NOBLES

MINNEHAHA · ROCK

Beaver Creek · Luverne · Adrian

Sioux Falls · Luverne · Magnolia · Worthington

Beaver Creek · Magnolia

Martin · Clinton · Kanaranzi

Hills · Steen · Ellsworth · MINN.

IOWA

LINCOLN · LYON

Canton · Inwood

Sioux R.

Duluth

Minneapolis · St. Paul

Luverne · Worthington

1940 U.S. CENSUS

Rock County, Minnesota	Population
Battle Plain township	486
Beaver Creek township	672
Clinton township	634
Denver township	429
Hardwick village	273
Hills village	450
Jasper village (in Rock Co.)	103
(in Pipestone Co.)	777
(Total)	880
Kanaranzi township	452
Luverne city	3,114
Luverne township	483
Magnolia township	399
Magnolia village	273
Martin township	750
Mound township	418
Rose Dell township	581
Springwater township	578
Vienna township	584
Kenneth village	148
Rock County total	10,933
State of Minnesota total	2,792,300

Employment Status, Class of Worker	M	F
Agriculture	2,356	34
Construction	138	2
Domestic service	2	133
Eating & drinking places	33	48
Finance, insurance, real estate	57	21
Food & dairy product stores & milk retailing	67	23
Government	46	21
Motor vehicles & accessories retail, & filling stations	77	3
Professional & related services	77	124
Wholesale trade	91	8

Cartography by Philip Schwartzberg, Meridian Mapping, Minneapolis

Foreword

When I first heard this book was going to be published, I was very excited. *Selected Chaff* is an intimate look at the history of Rock County during World War II. Many of these stories are the kind we want to pass on from generation to generation. Our local history is so important to all of us. We cannot forget those little stories about our community.

My knowledge of Al McIntosh came through my father, Charles W. Soutar, who was a friend of Al's. They were both "Scotsmen," which I'm sure enhanced their friendship.

Al came to Luverne from Lincoln, Nebraska, as editor of the *Rock County Star*. He was very active in many organizations. Being the son of a Presbyterian minister, he continued to serve the Presbyterian Church in Luverne in many ways, and was active in the Rotary, which met every Monday noon at the Manitou Hotel.

Al bought the *Rock County Herald* and combined the two papers to become the *Rock County Star-Herald*. Soon after this he began writing the column, "More or Less Personal Chaff." This weekly column gave his impressions of how our community was dealing with local and national issues of the time. He would walk down Main Street and visit with anyone he met. You needed to watch what you said, because it might appear in his next column. He often said "to be a good journalist, you had to forego having friends."

People considered him honest, even though they might not agree with his views. Al would hold a story until he felt it was right to publish it. He called himself an "independent," but people knew he was a "conservative Republican." Many people will remember the editorial he wrote on May 13, 1965; "A Tired American" sparked some controversy and won him national recognition.

Since my parents were friends, they received a Christmas card from the McIntosh family every year. The cards were filled with pictures of his family. They were called "Jean Mae's Merry Christmas Scrap Book." We are pleased to have them on display at the Rock County Museum. In addition to these cards, the Rock County Historical Society is honored to have in our museum a collection of his columns, his typewriter, and the camera he used as editor and publisher of the *Rock County Star-Herald*.

I am looking forward to reading this book and recalling many memories.

Betty G. Mann

—Betty Mann, president,
Rock County Historical Society
June 2007

Preface

Weekly newspaper columnists are happy to successfully plow through their writer's blocks by deadline time with all their names spelled correctly and a good portion of the truth intact. In his column, "More or Less Personal Chaff," Al McIntosh managed to do that, and much more. Documentary filmmaker Ken Burns has compared his storytelling ability to that of Mark Twain. McIntosh's wit, wisdom, and compassion seem ideally suited to boost the wartime morale of a community that experienced its fair share of suffering and sacrifice during World War II.

At times, the *Rock County Star-Herald*'s front page brimmed with headlines and stories of area boys missing or killed overseas, their smiling photos providing evidence of better times before their lives were cut short by war. Al McIntosh shines during these moments of deepest despair, when it seemed there would be no end to the loss of young lives. You can sense it in his voice, stubbornly determined and unabashedly patriotic; that of a man possessed. A gadfly in the best sense of the term, he challenged, cajoled, and spurred the locals to do their part, to buy war bonds, to salvage, save, and ration, to give voluntarily, and to stay personally engaged in the war effort. Like any great community leader, he raised their spirit by his own tireless example.

McIntosh was an eyewitness to the ebbs and flows of one county during the most terrible yet necessary war our world has yet seen. The process of selecting the best of these columns came with a heavy burden of honoring the memory of both a man and a community. A conscientious effort was made to include both the best and most representative column excerpts that reveal his growth as a writer and as a journalist.

Most of the selection was guided by a simple question: does the column move me? I found the answer to be more frequently in the affirmative as the war dragged on, when Al McIntosh had only his Chaff to move an entire county into action. If you're not careful, you, too, will get lost in these columns and be ready to sign up for the next scrap iron drive. *Selected Chaff* recalls a nation and a community that, when called upon to do so, joined together at home and abroad to fight the "necessary war." Even today, more than six decades later, the urgency in Al McIntosh's unique voice comes through loud and clear.

A NOTE ON SPELLING STYLE: Without the man himself here to guide our editorial hand, we had to use our imagination: "What would Al do?" Judging from the distinct style incorporated by his newspaper, it seems clear that he was a student of the simplified spellings first recommended in 1876 by the Spelling Reform Association. These word lists were adopted by the National Education Association in 1898 and, on the orders of Teddy Roosevelt, by the U.S. Government Printing Office in 1906. Despite these influential supporters, most of these spellings did not catch on in general usage and eventually fell by the wayside.

But I like to think Al McIntosh's spellings of words such as "altho," "cigaret," "employes," "thru," and others were simply a part of his total dedication to the war effort on the home front, perhaps meant to conserve ink for more important uses such as dispatches between Allied front line units. If for no other reason, we will follow his lead for the sake of historical accuracy in preserving a national treasure—the column excerpts contained herein.

—Steve Gansen, editor
June 2007

Acknowledgments

The editor and publisher would like to thank the following individuals who helped make the near-impossible happen—tracking down Al McIntosh's wartime columns and taking them from microfilm to layout in under a month:

Rock County Star Herald: Everyone, especially
Rick Peterson, Lori Ehde, and Sara Quam
Rock County Historical Society: Betty Mann
Rock County Community Library: Glenda Bremer,
Barb Vehey, and Jessica Van Batavia
**Minnesota History Center/Ronald M. Hubbs
Microfilm Reading Room:** Lisa Whitehill and
Jane Wong

And especially Tolly Noyes for her remarkably accurate key entry in record time.

ROCK COUNTY STAR

LUVERNE, MINNESOTA THURSDAY, DECEMBER 11, 1941

...tock Indemnity Fund To Be Crea...

...Take Steps ...d Incorporation

...Night* ...Fav-

...rer to be- ...illage this ...g Monday ...nts of the ...orporation. ...was named ...e as chair- ...d Rev. Wil- ...to serve as

...taken at the ...general atti- ...osed change of ...gible voters, 27 ...avor of incor- ...ed against and ...ned blank. The ...o official bear- ...change.

...mittee

...isting of William ...an; John Elbers ...was elected who ...and Rev. De Jong ...ll make prepara- ...a petition to pre- ...nty board. When ...s and presented, the ...ll grant the petition ...election board. Vil- ...vote on the incor- ...pecial election.

...s founding in 1888 ...was known as Vir- ...of Clinton township. ...idents of the village ...d for home rule in the ...of the town, modern ...ng have brought about ...changes which would ...convenient for resi- ...were incorporated. One ...this, according to re- ...matter of electricity. ...s served by a large public ...n who not only supplies ...the homes but also for ...lights. Under the present ...ate for operating the street ...now assessed against indi- ...ers.

...Has Advantages

...village were incorporated, ...ity company could bill the ...for the amount and elimin- ...ly collections. The company ...ld, has agreed to reduce in- ...al rates if a new arrange- ...to pay for village used cur- ...ould be made.

...er matters that proponents of ...ncorporation feel could be bet- ...andled by a village form of gov- ...ent than under the present ...ship system is that of police and ...protection. They also could re- ...the licensing of sale of to- ...co and beverages and utilize the ...ds derived therefrom for the ...nefit of the village and not spread ...em over the township as a whole.

...Miss Rose Dvoracek returned Sun- ...ay and the following day resumed ...er duties as an instructor in the ...public school here, after having ...pent the past week at her home ...in New Prague recovering from a ...short illness.

TAX RECEIPTS APPORTIONED

Report of November Settlement Made by County Treasurer

Personal property tax collections for the period from June 1 until Nov. 1 totaled $146,022.86, County Treasurer Paul Herreid reported in his annual fall settlement, completed last week.

At the same time, Mr. Herreid reported that money and credits tax collections for the period totaled $184.63; mortgage registry taxes amounted to $768.30 and grain tax collections were $41.75.

The Apportionment

The personal property tax collection has been apportioned as follows, according to Herreid:

State debt—$29,293.20; teacher's insurance and retirement—$1,136.00; county revenue—$15,869.93; county road and bridge—$15,947.13; county poor (transferred to county revenue)—$38.85; sanatorium—$999.97; county bonds and interest—$3,76; welfare—$6,963.86; old age assistance (transferred to welfare)—$2.94; county T. B. test (transferred to revenue)—$.35; county revenue, one-half penalty—$224.07; general townships, city and villages—$22,569.23; general school districts—$50,971.08; school—$211.03; current school, one-half penalty—$224.07; judicial ditch repair—$19.65; state loans, cities and villages—$8.83; state loans, school districts—$3,-502.74.

Townships Share

The townships received the following amounts: Battle Plain—$1,-426.30; Beaver Creek—$1,471.47; Clinton—$1,363.42; Denver—$1,301.-66; Kanaranzi—$1,293.14; Luverne—$1,475.16; Magnolia—$1,227.09; Martin—$1,480.18; Mound—$1,505.70; Rose Dell—$1,164.66; Springwater—$991.48; Vienna—$746.79.

Village apportionments were as follows: Beaver Creek—$849.84; Hardwick—$278.48; Hills—$1,056.58; Jasper—$215.35; Kenneth—$37.60; Magnolia—$188.75.

The apportionment to the city of Luverne totaled $4,505.58, which will be distributed to the following funds: Band—$175.36; fire department—$140.65; library — $735.68; sinking fund—$2,605.35; public improvement—$8.78; bonds and interest—$32.04; paving—$799.94; penalty—$17.78.

Dan Main Appointed Judge Here

D. M. Main, of this city, became municipal judge here Tuesday, following the receipt of official notice of his appointment from Governor Stassen. City Recorder Fitzer administered the oath of office to the new official Tuesday morning, and Mr. Main immediately went to work in the judge's office on the second floor of the city hall.

Main will serve until the April election, at which time the judge will be elected for a four-year term.

The new judge has been a resident of Luverne since 1902 with the exception of three years that he lived in Detroit Lakes, Minn.

He was employed by the E. A Brown company here until 1905 and then worked in the First National Bank for 20 years. Since retiring from the bank, he served as bank receiver and has been engaged in the real estate and insurance business.

Main is married and has three sons, Norman, of this city; John, DuPont, Wash., and Robert, stationed with the U. S. Army at Camp Callen, Calif.

SEE INCREASE FARM PRODUCE

Survey Shows Rock County Farmers Expect To Raise 27 Per Cent More Hogs

A survey completed by the Rock county AAA township committeemen indicates that Rock county farmers will market 27 percent more hogs in 1942 than in 1941, Chairman R. C. Juhl reported this week. This would step up the number of hogs produced in Rock county to 108,795 hogs for the coming year. Likewise there are indications that farmers will also increase milk and egg production.

Pork production for the state will be sharply higher as reported by Charles W. Stickney, chairman of the Minnesota AAA and chief of the U. S. D. A. defense board. Summaries for the state indicate farmers will market 25 percent more hogs in 1942 compared to 1941.

Anticipate Egg Increase

The anticipated increase in egg production indicated that Rock county farmers are planning on producing 294,564 dozens more eggs for 1942 or an increase of 18.5 percent over 1941. The survey for the entire state indicated an increase of eggs of around 28 percent. This would mean a total production for the state of 206,934,000 dozens for 1942 as compared to 161,667,000 dozens, the estimated production for 1941.

Milk production lagged behind the sharp increases for eggs and pork as reported in both the county and state. Rock county farmers are planning to increase milk production 6.5 percent over 1941. The increase for the state as shown by the summaries indicated an 11 percent increase for 1942.

New High in Production

County summaries received in the state AAA office, Mr. Stickney stated, showed that indicated production of eggs, milk, pork and vegetables will be the greatest in many years with some products reaching new production peaks. The sharp increase in production of foods needed in national defense will mean thousands of dollars in additional income to Minnesota farmers.

With more than 50,000,000 bushels of grain stored in the every normal granary on farms and in public warehouses, plus thousands of tons of tame and wild hay, farmers in this state are in a position to turn this great supply of feed crops into foods needed in an "all-out" defense program without great expense to themselves, said Mr. Stickney.

Small Child Suffocates

Tragedy struck in the Ralph Top home southeast of Beaver Creek early Wednesday, when their eight-week's old baby, Peter, was found dead in his crib. Coroner C. O. Wright said that death was apparently the result of suffocation.

According to Dr. Wright, Mrs. Top had fed the baby at 3 a. m. When she arose at 6:15 a. m. the child was dead.

THIEF TAKES CAR, WRECKS IT, STILL NO CLUE IS FOUND

Authorities Seek Person Who Escaped From Wrecked Car Near Garretson

County Sheriff Roberts and Minnehaha county peace authorities were puzzled last night as to the whereabouts of an auto thief who stole a car from the Oscar Erick... son farm in Springwater township... drove it about a mile, wrecked i... and left no clue as to his identit...

Owner of the car was Norm... McKinven, Martin, N. D., who h... been visiting at the Erickson fa... in Springwater township, a... and a half east of the South ... kota state line. McKinven, toge... with the Erickson family had ... home yesterday forenoon in the ... ickson car, leaving McKinven's ... at the place unattended.

The car was taken betwee... time of their departure and 12 ... m. when the wrecked machin... seen by Alvin Crosten, farm... that neighborhood, Sheriff R... said. The driver turned wes... the Erickson farm yard, ... half mile to the state line, a... turned south. About a h... from the corner, he evide... control of the car as it ... into the ditch, rolled over ... ally come to a standstill in ... fa field.

Although the machine ... wrecked, none of the win... broken, and there were ... of blood which would in... the driver had been inju... was made with doctor... Springs, Garretson and ... but none had treated ... might have been thus ... No other clues were... erts said.

TO L... AL... RO...

Fund... Ev... soon... ing ... co... we...

WILL TEACH METAL WORK CLASS HERE

Arrangements Made For Out-of-School Youth Defense Training

A course in general metal work for out-of-school youth, boys ages 17 to 25, is slated to begin in the local high school work shop next Monday, Supt. M. C. Munson stated this week.

Plans to include older men in the class fell through when the Public Employment Service refused to approve such a class. The service did, however, approve a class in airplane sheet metal work, but because the school did not have proper facilities for that particular branch of training, that alternative was abandoned.

According to Mr. Munson, the training course can accomodate up to 30 boys of eligible age. In the event that 30 enroll, there will likely be two classes daily, a three hour day-time class and an evening class of similar duration. A. L. Canfield will be in charge of instruction.

"The course offers an opportunity for a youth to learn the fundamentals of sheet metal work, welding and forging," Mr. Munson said. "This, we feel, should serve as an incentive to many to take advantage of the course as industry has many openings for men trained in this line of work, especially if they are young men. Anyone in the community who is interested in enrolling should see Louis Kohl, George Edmonds or myself sometime before Monday."

RURAL TEACHERS' AVERAGE SALARY SLIGHTLY HIGHER

There's a little more money in being a country school teacher in Rock county this year than there has been for several years past, Supt. Barrett disclosed this week.

In his annual report, relating to teachers in the ungraded elementary districts, it was revealed that the average monthly salary of the instructors was $85.55 as compared to $81.26 a year ago, and $77.29 in 1939. Highest salary paid is $95. Four of 62 receive this amount. Smallest salary paid is $75. Three in Rock county are employed at that salary.

The teacher having the record for the greatest amount of experience has taught school 26 years, 14 of which were in the same school. Two have 19 years experience each.

Movies of Kodiak On Dec. 16th

Final plans were announced by the Kodiak Kontributions Committee for the showing of colored movies of Kodiak Island at the Pix theater here next Tuesday, December 16. First show will start at 2 p. m. and will be followed by second and third showings of the films if such showings are necessary to accomodate the crowd.

The movies will be preceded by an explanation of the pictures, given by Ryal Miller, Sioux City, who took the pictures this summer while vacationing in Alaska. Following the presentation of the movie, Capt. George Fried, who recently returned from Kodiak, will be present to answer any questions the public may have about the island, and the men there. Each show will require approximately one hour and 15 minutes.

The committee declared this week that the movies would be open to the public and will be shown free of charge. Especially invited, however, are parents and relatives of men stationed with the army at Kodiak.

MANY ATTEND ... CREEK F...

Annual meeting ... Creek Farm Burea... at the Beaver C... auditorium Monda... a large crowd in... Mrs. S. Johans... cussed "Food For... Harry Leslie gave... is Ahead for th... James Dunn, pre... Youth Group d... organization.

John Gibson... director and ... director, Jame... to succeed Ha... retary-treasur...

Lunch was ... meeting.

HOG BUSINESS BOOMS; BOARS ALL SOLD OUT

Do Star Classified ads pull? You bet they do and you have the word of a dozen or more swine breeders in the county to prove it. During the past week, Harold Crawford, Beaver Creek; Dean Bell, Valley Springs; Phil Ordung, Robert Cook and E. S. Juhl, Luverne and Alvin Heime, Kenneth have ordered their "boars for sale" ads discontinued because their entire stocks had been sold.

Mr. Juhl said, "I could have sold a dozen more if I had had them." He sold 38 head privately this fall.

This is further proof that Rock County Star Classifieds have "pull" among rural readers. Use this inexpensive and profitable method of advertising often.

WHAT'S NEW IN GIFTS! READ THE SHOPPING GUIDE IN THE STAR

If you're puzzled what to give, we suggest that you read the Christmas shopping guide on page six of this week's Star. It's crammed chock full of ideas, something perhaps you'd never thought of giving. Look it over closely. Your Christmas shopping is easy if you do it The Star classified way.

FREE TICKETS TO CHILDREN'S MOVIE

Children who have not yet obtained their free tickets to the Civic and Commerce association's Christmas movie at the Pix theater on Dec. 23 are requested to ask for them at their favorite store and business place. There is nothing to buy or sell; all that is necessary is to ask for them. There will be several showings of the movie, giving all the children in the county an opportunity to attend. Children up to and including 14 years of age are eligible.

To Use Local Jai... Pipestone Co. ...

Pipestone county, whose jail was recently condemned by the state, will keep their prisoners in the Rock county jail, under an arrangement made between officials of the two counties. Before prisoners will be moved here, however, the county attorney of Pipestone county must petition District Judge Flinn to designate the Rock county jail as serving Pipestone county until they construct a new building for that purpose.

Permi... was gra... board of... meeting... Unde... being ... day fo... prisone... this d... In ... for ... coun... day ... in ... was ... we...

Expect to Start Work On Court House Annex

Verbal assurance that the proposed court house office building project would get under way here as soon as materials were on the grounds was given the county board this week by Allen Halseth, WPA area engineer for this district.

The project, designed to provide more office space for county officials, and at the same time providing work for WPA clients, has been approved. At present, Architect W. E. E. Greene is preparing lists of materials needed to commence the work.

Elected to serve as a materials purchasing committee were George V. Carstens, chairman of the county board, County Auditor Koehn and County Engineer Brown. They are now trying to obtain a priority on some steel beams necessary for the construction. Mr. Koehn said that the committee was optimistic that the steel could be had as they already have the necessary beams on hand now and require only a ... inforcing and lin...

would be used for such purposes as food stamp distribution, rehabilitation and employment services, attorney's meeting places and committee rooms.

The ground floor of the new building would provide a community room 40 by 60 feet, with a seating capacity of about 400. In the portion connecting the old and the new buildings, space would be provided for a kitchen, two rest rooms, an additional room for the janitor's apartment and coal bins.

The present plan calls for a sloping grade from the building to the street on the north with the elimination of the curb there. The slope would be black-topped and would thus be used as a parking space.

...s de- ...sug- ...r Life ...eneral ...s the ...fol- ...pinion ...eneral ...ing tin ...en this

...en we ...t down ...t for ...Wild- ...Three ...went on ...frantic- ...d the ex- ...banquet ...the head- ...f the

CHUNN NOT SEEKING MUNICIPAL JUDGESHIP

M. W. Chunn, who last week was listed as one of the men seeking the municipal judgeship of this city, this week declared that such a statement was erroneous. Mr. Chunn wishes it known that he was not a candidate for the office. In his 45 years here, Chunn said, he has never sought public office and now that he has retired, he has no reason to deviate from his previous policy.

Mr. and Mrs. Duane Backer returned yesterday from the Twin Cities where they had been since Sunday.

STORES WILL REMAIN OPEN FOR CHRISTMAS SHOPPERS NEXT WEEK

Ben Pelstring, president of the Civic and Commerce association announced yesterday that beginning Wednesday, Dec. 17, Luverne stores would be open evenings for the benefit of Christmas shoppers. They will continue to remain open through Tuesday night, Dec. 23, and will close at the usual hour on Wednesday evening, Dec. 24, so that employees can spend Christmas eve at home with their families.

STEEN SCHOOL PRESENTS PLAY AS PART OF ITS FALL ACTIVITY

December 1941

"Events are moving at such a dizzy pace that editorials and news stories are outmoded almost before the type is ready to be laid on the page forms for the press."

—Al McIntosh

DECEMBER 11, 1941

Events are moving at such a dizzy pace that editorials and news stories are outmoded almost before the type is ready to be laid on the page forms for the press. Outwardly, Rock county is as serene and peacefully beautiful as always. But, already, the shadow of war is over the county.

The banks had hardly opened for business Monday when they were instructed to freeze all accounts of any Japanese that might be customers. Railroads were instructed not to sell tickets to any Japanese. And altho war seems a long ways off, guards were immediately stationed at the Omaha railroad bridge east of the city. The men, Glen Balimes, Albert Krahn and Claus Pepkes, former section employees, are working eight hour shifts straight around the clock. The men are parked in their cars with their heaters on but some provisions may be made soon for their comfort in winter months.

Charles Merrill has received word from his son, Jim, in Chicago that his wife's brother was a seaman aboard the U. S. S. West Virginia, which was reported sunk in the first day's attack.

Also in the trouble zone, altho not at Pearl Harbor, was Miss Helen Houg, daughter of Mrs. Carrie Houg and a sister of Mrs. C. D. Millard. She has been stationed at Honolulu as a nurse in the Naval Dispensary. She had been there just a year and was scheduled for one more year, under normal conditions of service.

And in one of the hottest spots of all is Russell Ormseth, formerly of Luverne and a brother of Norman Ormseth of Luverne, who is with the Marines at Guam, reported taken by the Japs.

And Marvin DeLapp, formerly of Luverne, is aboard a submarine. When last heard from he was on the run between Manilla and Singapore. His brother, Franklin, was stationed at Pearl Harbor, attached to the U. S. S. Montgomery.

★ ★ ★

One of the first things we thought of Sunday after hearing the war bulletins was how thrilled Mrs. Frank Frakes had been Saturday over the letter she had received from her son, Marion.

Marion had just arrived at Honolulu and had sent a letter back by Clipper. The letter reached her just three days later at Magnolia.

"The Japs are acting pretty fresh," wrote Marion. Then he went on to say that if they could see what the navy and army had at Hawaii it would be wise for the Japs not to get too cocky.

The Magnolia boy said the trip over on the transport was a bad one as the men were over-crowded like the proverbial sardines. The officers fared better because, he said, 100 officers had more room allotted to them than there was for 2,000 men.

All kinds of rumors were flying thick and fast among the soldiers, wrote Marion, as to where they would eventually be stationed. Most prevalent guess was duty on the Burma road.

Where Marion is now, the Frakes' haven't the least idea as he was scheduled to leave that same night from Hawaii. Also from Magnolia in the same outfit is Orville Barclay, son of Melvin Barclay.

———— ★ ★ ★ ————

And wondering where her son, Lawrence, is now stationed is Mrs. Etta Dehmlow. She thinks he is at Hawaii but is not sure. He is assigned to the navy repair ship, Pelais.

In view of the fast moving developments in the Pacific we suggest you get last week's issue of Life and read the article on General Douglas MacArthur. It outlines the strategy that is, and will be, followed. If you had the same opinion that many of us had that General MacArthur was just playing tin soldier in the Philippines, then this article will open your eyes.

DECEMBER 18, 1941

The call for volunteers for civilian defense activities raises a question that all of us should consider—what can we as individuals do to help?

Probably you had the same reaction a few months ago that many others had. The news reels of women learning to be mechanics, air raid spotters pretending to scan the skies for enemy planes, practice blackouts in large cities—in many cases they looked far fetched and even ridiculous. But in the light of the past week's headlines we can render fervent thanks that some leaders had the foresight and courage to begin preparations for any emergency.

The local council wisely concedes that chances for any actual need here in this midwestern community are very remote. But it's still wiser to volunteer and help create a well knit organization which will never be used than to let ourselves be lulled into a sense of false security.

———— ★ ★ ★ ————

Latest precaution to be taken in Luverne is the addition of a night watchman at the armory. The night shift is handled by Earl Tunstall with Bill Steinfeldt continuing as day time custodian. Don't be playing any belated Hallowe'en pranks down there as they won't be playing "patty cake" if anythings bobs up in the way of trouble.

DECEMBER 25, 1941

More word direct from Kodiak—Mrs. Martin E. Jensen had a telegram from her husband, Capt. Jensen, that reported everything was fine with the men of Battery E.

However—Leon Opsata, sergeant with the outfit, is in the hospital where he is recovering from a leg injury sustained while playing football. The game, a team of sergeants opposing a team of privates, must have been a rugged affair judging by the accounts we have heard. The sergeants finally won, 18 to 0.

———— ★ ★ ★ ————

The whole town of Steen is as bare of waste paper and tin cans as your front yard because the children are gathering those articles up—and they really have cleaned the town. As their "defense project" they have appealed to everybody in the community to save the paper and tin cans. The youngsters are pounding out the tin cans and are going to make that contribution to the government.

There are some thoughtful youngsters in that Steen school. They remembered that Mrs. Fred Wiese had been ill at her home for over a week. So when they went out to sing carols they made a special trip to the Wiese home where they not only sang a program of carols but also presented Mr. and Mrs. Wiese with a Christmas box.

Rubber Drive Launched In Cou

WANT TUSSLE WITH JAPS NOW SO THEY CAN GET HOME AND BACK TO WORK

ROCK COUNTY STAR PHOTO

Back row, left to right—Martin Tufte, Sherman; Walter Clausen, Pipestone.
Luverne; Arthur De Buck, Luverne and Walter Clausen, Pipestone.
Front row, left to right—Alfred Loeffler, Sherman; Clyde Shepard, Luverne; Alfred Wahlert, Sherman; Elmer Rollag, Beaver Creek;
Theodore Hamann, Garretson, and Virgil Stoterau, Luverne.
(Other photographs on pages 2 and 3.)

"HURRY up, get this picture over with. We want to get at those Japs so we can get back here and get our work done!" That was the sentiment expressed by the above group of men, and others last week, as they prepared to depart for the Ft. Crook Induction center and for service in the army.

DISCUSS WAR RELIEF CHEST

Would Eliminate Constant Solicitation for Various Contributions

Five men, consisting of F. A. Leicher as chairman, R. C. Engan, E. A. W. Brown, Fred Herman and E. A. Grunke, were appointed as a temporary committee at a meeting Tuesday night, to draw up plans for some form of "war fund chest" organization. It plans materialize, it calls for war relief needs hereafter would be met from funds contributed by the public to the organization.

Plans to form such an organization came as an outgrowth of various drives for contributions which have been conducted in the past and which are anticipated in the future. If it becomes a reality, the organization would direct a campaign for contributions, instead of calls for charitable and relief purposes. Then, when some organization established a quota for a war purpose, the call would be met with funds from the "chest," and residents of the county would not be required to make individual donations to every campaign launched for such purposes.

Although no definite plan was devised, the prevailing opinion of those present seemed to be in favor of some such program, as each individual would be called on for an amount large than he would ordinarily make a solicitation. The organization making a solicitation was agreed that a person would be asked that he could afford to do so, but no solicitor would thereafter call on him for a whole year.

GOVT PAY

Hope...

FORMER ROCK COUNTY MAN FOUND SLAIN

Robert Engle, Formerly of Battle Plain Township is Murder Victim

A former resident of Rock county who had spent his boyhood and young manhood days on a farm in Battle Plain township was the victim of a strange murder case in Thurston county, Nebraska, on June 1.

According to word received from the sheriff at Pender, Nebr., by County Attorney J. Robert Engle, about 60, who until a few years ago owned and land east of Hardwick, this badly decomposed and shot riddled body was found by Thurston county authorities in a shed beside the road 12 miles east of Bert Bartelle in a wooded region six miles east of Winnebago.

Friends, seeking partial clothing for Bartelle, who had died of pneumonia in Walthill, Nebr., were rummaging through the dead man's modest home when their attention was attracted by an odor from the shed. They forced the shed door open, and there discovered Engle's body, with his left side of his head blown away by a shotgun charge. He was tightly trussed with wire and rope, and a loaded single bar reled shotgun was found near Bartelle's truck parked near the house.

Dead Several Weeks

According to word received by Sheriff Roberts, Engle had been dead several weeks. He had been last seen when a motorist picked him up on a road near Winnebago and took him to near Bartelle's home.

The fact that Bartelle died before he could be questioned, ended as far as is known, all possibilities as of ever solving the mysterious crime. Bartelle had been brought to a hospital with pneumonia, but refused to remain, because he said he had to return to his home to look after his property. Three days...

(Continued on Page Eight)

AIR WARDENS MEET MONDAY

Will Formulate Plans for Workable Air Warning Service in County

Preliminary steps to the formation of a workable air raid warning organization throughout the county will be taken Monday night, when a special meeting for appointment of air raid wardens will be held at the Luverne high school auditorium. The meeting, called by Dan Main, chief air raid warden, and Bryan McRobert, air raid warden instructor, will begin promptly at 8 p.m.

Although it is generally agreed that little danger from air raids exists here, the fact that there is all-out war in progress makes it necessary to be prepared for the worst, according to Chief Warden Main. If an air raid warden organization would accomplish nothing more than to be prepared to meet other emergencies such as may result from storms, or other disasters, the efforts of all those who participate will be well worth while, declares Mr. Main.

Instruction Meetings

Monday night's meeting will be preparatory to a series of instruction meetings to be held in the future. Plans will be laid for future activities and all rural wardens who have not as yet been fingerprinted will be at that time. All men who have been notified are urged to be present.

Mr. McRobert, who will serve as instructor, recently completed a training course for air raid wardens at the University of Minnesota. He will be supplied with instructional material for distribution to the wardens, and will direct the education campaign that will be launched to acquaint the public with important details of civil air raid protection.

Those who have been appointed wardens and others interested in the work, are asked to listen to special broadcasts on the subject every Saturday night at 6:30 over WOOD.

Senator Frank J. Sell Files For Re-Election

WORTHINGTON LAWYER TO OPPOSE SEN. SELL

James G. Mott, Worthington attorney, who was speaker here at the Memorial day exercises, will oppose Senator Frank J. Sell, Adrian, for the state senatorship serving Rock and Nobles counties. It was announced this week. Mott, as ex-service man, and resident of Nobles county for many years, served as county attorney there and has also served as attorney for the city of Worthington.

Senator Frank J. Sell, Adrian, has filed for re-election as state senator from Rock and Nobles counties, thus becoming the fourth incumbent official representing this county to make public the fact that he was again seeking office.

In announcing his candidacy, Senator Sell stated that he have tried to make my record one of helpful service and constructive action for every principle of my constituents of the district and to our state."

In reviewing the 12 years in the senate, he cites the following accomplishments:

1. I helped provide employment for men who were unable to find private work by securing approximately 75 miles of new trunk highways. Secured nearly 80 miles of paving, as well as many miles of oil paving, providing employment elsewhere could not so work. This would not be.

2. Was author of the Minnesota Labor Relations act and helped collect several thousands of dollars for laboring men.

3. Has cooperated with representatives of farm organizations and farmers in behalf of agriculture, and has been glad to help business organizations and better business.

4. Voted payment of state school aids in full to lessen local taxes on property.

5. Worked with conservation groups in Rock and Nobles counties to insure fish for stocking lakes and ponds.

His election platform follows:
Long range conservation policy, with the legislature encouraging or one with mining of low grade iron ore, prolong mining industry and to insure employment for thousands of men.

No increase in tax levies by Legislature, but a policy to conserve present funds to help shock in giving employment wherever possible at that time.

Tax exempt securities should be discontinued, with all owners to be invited to exchange their tax exempt securities for a new special series of taxable defense bonds.

Firmly opposed to centralization of township, village, city or local school government. Policy of dividing gas tax equally between counties and townships should be...

(Continued on Page Eight)

CAR CATCHES FIRE; PASSERBY COLLIDE

A minor blaze that resulted from defective wiring in the car owned by Clive Bendt, Hardwick, caused considerable excitement on U. S. No. 16, about two miles south of Hardwick Saturday night, although it did very little damage to the Bendt car.

Bendt and his family were driving home from Luverne when he noticed smoke. He drove over to the shoulder of the road and began to extinguish the blaze.

Meanwhile, Oscar A. Olson, Luverne, came from the south, and Irene Dill, Magnolia came from the north, meeting almost at the point where the Bendt car was stalled. Olson, according to Sheriff Roberts, turned out to avoid hitting the Bendt car, and in so doing, sideswiped the Dill car, damaging both cars slightly. No one was injured, although Bendt was taken to Luverne for treatment of his burns.

FARM BUREAU PICNIC CANCELLED THIS YEAR

There will no Rock County Farm Bureau picnic this year, County Agent King announced this week. At a meeting held here, Farm Bureau officials agreed that because of the shortage of farm help, and the necessity of conserving tires, the picnic would be cancelled for the duration, or at least until existing conditions improve.

FOURTH OF JULY PICNIC PLANNED

Old-fashioned Fourth Will Be Held Here With Fun for Everybody

The Luverne Civic and Commerce Association is planning an old-fashioned "Fourth of July family picnic" according to Elmer Piepgras, president.

The picnic will be held in the city park. There will be some sports events, races and contests. A local speaker. Piepgras emphasized that the affair, which is planned for all, is purely "a local" picnic—no carnivals or other attractions planning an old time open.

"We are planning an old time picnic," he said, "where you and your family can come and enjoy a safe and sane Fourth of July with your family and your friends. Everyone is invited."

Former Steen Resident Hurt at Pearl Harbor

The following article, concerning W. H. Rockman, well known in the Steen community, and brother of Mrs. W. C. Lauck, of Bigelow, who injured in the raid on Pearl Harbor...

Bob Leicher left Monday morning for Spokane, Wash., where he will deliver a new fire truck manufactured by the Luverne Fire Apparatus company. He expects to return by train next week.

MAY BUSINESS V DROPPED 11 PER

Business volum month of May in Luverne was 11 per that of May, 1941, the debit figures the Federal Rese Minneapolis. On hand, business for months of 1942 w similar January ried a year ago closed.

Throughout the next volume months of the 9 per cent of the for the like while for the 1942, busines 1941.

Since bank most part are checks a Against th since given in use for ed a s busine

FIVE

Of Rock Ad Fo ar ha th FH th

THIS GROUP PART OF COUNTY'S LARGEST DRAFT CONTINGENT

1942

"And so at last—the first of those dreaded envelopes from the war department bearing the grim news that two Rock county men who unflinchingly faced their inevitable fate at Corregidor must be considered 'missing in action.'"

—Al McIntosh

JANUARY 1, 1942

Some of the 80-mile-an-hour highway smart alecks who once snickered as they roared past Fred Larson and his horse and buggy may be tickled to death to hitch-hike a ride with him yet.

It is wonderful in what good spirit everybody accepted the news of the tire rationing plan. I only heard one bit of grumbling and I doubt if that was sincere. Most everyone takes the attitude "we've been eating a full dinner table so long we've taken everything for granted and are spoiled." A return to the "horse and buggy" days won't hurt anyone of us.

The easiest way to look at it is to remember the old poem "for want of a nail the shoe was lost," etc. It would be terrible to think of American soldiers trapped in a desperate spot because their countrymen were unwilling to make the sacrifices which would mean the difference between life or death.

JANUARY 8, 1942

Just One Year Ago!

Time is a funny thing. In one way it seems but a few short weeks and in another way it seems like five years since those 133 Rock county men assembled on a Monday morning at the Luverne armory.

They were due to leave in ten days for a "year's training at March Field, Cal." That's what they were told and that's what they believed but little did they, or anyone else, think that 365 days later would find them manning one of Uncle Sam's most strategic island outposts. And that upon their courage and alertness would depend the welfare of millions of Americans.

That was a busy and hectic ten days for Battery E. There was something make believe and strange about the whole affair. Some of the out-of-town men were sleeping nights at the armory while the town men were allowed to go to their homes. And even the boys of Battery E would be the first to admit it today but they did look pretty much like a rag tag and bob tail outfit when they assembled. There weren't enough uniforms to go around. Some little chaps had overcoats that bounced around their shoe tops while some of the tall boys had coats that flapped about their knees—while others still had nothing to wear but their civilian attire.

Some of the sidewalk smart alecks who yelled allegedly funny remarks as the men marched down the street to the restaurants for their meals would have their eyes opened if they could see them today—trim, erect, heavier and tough—nothing sloppy about them now but first class hard hitting fighting men, a credit to the country's uniform.

Then came the Military Ball with Adjutant General Walsh making a special, hurry up trip from the cities to pay his official respects, the presentation of Phyllis Brooks as honorary colonel, the union church service and then the going away.

There were a lot of long faces down there at the depot—and there were a lot of people who were all smiles, altho you knew they didn't feel that way inside. There were a lot of tear-stained faces as a number of Luverne girls wept bitterly as they said their goodbyes "for a year."

The band played Auld Lang Syne, several times during the awkward and prolonged wait, but it turned out to be more fitting after all in the light of events than if it had been the Beer Barrel Polka. The long wait came to an abrupt end. Col. "Andy" Anderson, who had been running around like a mother hen seeing that all his "chicks" were properly entrained, climbed aboard. And then the engineer slammed the throttle over wide and the cars began to flash past. We can still see, in mind's eye, "Marty" Jensen, George Fried and the other officers standing in the open door of the baggage car waving their final goodbyes.

Probably the most vivid recollection for many is the union service held at the high school. It was a most solemn affair, not a sound except the shuffling of feet broke the reverent hush as the men marched in to take the places reserved for them—the simple but sincere and dignified service. "Marty" Jensen going up and shaking hands, in behalf of the battery, with the five pastors. There were a lot of people in that auditorium that morning who were fighting hard to get rid of that lump that kept strangely choking up in their throats.

We will never forget the sight as the men marched away from the high school after the service. There was a feeble winter sun and its slanting rays on the frosty day played funny tricks in making almost individual halos, it seemed, about the heads of the men as the outfit swung down the street.

A year has passed and many things have happened since. When newspapermen get to suggesting things they are out on dangerous ground but it would seem to me that it might be fitting and proper for this community to hold another union church service at the same place. Not just for the men of Battery E, but for those other men who are serving elsewhere in our armed forces. Wouldn't it be proper for everyone to meet and offer up a united prayer for the safety and happiness of all these men. They can't be here but I think they would appreciate the united effort.

——— ★ ★ ★ ———

Jess Frakes, the contractor whose log of travel with the navy reads like the itinerary on a world cruise, has sadly resigned himself to the belief that his contribution to national defense will be "hoeing corn" next summer.

Jess did "3 years, 9 months and 10 days" with the navy—winding up in 1930 as a first class yeoman. The other day, to keep in line with the true Frakes' tradition of wearing a uniform, he tried to get back in the navy. But the navy wouldn't take him altho Jess will fight if you say he's not as good a man as he ever was. Trouble was—he's short some all important teeth. He even offered to stand the expense of having some plates made but "no dice" said the recruiting officer as Jess still fell short of dental and optical standards.

And teeth tripped Bryce Connell, too, the other day when he tried to join the navy. And his brother, Jim, was just as determined to enlist but it seems he needs a course in trigonometry to pass requirements for the desired branch of the service. So it looks as if it is "back to school" for Jim.

JANUARY 15, 1942

As the radio quiz show announcers would say—"here is the four-dollar question—is it against the law to meet a car on Luverne streets without dimming your lights?"

If you are one of the ten per cent who know the right answer—that this is one of the laws being enforced to the last letter by the highway patrol—then you are in line to save some money.

Speaking of the highway patrol there was a heated, altho brief, scrap in the drawing of one of the resolutions at the recent annual meeting of the Rock county Farm Bureau.

As first drawn, one resolution condemned the "Hitleristic tactics" of the highway patrol, but some of the cooler heads prevailed and the wording was modified. The members were satisfied in passing along a rebuke to the officers for some of the rough-shod tactics they have employed.

★ ★ ★

In the mail comes a letter from Jarnet Johansen, now a private in Camp Polk, Louisiana.

"This is sure some country," he writes. "It rains at least twice a week and when it gets cold here you can't seem to put enough clothes on. I'd rather be in Minnesota at 25 below than here at 20 above." (And knowing how that Louisiana cold knifes thru you, we second the motion.)

Jarnet likes army life a lot better than he ever expected and thinks the officers and men certainly are patient and friendly. How they hold their tempers at times he can't understand.

And from Howard Heiges at Kodiak comes a letter to say that the weather up there is pretty much like that of Minnesota now. There hasn't been much snow but it was snowing hard as he wrote.

Altho Kodiak may not be the most pleasant place in the world, Howard says things can be tougher anywhere a person may be.

★ ★ ★

Also in the mail comes a chiding letter from Private A. O. Bierkamp ("Buck" to the thousand assorted friends he has in Rock county), rebuking tardiness in answering a previous communication.

Now at Camp Robinson, "Buck" will take 20 below Minnesota weather anytime in preference to 10 above in Arkansas where the cold knifes thru you. His hope is to move soon to a pyramidal tent with five other fellows as the gas heater in his present tent was evidently designed for Florida weather.

Arlo reaped a financial harvest last fall laying bets on the Minnesota football team, profiting by the envious desire of others to see Minnesota "get knocked off." But the football season is over and Buck is finding it slim going now financially and he is urging a concerted appeal to congress for a raise in pay for soldiers as he only has $6 left until February 6. (Are you reading this, Ott?)

And from H. B. Creeger at Bradenton, Fla., comes a glowing account of his garden. He writes in mouth watering terms of his beans, cabbages, lettuce and radishes. Temperature at Bradenton has been most enjoyable, if anything a bit too hot. The county had its first blackout and it was a "100 per cent success." Creeger had a new experience the other day and he still isn't sure whether he cares to make a habit of it—walking along the shore, picking up oysters, opening and eating them on the spot.

——— ★ ★ ★ ———

Don't spend all your time watching the president in the news reels. If you do you're missing 95 per cent of the drama, like the football fan who forgets the line play and only watches the man with the ball.

Forget the president and keep your eyes on the secret service men. It's fascinating to watch how (they're the men who always stand at each side—and down in front), they constantly scan the crowd in front of them.

——— ★ ★ ★ ———

If you want to know the reason the British barred Cecil Brown from the air then get last week's Life magazine and read the blistering article he wrote on the Far Eastern situation.

——— ★ ★ ★ ———

And another bit of good news from Hawaii came in the wire from Kenneth Olson. "Clarence Dybedock and I unhurt." Kenneth, who has been in the navy three years, is the son of the late Mr. and Mrs. Albert Olson of Luverne. He sent the message to his cousins, Mr. and Mrs. Archie Olson.

And Sergeant Willard Schwartz, who left Kodiak on December 6, thinking that he was on his way home, arrived in Seattle January 1, after a round-about-trip. Now at Fort Lawton, the Luverne boy is awaiting further orders.

Two boys well known around here, Private David Jones and Private Marshall Randolph, have had a big part in the printing of the official Kodiak paper. Their printing experience has proved invaluable, (Marshall is the son of John Randolph, Edgerton publisher) in the publication of the attractive news sheets, now rechristened the "Kodiak Bear."

———— ★ ★ ★ ————

And tickled to death to get word from his son, Harold, was S. F. Roemeling. The Rock county boy wrote the letter, which came last week, on Christmas day from his station at Schofield barracks in Hawaii.

———— ★ ★ ★ ————

Dick Wildung has signed up with the U.S. Naval Reserve but it is not believed that his scholastic plans will be interrupted.

JANUARY 22, 1942

The spirit that prompted the gift of a boy's most precious treasure should spank some of us who haven't responded to the Red Cross appeal. Did you know, and it's hard to reconcile with Rock county's traditional record of open handed giving, that only 300 people have responded to date. What would you rather have— a campaign with door to door solicitors or one where you give voluntarily—because of a great need. There aren't any solicitors— why don't you slip that check in the mail today?

———— ★ ★ ★ ————

Don Roemling, who left for the army last week, had worked two years for the Ralph Arends family in Springwater township. Don was a prime favorite with the youngsters.

The day before Roemling left, six-year-old "Buzzy," talking to his mother, said, "When's Don going to fight?"

Mrs. Arends explained that Don would go to a training camp first and that she didn't know how long he would stay there.

"I'm going to give him my knife," said Buzzy. Offhand, that doesn't sound unusual but that knife was the youngster's prize possession: a Christmas gift from an uncle.

So that night after Buzzy went to bed Don came over to say farewell to the family. Buzzy overheard the conversation, jumped out of bed, slipped downstairs and made a solemn and tearful presentation of his gift.

JANUARY 29, 1942

Most people are scratching their heads trying to remember all the deductions to which they are legally entitled in order to cut down the size of their income tax payment. But here's a story that's different.

A Hardwick man came in to Millard the other day for help in having his income tax return made out. Cliff went over the figures, filled out the return, and then told him that no tax payment was necessary.

"I don't care what the figures show," retorted the man. "I want to beat Hitler so bad I'm going to pay a tax anyway." And he sat right down and wrote out a $20 check.

So the collector of the internal revenue today has an income tax report showing no payment is due but with the return is the $20 check and a note of explanation.

FEBRUARY 12, 1942

Many a person gave prayerful thanks that Rock county men, serving in the armed forces, were spared in the Japanese attack on Pearl Harbor that Black Sunday, December 7.

But now—over two months later comes word that a Rock county man was injured that day. It was Walter Rockman, formerly of Steen, who was a member of the Marine Corps. Rockman was off duty at the time he was wounded so he must have been hit at the very outset of the attack.`

The former Steen man lost two fingers and his arm was badly injured. Brought back to the United States on one of the first boats to return after December 7, Rockman was placed in a San Francisco hospital. An infection set in and it's believed it may be necessary to amputate the arm.

He is a son of Fred Rockman who has lived at Bigelow, Minn., the past few years.

———— ★ ★ ★ ————

Archie Matson has been in the army now nearly a month and he thinks it's a lot of fun, according to a postcard he sent the Star.

Archie is at the Engineer's Replacement Training Center at Fort Leonard Wood, Missouri. The Luverne delegation was scattered after the men left Fort Snelling, writes Archie. "My frame is plenty sore from these workouts," he concludes.

He didn't have them then but he's a cinch to have them now. The doctor at Camp Robinson, Arkansas, diagnosed "Buck" Bierkamp's swollen jaw as a case of mumps so he ordered the Luverne boy to the hospital—and put him in the "mumps ward." Later they discovered that Buck didn't have the mumps and he was released—but he's expecting to be back there any day now with the "lump jawed brigade."

And instead of 28 men leaving for Fort Snelling Thursday there will be only 27—and altho that 28th man is anxious to go the other 27 will be tickled to death he didn't—because Gordon Tobiason has the mumps.

———— ★ ★ ★ ————

It's amazing the way the school children have purchased defense stamps in Rock county. The remark was made the other night that the children have put the grownups to shame—their purchases nearly equaling those of their elders.

An eighth grader from Sherman, Gene Solem, got so enthusiastic the other day that the youngster turned in the following poem. Some might criticize the "meter" of the poem—but not the spirit. Here 'tis.

"Everytime you a buy a stamp
You slap a Jap into camp.
"Buy everytime you have a chance
And we'll beat the Axis prance.
"Remember Pearl Harbor—forget golf
till we beat that man, Adolph.
"When we beat the Axis three
The Japs will climb a Cherry Tree."
—GENE SOLEM

February 19, 1942

Stener Holland, oldest son of Mr. and Mrs. Ole Holland, died in France during the World War I from influenza. He was a member of the medical detachment. Last week the Holland's youngest son, Russell, left with that delegation of 28 men who entered service in World War the second.

———— ★ ★ ★ ————

From Los Angeles comes an interesting letter from Mrs. Nora Iveland Erickson—one that will make the local fishing fans green with envy.

The favorite fishing places of the Ericksons have been taken over by the army, she writes, so they have had to seek new locations for the weekly fishing excursions.

"At Oxnard beach," she writes, " she had' quite an exciting time surf fishing and caught over 50 big, nice, silver perch.

Mrs. Erickson tells of the army beach patrols and of the tiny, sturdy, "jeep" cars roaring down the sands at 40 miles an hour and "sometimes the waves would hit them, sending the ocean spray in all directions."

"Above," she writes, "the airplanes drone back and forth, on guard, at all times. Uncle Sam is watching, and what a pleasant feeling it is."

They always pack a lot of extra lunch and the soldiers are glad, not only to have company in their lonely outposts, but for the special food.

Recently Mr. Erickson went deep sea fishing and came home with two gunny sacks full of fish, big barracudas and bonitas—and in addition won the jackpot, catching not only the first but the largest fish. The trip cost $3 but the jackpot totalled $5.25 so he came out with a neat profit—to say nothing of the sport with the water fairly "churning" with fish.

Mrs. Erickson laments that she can't understand why she, a "viking born right near the fjords of Norway must have an annoying and disgusting thing like sea sickness"—which prevents her from going on the deep sea fishing excursions.

Mrs. Erickson closes by confessing that her greatest ambition would be to be allowed to man a machine gun on the breakwater and when not shooting Japs be allowed to fish.

FEBRUARY 26, 1942

Maybe Jay Helgeson has been reading too much war news and his nerves might be a bit jumpy—but when you see him ask him if he's been "held up" lately.

We'll explain to you what all the commotion was down at Nelson's this week.

It happened when Jay, whose glasses aren't always correctly focused, waited on Mrs. Thorvald Friestad, who happens to be quite hard of hearing.

Mrs. Friestad came in to look at some men's furnishings and Jay went over to wait on her. She couldn't hear what he was saying so she reached into her pocketbook for the hearing aid she uses.

Jay admits his vision was a bit fuzzy as he hadn't properly adjusted his glasses, and he had the awful feeling that the woman, who was a stranger to him, was fishing a revolver out of her bag.

So quick as a flash Jay reached out his hand and batted the purse from Mrs. Friestad. The hearing aid went flying thru the air and Jay jumped about 56 feet (if you believe what some of his friends claim).

Jay might have thought he was scared but imagine how Mrs. Friestad must have felt having a salesman turn without warning and put on an act like that. When they finally got everything all explained they laughed till their sides ached.

———— ★ ★ ★ ————

We received the new "Kodiak Bear," official paper of Fort Greely and it's bright, breezy and full of news. Incidentally—two boys who are well known here, Marshall Randolph and David Jones, worked 26 hours straight getting the paper out.

The "Bear" was formerly the army's only "hand set" paper but it is now printed in Anchorage, by "remote control." When the editors want pictures, and they have a number, they have to send their pictures all the way to Seattle to get the engravings.

One Luverne woman took it upon herself to soundly berate the Civic and Commerce Association committee because the moving pictures and sound records, being sent as a Christmas gift to Kodiak, didn't reach the boys on Christmas day as expected. The committee were quite upset about it—they certainly did all they could to get the packages there in time.

Now they are vindicated because the "Bear" reports that the incoming holiday mail at Kodiak totalled 90 tons in the two week period . . . so much that the men couldn't keep up with the unbelievable flood of letters and packages.

And the camp paper goes on to report the informal birthday celebration honoring Col. Wm. Frazer, the commanding officer. The men staged a rumpus outside headquarters to attract the attention of the C. O. He marched outside to see what it was all about and just then the band broke into "Happy Birthday."

And then, we'll quote the Kodiak paper, "Suddenly the ceremonies were interrupted by a loud shout from the steps of the station hospital.

"Happy birthday, Colonel," called Lt. Col. Andrew A. Anderson, saluting with one crutch while he supported his mending leg with the other. It was Colonel Anderson's first public appearance since he fell and broke his leg more than two months ago. The music of the band was too tempting even for a man under Nurses' orders to stay flat on his back."

And the Luverne boys have started the "Whirlwind Club" with the following officers: Arvin Dorman, president; John Stavenger, adjutant; Ole Hornman, treasurer; Marvin Boelman, notary public; Wallace Haakenson, staff driver; Harry Shadwinkel, mess officer; Donald Obele, janitor; Dick Loger, sergeant at arms; Jim Taige, clerk; Mervin Denzer, doctor; Emroy Lange, attorney; Harvey Buus, mailman.

And we see where Warren Herreid wins the title of being the "champion letter getter of the outfit."

March 5, 1942

In a newspaper office an anonymous letter never receives a second glance before it is tossed in the waste basket because the opinion of anyone lacking the courage to sign their name isn't worth bothering with.

What sort of perverted pleasure or satisfaction do writers of anonymous letters get from their handiwork anyway? If they do get pleasure as a result then they will probably gloat in the fact that one of the letters caused an elderly Luverne woman to weep bitter tears of grief last week.

The letter read:

"You and all your boys better all donate to the Red Cross or something will happen. Signed ... The Committee." That took a lot of courage ... to threaten an older woman and not sign one's name.

It was only by chance that the matter came to light and Ned Brown was pretty grim and tight lipped about the matter. He assured her that the Red Cross wasn't making any threats to get donations, and that anytime the Red Cross sent any communications they would be on official printed stationery and SIGNED.

Brown was angry because the Red Cross drive, which he headed, reached its goal after as fine a campaign as ever had been staged anywhere.

No high pressure efforts were used and it truly was a free will offering for a worthy cause.

What the motive was behind the letters Brown doesn't know—whether someone is seeking to cause grief to people or whether it is a crude attempt to create antagonism towards the Red Cross.

———— ★ ★ ★ ————

Here's a coincidence. Some weeks back among the mail bag were letters from two Rock county boys now in service, Arlo Bierkamp and Jarnet Johansen. In the mail this week, on the very same day, came letters from the same pair.

Jarnet is taking radio training now. The one thing he wishes is that more Rock county boys would be sent to Camp Polk, the only man he has seen so far is George Sathre of Kenneth.

Arlo has been moved to an armored division training camp at Fort Smith, Arkansas. As soon as pay day rolls around "Buck" says he is going over and investigate the town of Fort Smith which, he says, is reported to be a "pretty fair town," of 35,000.

"Made out my income tax for 1941," says "Buck," "and am sure I won't have to pay any for 1942 at my present salary."

"If I could get a job helping build this camp I'd be okeh," he adds, "really the wages are out of reason. Makes a fellow kind a sore when they can pay those men more in a day than we make in a month."

MARCH 12, 1942

Go along to see "A Yank in the R. A. F." starting Sunday at the Palace. It's way above average.

And for signs of spring it should be reported that Jack DeBates of Hardwick was digging fish worms on Feb. 27. Ed Elbers and his brother were going to bring them in for proof to us—but so far they have failed to show up. And the first two men to be already at work in the fields are Nick Wilroth and George Mann.

———— ★ ★ ★ ————

Mrs. Albert Birdsey is happy because she has received the first word in a month from her son, Ernest, an army radio operator. She received the brief message, "we landed safely," but she has no more idea on what convoy he was, or his destination, than you have. And Mrs. Etta Dehmlow is also thrilled because she's had reassuring word from her son, Lawrence, altho she fears he has been slightly wounded.

———— ★ ★ ★ ————

The nation is honoring the name of Ed O'Hare, Chicago, as being our greatest wartime aerial ace—for knocking six Jap bombers out of the sky. O'Hare is an old friend of Mrs. G. N. Getman—he used to date steadily her very best friend.

And we should report that our "suicide squadron" was not in force at the roller rink last Thursday night. Among the casualties were Einar Lorange, who sprained his wrists so bad he couldn't ply his trade of meat cutting for days; Gordon Remme, who sprained his thumb; "Bud" Sherman, who suffered a back injury when he, Mrs. Stan Remme and Mrs. G. N. Getman crashed together. All of them were "out cold" for a second or so—and Sherman was so sore the next day he didn't dare sneeze he ached so badly.

MARCH 19, 1942

Back in the "States" again is Lt. Col. A. A. Anderson. The man who headed the Luverne national guard unit has had a miserable time since he fell and broke his leg over four months ago at Kodiak.

Nobody who knows "Andy" would ever believe that he patiently folded his hands and waited uncomplainingly for time to heal the injured limb. And the fact that his recovery has been slow and unsatisfactory didn't help the situation any.

The colonel has been brought back to Barnes General hospital at Vancouver Barracks in Washington for further observation and treatment. He has been due there for over a month but his departure from Kodiak was delayed from week to week for various reasons.

If recovery isn't more rapid there is a possibility that the colonel may be invalided home and released from service.

———— ★ ★ ★ ————

"Just a few lines in haste and let you know I am still alive and putting in long hard days of work," scribbles Ray Fritz, sending in the renewal for his Star subscription.

Ray has been gone from Luverne just about a year now and he has certainly led a whirlwind existence in defense work since then, putting in light and power equipment at a California advanced flying field; installing light and power equipment at a big motorized equipment supply depot. For the last two months he has been installing power equipment on navy mine sweepers.

"Believe you me," writes Ray, "there's lots of electrical equipment goes on one of those boats so have been doing the best I can to keep 'em flying, rolling and sailing and buying defense bonds.

"Enjoy getting your paper every week, but sometimes delayed in reading it, on account of long hours of work and so tired when I get to hotel I crawl right into bed."

If you would like to write him—and he'd appreciate a letter—send it to Ray Fritz, Hotel State, Stockton, Calif.

———— ★ ★ ★ ————

Speaking of Ray reminds us that his dad, Frank Fritz, came in not so long ago with a "score-card" on the duration of the last seven wars in which the United States has been engaged. It will save a lot of guessing and thumbing the pages of history books in case you get in an argument—so better clip it out.

Our war for independence started April 19, 1775; officially ended at noon April 19, 1783. War of 1812—begun June 18, 1812—ended January, 1815. War with Mexico—started April 25, 1846—ended September 14, 1847. Civil War started April 15, 1861—ended April 9, 1865. Spanish War began April 21, 1898—

ended August 13, 1898. We entered World War I April 6, 1917. The Armistice was signed Nov. 11, 1918. Our longest war was about eight years in length—and our shortest war was ended in less than 6 months.

MARCH 26, 1942

Two very polite little men walked into Clyde Stephen's store last Monday morning. One of them said, "give me a couple packages of Camels."

Clyde took one look, turned on his heel and walked away quick before yielding to a temptation to throw a meat cleaver, and snapped "we don't have any Camels."

The men walked out but that didn't end it. The more Clyde thought about it the madder he got. So when we walked in later, he said, "say, what do you mean printing a story last week that there aren't any Japs in this county?"

It seems those little men who wanted the Camels were Japs. They are employees of a chick sexing syndicate and still are permitted by our government to travel around the country working for the hatcheries that used to employ them.

There are a lot of people who will have to suffer for the sins of a few but it does seem that our country is easy going and tolerant. We can't imagine the Japs permitting any Americans in Manilla or Tokyo to travel round going about their regular business.

APRIL 2, 1942

Nothing can be said about it yet for fear of taking the edge off a very sweet surprise for some loved ones. But some men in uniform must be commended for their thoughtfulness.

——— ★ ★ ★ ———

Proud as could be when he visited Tuesday in Luverne was A. C. Halls, Garretson city attorney. And he had a right to be for he had just received in the mail a Silver Star award for Gallantry in Action during World War I.

A brother of County Commissioner Halls the Garretson man is a former Hills boy. Halls was showing the medal to County Auditor Koehn.

According to Walter Simmons who writes "Maybe You've Heard" in the Sioux Falls Argus Leader the medal is belated recognition for the bravery of Halls, then a corporal in Co. 1, 305th Inf., 77th Division, in the Meuse-Argonne sector. The Silver Star award, according to W. A. S., ranks just a little below the Distinguished Service Cross.

———— ★ ★ ★ ————

The "Kodiak Bear" has excited real curiosity in many places. It has been widely quoted in many daily papers and last week we received a request for a copy from the Minnesota Historical Society, after the curator had noticed a comment about the new paper in Chaff.

APRIL 9, 1942

If you have a "BOY IN CAMP" then don't miss this week's Saturday Evening Post. The cover is a work of art and good for a dozen chuckles—and incidentally it's a good hint as to how much he appreciates getting the home town paper REGULARLY.

———— ★ ★ ★ ————

Not talkative but still telling enough to make a fascinating story was the American boy who stopped in at Long's Roadside Inn the other night en route home to Los Angeles for a 60-day furlough.

A former enlisted man in the U. S. army the young man transferred to the Canadian forces and for two and a half years has been in the British forces. He told Martha Krahn that he never thought that he'd get home as the convoy in which he was traveling was attacked by subs. The tanker, proceeding ahead of them in the convoy, was blown up by a torpedo.

APRIL 16, 1942

The memory of that "bosun's whistle" is stirring Roy Paulson to action. Roy has served several hitches in the navy and regardless of the café, his wife and youngsters, he thinks he'd like to be back in the navy for the duration. Roy would like to go back with his old rating, which was musician first class.

———— ★ ★ ★ ————

We have the uncanny knack of always managing to say the wrong thing at the wrong time.

Walking back from the coffee shop last Thursday morning where we'd heard the grim news over the radio that Bataan had finally fallen we met Ben Padilla walking home from his night's work. The roly poly baker was minus his customary infectious grin and his face was long and sober.

"What's the matter, Ben, lost your best friend," we asked.

"My brother was at Bataan," he answered quietly.

What can one say at a time like that?

Then—after we'd walked a few moments in silence Ben said in a grim voice, "it's a hard thing to say—but I hope Jake died fighting bravely rather than be captured by the Japs."

———— ★ ★ ★ ————

Looking thru an eastern daily paper last week I noticed a picture of a husky English bulldog and a youngster. The picture's caption read that the dog can be both gentle and tough just as the Armies of the United Nations are proving they can be. The nine months old youngster, helping himself to a ride on the bulldog, was James Goeske, son of Mr. and Mrs. John Goeske of Luverne. The picture, which was reprinted all over the country, was taken at Fort Sheridan, near Chicago.

———— ★ ★ ★ ————

And if you've never seen Abbott and Costello you don't know how many laughs you're missing—so don't miss "Ride 'Em Cowboy" starting tonight at the Palace.

April 23, 1942

Not to start any feud with our neighbors in Nobles county but it is a fair question to ask "are Rock county young men healthier specimens of manhood than those of Nobles county?"

Early arrivals at Worthington Sunday reported that the number rejected from the delegation Nobles county sent to Fort Crook would run approximately 50 per cent.

The boys rejected because of physical defects shouldn't feel too gloomy about their chances for living to a ripe age. They can take comfort in the following news we read from Glendale, Calif.; "E.J. L. Merchant tried to enlist in the union army at the start of the Civil war. He was rejected. Friday he celebrated his 101st birthday."

APRIL 30, 1942

A lot of people who patriotically hammered their fingers to a pulp and ruined their tempers straightening out old tin cans breathed a sigh of relief when they learned that the government isn't greatly interested right now in gathering up old tin cans. It seems that the tin percentage is so small that nothing much will be done with the drive until more efficient methods of reclaiming the tin are devised.

That belated news doesn't bring any happiness to Louis Ahrendt for he had been one of the busiest toilers in the tin can drive staged by the cub scouts. Louie isn't complaining but the drive wasn't very profitable—for him.

He had loaded the collection of tin cans in a borrowed trailer and started down town to dispose of them. On the way the trailer came unhitched and the tongue rammed into the rear of his car, smashing thru the trunk.

So the score now stands . . . "to cub scout treasury from sale of tin cans, $2.45" and a local garage bill reads "to Louis Ahrendt, repairs on car, $10."

———— ★ ★ ★ ————

And he looked to be such a nice fellow.

These days everybody is leaning backwards to be helpful to men in uniform. So the other day when a sailor stopped in to inquire where he could find the local Red Cross chairman we did more than pointing out the direction to Ray Engan's office—we got busy on the phone and called Ray away from his lunch in a restaurant.

The fellow explained he was on leave from the San Diego training station to see his sick sister in Ortonville and that he had hitch hiked this far from Sioux City.

Engan hastily swallowed a mouthful of scalding coffee and was waiting with the royal purple welcome carpet unrolled for the seaman. Now, Engan declares he was just a shade skeptical about why the fellow didn't have a ticket for the entire trip but even so he advanced Red Cross funds to the extent for a dollar for meals and $3.73 bus fare. Always skeptical Ray watched to see that the fellow did get on the bus.

Monday night at the Red Cross executive meeting the chairman explained the expenditure and asked if he had done right in advancing money.

"If there are mistakes to be made concerning men in uniform it is better to make them on the liberal side," the committee decided.

Was Engan surprised to pick up the Argus-Leader the next night and find that his sailor friend had landed in the "Pipestone pokey."

That boy wasn't home on leave—he is a deserter.

Credit for the apprehension of the sailor must go to another Red Cross chairman, L. H. Himmelman of Pipestone. He had received a similar plea from the same fellow. Evidently the sailor was cashing in bus tickets all along the way and making a good thing out of it. So Himmelman advanced money. This time the sailor was trying to get to his "home in Yankton." Was Himmelman surprised the next morning to see the sailor and a girl taking out a marriage license in the county clerk's office at Pipestone. (Who said sailors weren't fast workers.)

The sailor was married to a Sioux Falls girl in a Pipestone church parsonage. By the time the Red Cross chairman had received word back from San Diego that the youth was a deserter, the couple had left Pipestone but they were soon arrested by police in Sioux Falls.

It looks as if we had Ray in training to be the head of the Naval Relief Association in Luverne—the only thing we're afraid of is that he'll (try to) bill us for that $4.73.

Engan said, this probably won't be the only mistake made this way but it's better to make ten of them than run the risk of turning down one honest man in uniform who really is in a hurry to get to his home."

He doesn't mind missing part of his meal but he doesn't want to be called out of the bath tub the next time a service man wants financial assistance.

MAY 7, 1942

About a month ago Louie Cohen was admiring a necktie Harold Glaser was wearing. He admired it so much that Glaser said, "you like it?"

"If you'll give me that tie I'll buy you the best one that money can buy when you get back from the army," replied Cohen. And then he forgot about the whole affair.

The day after Glaser left for the army Cohen came home and found a package in the mail box, wrapped in Christmas gift paper. It was the much coveted necktie—Glaser hadn't forgotten.

———— ★ ★ ★ ————

Despite the barrage of publicity that heralded the sugar rationing plan one wonders at the actions of some people (whether they've yet heard that there is a war going on) who went in to their grocers and tried to buy the sugar, the one week that it had been announced that none would be sold.

They are calling Superintendent of Schools Barrett and Superintendent Munson the "sugar daddies" of Rock county this week for they have certainly done a grand job in setting up the registration machinery.

The staff of teachers and volunteer workers certainly did a grand job of handling the registration. There was no fuss and feathers about it and no loss motion.

———— ★ ★ ★ ————

Don't ever think that Capt. Martin Jensen isn't idoled by his men. It seems that "Marty" is always on the lookout for the welfare and happiness of his men. And he doesn't stop there . . . but tries to keep the home folks feeling happy. We are reprinting, word for word, a letter that the captain enclosed in a letter that Corp. Jake (Bud) Voorst sent to his brother and family, Mr. and Mrs. Gerrit Van Voorst at Steen. It tells the story better than anything else. Here's the letter:

"Just a word from the captain:

"Being that I censor all the mail that goes out of the battery, I also like to steal the opportunity to drop a line to some of my boys' parents.

"We are getting along just fine and so is Bud. He is a great guy to keep the boys in his platoon in good spirits, a good soldier and we all like him.

"Some day I hope to meet his parents and we hope to have this thing settled soon.

"Don't worry about us as we are in swell shape to meet any emergency.

"We eat well, sleep well, have some fun and we'll fight well when the chance comes."

(signed)

Capt. Jensen.

"Marty" didn't know that "Bud" doesn't have a father, just his mother, but it shows that his interest in his men is true and deep.

MAY 14, 1942

Mrs. Albert Birdsey calls to say that she had the happiest Mother's day of all when she received a special greeting Sunday from her son, Ernest, who is now in Australia. And there was a special reason for that big armful of roses that held a special place of honor in Etta Dehmlow's window this week. They were her Mother's day remembrance from her son, Larry, who telegraphed the order from his station at Honolulu. And Mrs. Ed Kelbert is happy because long overdue news has been received that her "missing" brother is also in Australia. And Roger Kelsey the producer of these Helzapoppin class plays, phones the information (which he claims from reliable sources) that a number of Minnesota boys, up until now seemingly forgetful with their letter writing to the folks back home, have just landed in Australia.

MAY 21, 1942

A few years back a favorite target for jokes was the radio "ham," the amateur short wave radio operator who sat up till the "wee small hours" calling "C. Q. . . . C. Q." in the effort to strike up radio conversations round the world.

But the war has quieted all those jokes for most of those same "hams" form the nucleus of our communications web that connects our far flung forces. And for those who still remain a ban has been placed on the conversations . . . but they can still listen.

And to one "ham," Sidney Wiese of Los Angeles, Mr. and Mrs. Mike Ormseth of Canby owe a great debt . . . for he brought them great news, the best of all, that their son who had been given up for lost is alive and well. The government had posted him as among the list of probable prisoners of war.

Their son, Russell, who is a brother of Norman Ormseth of Luverne, was one of the gallant band of marines who fought the Japs to the bitter end at Guam.

Nothing has been heard from him since the fall of Guam. Then the other day Wiese was sitting at his set. He was listening to a program staged by the Broadcast Corporation of Japan which was sending several Mother's Day greetings from prisoners of war.

And then the "ham" picked up this message addressed to the Ormseth family:

"Am perfectly well and feeling fine. Have not been injured in any way. Don't worry. Hope to see you in the near future . . . signed . . . Russell."

Wiese wrote immediately to Mr. and Mrs. Ormseth and he said, "not knowing whether anyone in your section would hear this or not so I am trying to relay it to you."

Another "ham," a San Diego woman, also had heard the broadcast and relayed the good news.

Somewhere we read about the way the Japs first broadcast these messages from prisoners of war. For fear the men might slip some important military information into their greetings the Japs first made transcriptions which were later broadcast. People who heard these programs declared that the men sounded exceedingly listless and parents maintained that voices didn't sound natural. It was then discovered that the Japs were playing the records back at too slow a speed.

Some people at first believed the boys had been drugged by the Japs because the voices didn't sound natural. The broadcasting of messages by prisoners of war is just a scheme of the Jap Propaganda ministry to get Americans to listen to their broadcasts.

And speaking of transcriptions—Gordon Hawkinson, who is stationed in New York, has a new wrinkle to save himself the effort of writing letters to his parents, Dr. and Mrs. J. W. Hawkinson. Gordon goes to a studio and has a record made of what he wants to say. He mails it back and his parents play it on the family phonograph.

——— ★ ★ ★ ———

For the sake of the safety of your boy when he writes you that he is soon to leave for a coast port to sail for an "unknown destination" keep that information to yourself until he has landed safely.

Every so often a card comes in from a camp postmaster asking us to change some soldier subscriber's Star to an address in care of the postmaster of New York City, or some other port. To publish or not to publish—that has been the question. Many newspapers have been publishing that information so to clear it up Irid wrote the Office of Censorship and a reply from Nat Howard cleared up the whole matter.

We're always happy to have you send in information of your son, and his activities in the armed forces, but we suggest you use the following yardstick as to when you should give out information:

1. If he has recently been inducted at Fort Snelling and then has been sent to Jefferson Barracks, Mo., let us know. That's appropriate for publications.

2. If for example, he has been at Camp Wolters, Texas, and has been transferred to Camp Croft, S. C., and his address is Co. B., Inf. 34, that is appropriate for publication.

3. If you have received word from your boy that he would like to have mail from his friends and you send in his camp address that is suitable for publication.

4. If he should write that he has now been transferred to Port Angeles, Wash., and expects to leave soon for an unknown destination keep it to yourself. It's not appropriate for publication.

5. If he should be home on furlough and should receive a call telling him to report to New York, or some other center, on a certain date to leave for foreign service . . . then mum's the word. It's not appropriate for publication.

6. If you should receive word that your boy has landed in Ireland, Australia or any other place tell the world about it. It's appropriate for publication.

7. If you should hear that he is leaving by boat for an unknown destination it's not appropriate for publication.

8. If he's stationed at, say Hickam Field in the Hawaiian Islands, such an item is suitable for publication.

———— ★ ★ ★ ————

Youngsters who have been hoping their mothers will ease up on the scrubbing of faces and ears because of a soap shortage have bad news ahead. There won't be any rationing coupons for soap because the industry is going full blast—not to make soap but rather for the by-product of soap, glycerine, which is an important war need. As a result soap stocks are piling up at a terrific rate.

———— ★ ★ ★ ————

One of the stories which will rock the nation's capitol is due to crack wide open any day. An eastern senator, who happens to have an important say-so in naval affairs, has been accused of being connected with a foul dive in Brooklyn where American sailors were prey for pro-enemy agents.

———— ★ ★ ★ ————

Comedians whose secret delight is to slip a vulgar, double meaning, joke into their radio programs are only digging their own financial graves. Even the best of them have been doing it. Bob Hope and Jack Benny slipped over two raw ones a week ago and it's a wonder church organizations who strive to maintain standards of decency in screen and air entertainment haven't made a bitter protest.

———— ★ ★ ★ ————

Recommended as good entertainment is "To the Shores of Tripoli" starting Sunday at the Palace.

———— ★ ★ ★ ————

Be sure to read "Remember Pearl Harbor" in this month's Reader's Digest . . . it's the best account of December 7 yet to appear. Then turn to "America's Enemy No. 2, Yamamoto" and get a chill. The youngsters won't remember but the grown-ups will— "The Frenzied Home Front 1917-1918."

MAY 28, 1942
"MISSING IN ACTION"

And so at last—the first of those dreaded envelopes from the war department bearing the grim news that two Rock county men who unflinchingly faced their inevitable fate at Corregidor must be considered "missing in action."

While the news is bad we all still must have hope and faith that these two men, Leonard Larsen and Frank Lane, are still alive and well. Should the worst come to pass then their parents, Mr. and Mrs. Sven Larsen and Mr. and Mrs. Fred Lane, have the consolation that the brave spirits of their gallant sons will live forever. Because theirs was the type of bravery that will serve to inspire generation after generation of Americans.

Larsen had been in the Philippines for about three years. He had previously been employed there by the Standard Oil Company. Lane, who is only 20, enlisted in the regular army Sept. 11, 1940, and left for the Philippines on Oct. 8 that same year. He was a member of a coast artillery outfit and was located at Ft. Drum, an island in Manilla Bay.

The following is an excerpt from the letters received by the families from the U. S. War department:

"I deeply regret that it is impossible for me to give you more information than is contained in this letter. In the last days before the surrender of Bataan there were casualties which were not reported to the war department. Conceivably, the same is true of the surrender of Corregidor and possibly other islands of the Philippines. The Japanese government has indicated its intention of conforming to the terms of the Geneva Convention with respect to the interchange of information regarding prisoners of war. At some future date this government will receive through Geneva a list of persons who have been taken prisoners of war. Until that time the War department will consider persons serving in the Philippine Islands as 'missing in action' from the date of surrender of Corregidor, May 7, 1942, until definite information to the contrary is received."

The letter was dated May 20, 1942, and was signed by the adjutant general in Washington.

———— ★ ★ ★ ————

The Kodiak bear is one of those animals you'd prefer to meet in the form of a rug rather than "in person." You'll think so when you see the two trophies of a Kodiak bear hunt just sent home by Lt. Col. A. A. Anderson. The big fellow probably weighed anywhere from 1,100 to 1,500 pounds (strictly our own amateur guess) and didn't have a pleasing personality, judging from the ugly face and wicked claws. The smaller pelt is that of a cub . . . but you wouldn't want nothing less than a high-powered rifle even for the little chap. Mrs. Anderson had the trophies taken down to the Luverne National bank for display.

———— ★ ★ ★ ————

Several of our local "sweet young things" who have been bitterly complaining about the shortage of men had a field day Tuesday when the "army" arrived. Or rather, a detachment of about 17 men from Turner Field, Albany, Georgia, who stayed here over night. Where they were going is a secret—and even some of the men declared they hadn't the slightest idea what their destination, or next stop, was to be.

We couldn't help grinning when we noticed several of the girls walking on the "double quick" to get to where the soldiers had parked their trucks. They were determined to show them that "southern hospitality" can't keep up with Luverne's.

But providing the real excitement for everybody was the "jeep" which was the "star" of the show. Nobody paid much attention to the big trucks but they were excited at their first peep at a jeep. Several privates were detailed to watch the equipment and they had their hands full, answering questions. They could have used a few more men to keep the excited youngsters away. We presume they stayed there all night, on guard, but we didn't think we owed it to our readers to make a detailed report on that question.

JUNE 4, 1942

When it comes to family war records you have to go a long way to top that of the Smook family. Back in World War I days there were six Smook brothers all wearing this country's uniform. There was Harm, who saw service overseas; Lee, Otto, John and Joe who were in the army and Jake in the navy. Lee and Joe were wounded in the Battle of Argonne. Six brothers—who fought for this country a quarter century ago.

But the story isn't ended yet. Over at Ellsworth lives their sister, Edna, who is Mrs. Peter DeBoer. She now has four sons in service and by July 1 she will have two more boys putting on the uniform for Uncle Sam, six in all. The boys, John and Jake, are in the navy; Harm and Henry are at Kodiak; Pete is joining the naval reserve as soon as school is out and Hilco expects to go in the selective service call in July. Top that one!

JUNE 11, 1942

Reading the item in last week's CHAFF about Mrs. Peter DeBoer who had six brothers in World War I and who has four sons in service now and two more going prompted a phone call about the claim that Mrs. Jake Wahlert can make.

She has three sons in the army now. Arlo is stationed at San Francisco, John is at Fort Bliss, Texas, and Alfred left Tuesday with the June contingent. Seven other sons and four sons-in-law are registered and are prepared to enter service when called. Five of these sons live in Ohio and one in Minneapolis.

"Who can beat that record," asks the caller.

——— ★ ★ ★ ———

Hardly a military action takes place nowadays that some acquaintance of yours doesn't take part. Word has been received that a Garretson young man, Gerhard Ellefson, son of Mr. and Mrs. Iver Ellefson, was one of the Americans who took part in the bombing expedition of Tokyo. Gerhard is an airplane mechanic and had been overseas since shortly after the war's outbreak.

——— ★ ★ ★ ———

One selective service registrant certainly went the limit in keeping the draft board posted on his change in dependency status.

Arnold Qualley tells of the man with a 3A classification who remembered the ruling that all registrations report to the board any changes in status. This young man phoned long distance from a Sioux Falls hospital to report immediately to the board that he had just become a father.

JUNE 18, 1942

Speaking of the campaign to salvage old rubber reminds us that Louie Cohen was giving most of his service station operator friends a bad case of the jitters Monday.

Louie would call up on the phone, trying to disguise his voice, and ask "are you paying for old rubber." The filling station manager would say "yes."

"Okeh," Louie would say, "I'll bring you over four or five ton and leave it on your driveway."

The service station men had heart failure because they knew Louie was just the kind of a kidder who would think it very funny to dump four or five tons of old tires and rubber on their driveway. It would make more of a mess to clean up than a two foot fall of snow.

———— ★ ★ ★ ————

When you see Al Luethje just ask him how the flag market is today.

Unlike the author of our national anthem, Francis Scott Key, who told how he kept his all night vigil during the gloom of the night to see "if our flag was still there" Luethje knows that his flags are "still there" . . . at Nelson's.

It goes back to the day when Al was making up an order. There was one flag in particular (and not a cheap one either) that he liked real well. He thought he'd gamble and order four of them. Was Al dismayed when the shipment arrived and he found that he'd made a blunder. Instead of writing "4" on the order he had scribbled "four dozen."

July 2, 1942

It has always been my contention that you, as a reader, are not the least interested in the goings and comings—or doings—of any member of The Star. (But in the interest of history we should report that our Master Gabrielson, the "devil" won $25 at bank night a week ago . . . and he has stubbornly resisted all our entreaties for a loan.)

But in the further pursuit of historical fact we should report that McIntosh has now realized one of his frustrated childhood ambitions—namely blowing a train whistle. (The other ambition was to own an electric train—which when we were a boy was much too expensive a proposition for any but the wealthy. Gerry Getman must have shared this same sorrow because two months after "Tommy" was born Gerry got his son a fine electric train for a Christmas present.)

This all started two weeks ago when we were riding on the Chicago bound Zephyr out of St. Paul heading east for the National Editorial Association convention. H. H. Urbach, the mechanical big chief of the Burlington, learned we were on the train and wired the conductor to invite us for old time's sake (having made with him that world's record non stop run on the Zephyr from Denver to Chicago) to ride the cab.

We nearly knocked the startled trainman down rushing up to the "head end," clamboring over the mountain high piles of baggage and threading thru the narrow aisle beside those roaring 1,800 horse power diesels.

We've ridden engine cabs before but the sensation of the Zephyr cab is strangely different. One has the feeling, sitting high in the air above that shovel nosed "cowcatcher," that one is sitting on a front porch rocker while the countryside rusted at you easily and smoothly. Then you look down at the speedometer and see the needle hand bumping against the 95 and 100 mile mark and you say to yourself, "brother, we're really traveling."

Like a bashful youngster, we confessed to the diesel engineer that we'd always wanted to blow a train whistle, particularly that air blasting, deafening, throaty sob of the Zephyr's horn.

"Son," he said, "if that's all you want, grab hold and blow it till you're blue in the face." (And did we blow heck out of that Zephyr horn for two hundred miles, every time we saw a post marked "W" and many times when we only imagined we saw one.) And we'll admit we showed off a bit when we flashed thru a town at a 70-mile an hour "slow" clip.

Blowing the Zephyr horn is more of an art than we first realized. The Burlington wants two long blasts, a quick short, and one final long blast . . . all this to start precisely as you "hit" the whistle post and ending as you roar past the crossing. I'm afraid Mr. Simmons was disgraced and embarrassed by our amateur efforts at first, for all we accomplished was more of a toot like a hiccup.

Well—that's accomplished. Now if anybody has an electric train they'd like to donate—we could lean complacently back and say "what else is there in life to live for?"

We felt guilty on this trip whenever we saw editors scrambling to typewriters to record for posterity their impressions of the beautiful scenery of Quebec province. But we quickly consoled our lazy self with the thought that nobody back home really was interested in a story of our traveling.

Seriously—after 4,000 miles one realizes how little we in the quiet midwest realize the tremendous labor pains this country and our sister nation, Canada, are going thru to produce the materiel needed in this life and death struggle.

There are heartening signs, the big airport where you see Ford bombers parked on the runway . . . and then Willow Run, the biggest plant in the world, which staggers the human mind in attempting to comprehend its scope.

Trains, depots and streets of our cities, and those in Canada, are jammed with men in uniform, all going "somewhere" in a terrific hurry. And America still is best symbolized by lights at night and puffing steam shovels, fulfillment of the promise that this nation would work night and day to produce the stuff in "time" to beat the axis.

We can honestly say that Canada—and we saw close range what she is doing as we toured her war industries plants—is carrying her share of the load and then some. Their slogan there is "THE MEN ARE THERE—NOW—IT'S UP TO US."

The Canadians are doing their job with a minimum of fuss and feathers but they're doing a big job—in a big way.

In Montreal we saw one plant, not a very big one at that, but still it employed 2,200 people, producing "X" amount of guns of just one type alone each month.

We know that total but it shouldn't be printed—but Mr. Axis wouldn't like to be reminded how big it is . . . and how much bigger it grows each month. And when they tell you that each one of those naval anti-aircraft guns, which fires 100 rounds a minute (they call them Chicago pianos) requires the manufacture of 5,000 parts then you realize what a staggering job it is for a nation to get underway.

Dorval, outside Montreal, was one of the tour's highlights. This is where the "ferry command" headquarters is located, where big bombers hot from American factories bounce in to a 90 mile an hour landing, piloted by American civilians. Without waste motion the R.C.A.F.* command takes over, readying the ships for the ocean flight. Long lines of bombers surrounding that field, plus the knowledge that they don't stay there too many hours, thrills one with the realization that here is a production that is beyond the "paper planning" stage.

Every few minutes you see one of those big ships, usually one of those wicked looking four motored "Liberators," the kind the axis hates, roar down the runway. You know it's bound for Newfoundland . . . just a matter of a few hours and it will be heading high above the clouds in the Atlantic crossing.

We were talking at Dorval with a U.S. Marine Corps major who had been assigned to the N.E.A. tour.

He was saying "four times as many men are killed in taking off and landing these big bombers as are lost in combat," when we heard the alarm bell clang and we looked out to see a big bomber crashing nose on and over in its takeoff.

Hardly had the dust settled before ambulances were at the scene and attendants were removing the injured crew.

Dorval is no place for casual visitors . . . "You're lucky to see it," said one Canadian. Visitors were checked in and out, and watched just as carefully as the U.S. mint handles gold bars.

We talked to a ferry command pilot, an American who formerly had an eastern airlines run, the next morning in front of the hotel.

He was slightly sour on the way the English treated the "ferry command" pilots during their brief stay in England. The R.A.F.,** he thought, was snooty.

We later mentioned this to a high Canadian official.

"Well," he said quietly, "let's turn the picture round and see it from the other side. The U.S. civilian pilots are dragging down $1,000 a month for making those crossings—and they're doing a magnificent job. Then they turn the ship over to an R.A.F. pilot who is going to risk his life, and that of his crew, in a raid over enemy territory. That man is drawing about $37.50 a month, not quite a twentieth of what the American gets. Can you see maybe why some of the boys might be a bit chilly?"

* Royal Canadian Air Force
** Royal Air Force

And we had to acknowledge the logic of his answer.

——— ★ ★ ★ ———

(If Hillebrand can set all this in time for the paper, he's a miracle man on the keyboard. And if you don't want this continued in next week's Star you better make your protest known early . . . for it's an easy way for lazy McIntosh to fill up CHAFF. But I would like to tell you a bit more next week about what Canada is doing in war production. It's truly inspiring.)

July 9, 1942

Right now the question of conscription constitutes political dynamite in Canada. A few months ago Canada, by national plebiscite voted in favor of conscription to raise an army. The actual debate on such a measure is now shattering the peace of parliament. The French are bitterly opposed to the provision which would permit the sending of men beyond Canadian boundaries. They say they oppose it in principle altho they maintain their devotion to the cause of the United Nations.

"It may be that we're like some Americans," they say, "who voted dry but drank wet . . . we'll fight conscription as a principle but we'll enlist for a cause."

The average Canadian (non French) tries to smooth it over like this:

"We really don't need conscription to get men for the army. When you consider the littleness of our country from a standpoint of population, when New York City has over half as many people as we have in the entire country, and then see the size of the army we've raised by enlistment we don't think we need conscription. In proportion to population we've raised a bigger army by volunteer methods than you have by conscription in the U. S. As it is we've more men available right now than our camps can train."

Be that as it may the French problem is not so different, (because the memory of the French-British struggle for Canada hasn't been entirely forgotten) than that of our southern soldier boys, mindful of the north's victory, who bitterly resent being assigned to "Yankee" outfits.

But Canada's internal problems are not serious. In a steady stream she is sending men and materiel to the war fronts of the world. And she finds common cause with the United States.

Probably the best illustration of the unity of viewpoint and goal was given us the night on shipboard when the tragic news of Tobruk's fall had been received.

When it came time for the orchestra to close its program it played the Star Spangled Banner. The Americans stood at respectful attention and sang their national anthem. And then the final number was played—"God Save the King."

I looked around the room—here were Canadians singing their anthem while Americans sang the words of "America."

And the thought came to me . . . here is the symbol of two mighty countries . . . they're both singing different words but the melody is the same and the harmony of both groups is truly perfect.

JULY 16, 1942

Probably the most intolerant of all are the "reformed sinners." Take Bill Wendt for instance. Why we can remember when he looked like nothing more than an overstuffed department store Santa Claus. And lately because he has achieved what might be referred to as a svelte figure (secretly we suspect he purchased one of those marvelous rubber reducing girdles before priorities hit) he has been getting unbearably uppity and critical about other people's waist lines.

We tried not to hear when he whistled every time he took a sidewise glance at our "pleasingly plump" waist line. But he's going too far when he starts bellowing across the street, for all the world to hear "if you'd ever fall down you're so fat you'd rock yourself to sleep."

———— ★ ★ ★ ————

Which leads us indirectly to the topic we had in mind. There is one way to reduce in a hurry . . . and that's to get on one of these defense projects. Have you noticed how thin and tired looking some of these chaps are who are supposed to be picking off some of the "easy money." When you talk to them it doesn't sound as rosy as one would imagine.

Take Lawrence Foight, for instance. Lawrence has lost an even 20 pounds since he started as a plumber on that air base job at Sioux Falls.

Even tho he looked miserably hot and tired the other night when he was hurrying home to a late dinner we stopped him and asked him about it.

(We were curious because we knew Lawrence, who a year ago was "pumping gas" for $60 a month, has made as much as $117 a week at Sioux Falls.)

And when we looked at his tired eyes we knew that he was really earning the money—even tho the wage scale seemed exaggerated.

Foight is honest enough with himself to know that such wages can't go on forever . . . but while they do he is doing his best to "lay by a few shekels every month and pay up my bills . . . and if I'm lucky enough to own my own home." When "Sioux Falls is finished" he hopes to move on to a Utah contract.

The fellow who can live in Luverne and work in Sioux Falls is in luck because he doesn't buck the high cost of living.

"The fellows over there," he estimates, "pay about $18 a week for a room, and meals come high because you're hungry when you work hard. One fellow spent $1.40 for a steak supper . . . why that's an hour's work right there."

There isn't any loafing on the Sioux Falls job, says Foight. If they see anybody sitting around they find something right quick for him to do . . . and if he doesn't do that he's canned.

We should point out, in fairness to all concerned, that unlike some of the fellows who have qualified as experts merely because they said so Foight had had years of previous experience as a plumber.

———— ★ ★ ★ ————

Then we talked to Jess Frakes, the contractor who has built so many new homes in Luverne the past three years. Jess is just back from the Rapid City air base job . . . and he's thin and gaunt too.

(Of course having that "Foxy Grampap" look results from the fact that Jess is still minus his upper teeth. And is he mad at the navy. He had those teeth all pulled so that he could get back in . . . now that he had them all yanked the navy revised the regulations . . . he could have gotten by if he hadn't been so impatient.)

Jess got $1.12 1/2 an hour on the Rapid City job . . . but he figures he could have been a lot of money ahead by staying in Luverne and working for 80¢ to $1 an hour wages, even tho his checks out there ran $88.88 a week.

The Rapid City job wasn't a high pay job, as contracts go, says Frakes. It was a non-union project and he doubts if over 300 men on the job got as much as $1.12 1/2 an hour.

Jess is reluctant to talk about the job but one reads between the lines that he thought a great share of the men on the job were men who, in private employment in the "old days," wouldn't have been honestly worth 35¢ an hour. And he evidently doubts some of the inspectors honestly knew what it was all about . . . altho there were a lot of competent, hard hitting, men on the job.

"By the time I got thru paying for living quarters and for food I couldn't figure where I had made as much money as one would think from an $88 check," said Jess.

Ralph "Dutch" Herrmann thinks it's "nice work" at the air base and the one time cafe operator says he hasn't bumped into any "slave drivers." Dutch hopes to follow the defense projects round the country if they take him.

No wonder there's a scarcity of harvest hands when youngsters fresh from the high school classrooms can get common labor jobs at $40 a week.

JULY 30, 1942

Uncle Sam lost one of his most faithful war stamp buyers when little Paul Moeller was tragically killed. Es Connell remembers how proudly Paul was talking Saturday about how many stamps he had purchased—and how many more he hoped to buy.

The accident came at a time when the Moeller's grain had been cut but not shocked. Tuesday night a few friends from Luverne thought they would go out and shock a while. They hadn't hardly arrived when a delegation of Hardwick men arrived. It seemed every time they lifted their heads there was another carload of men arriving.

By the time they all got going, 39 men in all, they went thru that grain field like a cloud of grasshoppers in South Dakota. (In former years.) In fact they did the work so fast that the last four men to arrive didn't have a chance to even pick up a bundle.

And while we're on the subject, orchids are in order for the friends and neighbors who helped the Lawrence Boisen family. Mr. Boisen was ill . . . that was all the word that was needed . . . and help arrived by the carload.

There's no getting around it—Mr. and Mrs. Rock County are the finest people in the world.

———— ★ ★ ★ ————

There's been a rumor going around that ought to be brought up short right now. It was to the effect that Louis Shelby, who is married and has four children, had been given a 1A classification and was to leave with the next selective service contingent.

Several men rushed home and told their wives, "well, if they take Shelby, who isn't any spring chicken and probably was in the other war, anything can happen."

The draft office admits it was a mistake and regrets the error. Shelby's card was filled in as 1A instead of 3A altho the book bore the proper classification.

How did Shelby take it?

"Oh," he said, "I wasn't worried—I figured it was all a mistake so I never went up to see about it." He might have been unconcerned but a lot of other chaps were in a dither.

August 6, 1942

Here's one for the books. The British believe that music speeds up production in war plants. But they've banned the playing of "Deep In the Heart of Texas" over the factory loud speaker systems. It seems that when it came to the hand clapping part the workmen would bang with their hammers on the machinery with the result that several costly machines were badly damaged.

August 13, 1942

A heartbreaking disappointment for a brother and sister occurred recently on the west coast during the visit there of

Mrs. Grant Curry. She has two brothers in the navy. Floyd who is in training, and Albert who was a participant in the Midway and Coral Sea naval engagements.

It was understood that the fleet was returning to its west coast base and every day Mr. and Mrs. Curry drove to a high point where they could look out for miles to sea. But not a glimpse of the big "battle wagons" coming rolling home.

Come the day of departure to Luverne. Just to be sure the Currys drove to their lookout point . . . it was a foggy day but there wasn't a sign of any ships. So they started home. It wasn't an hour later that Albert, knowing that his sister had been visiting in the port city, called. The fog had obscured the Curry's view of the fleet. Albert won't like this in print but they say he was so disappointed that he just about broke down and wept.

AUGUST 27, 1942

Mention of a Luverne boy turns up in the latest issue of the "Kodiak Bear" to come to our desk. Here is the way the army editor prints the story:

M. P. QUESTIONS
PINT-SIZED DOLL,
GETS FOOLED

Sgt. Max Schlader of the Gophers had a good laugh on an M. P. recently as he was coming back to camp from town. While in town the Sergeant had purchased a pint-sized doll for his little daughter.

He tucked the doll under his blouse near his armpit. The M. P. at the guard house began his search and thought he had found something when he noticed the "hump."

"What have you there? A doll?" he asked.

"Sure," Schlader replied, producing a big smile.

He then produced the doll.

The M. P. was speechless.

———— ★ ★ ★ ————

Worth reprinting in part is the satire turned in by an anonymous humorist on The Kodiak Bear staff entitled "What To Do In Case of Sunshine."

In a takeoff on the elaborate instructions issued the folks back home on what to do in a "blackout" the article reads as follows:

"Sometime during July, August or September, designated as the "summer" months, we may anticipate a burst of sunshine on Kodiak Island.

This possibility is confirmed by recent scientific studies, as well as by local legend and inscriptions found on ancient Aleut artifacts.

"If it comes we MUST be ready! The U. S. Navy weather bureau and volunteer observers are maintaining a 24-hour vigil and it is probable that advance warning will be given.

BE PREPARED

"But it may strike with alarming suddenness and catch us completely by surprise. WE MUST BE PREPARED FOR ANY EVENTUALITY.

"The prospect of sunshine NEED NOT be an alarming one. With proper preparation—and more important, WITH A PROPER MENTAL ATTITUDE—it may well prove a harmless and exciting experience.

"In many parts of the world sunshine is a FREQUENT OCCURRENCE and the natives have learned to take it in a matter-of-fact way. In some states of America, such as Florida and California, it has even been turned TO ADVANTAGE by the ingenious inhabitants, and many are the boasts made of its therapeutic values.

THEY'RE ACCLIMATED

"By taking a little at a time, the habitués of certain coastal beach resorts have immunized themselves and FRISK ABOUT FREELY in the brightest sunlight without protection. There are photographs on record showing these hardy people, of both sexes and in various stages of undress, gamboling with evident delight under CLOUDLESS SKIES.

"Here at Kodiak, however, our greatest danger is APATHY."

Then the writer prepares a technical manual on what to do in case a "blue patch in the sky" is noticed.

"Sunshine," he writes, "will be identified by a glaring brightness such as might be made by a 500 watt bulb in a clothes closet or other small room."

The organization of sunshine relief details, the proper emergency treatment for sunburn (coating the skin with bear grease) and the formation of "sunproof shelters" where "men and children come first" are but a few of the laughs furnished by the author.

"Remember," he concludes, "that a basement, if shaded, makes a good temporary refuge—but if sunlight comes we must meet it calmly and coolly. It may come any day, it may never come. But if it does come, ABOVE ALL KEEP YOUR HEAD."

SEPTEMBER 3, 1942

Too late for the "Land, Sea and Air" service men's column arrives the Kodiak Bear with some mention of Rock county boys—including the fact that Sgt. Bernard Eberlien has been made a staff sergeant; that Pvts. Arthur Tangemann, Marbert and Marmon Tunstall have been transferred to another Greely outfit; that Pvt. Emery Lange is now serving with the Quartermasters.

—— ★ ★ ★ ——

You won't want to miss one of the great pictures of the year "Mrs. Miniver" which is coming to the Palace.

—— ★ ★ ★ ——

Waging a one man campaign to see that all the visiting soldiers from Sioux Falls get rides back to the air base in plenty of time Ed Storaker points out that soldiers are expressly forbidden to do any "thumbing." So when you see a soldier standing patiently by the highway, but not making any gesture requesting a ride, remember he wants a lift but doesn't want to break regulations.

—— ★ ★ ★ ——

The luck of the Frakes boys still holds good. If you don't think so read this one.

Dale served two years on the Oklahoma—which was sunk at Pearl Harbor. Before that time Dale had been transferred to the Ingraham—one of the navy's newest and finest destroyers. That was the destroyer lost a week ago. But last June the Magnolia boy had been transferred to the Mervine.

Gordon Frakes, his brother, was assigned to the Sturtevant as his first ship. The Sturtevant was sunk but by that time Gordon had been transferred to another unit of the fleet.

——— ★ ★ ★ ———

They went away as a pair of skylarking, care-free boys, and they came from Kodiak to Luverne as MEN. We're speaking of Merv Denzer and Homer Craig, a pair of doggone good sergeants now on their way to officer's training school.

You can see why the army has recognized their ability and is sending them for the boost up the promotion ladder. They're keen-eyed and hard muscled. You can see what the long dreamed of trip back home meant—and thru their words you can interpret the longing for home of all the men in far away posts. But no one, they say, thinks of coming home until the job is done. When they knew that they were going to be transferred to this country, Merv and Homer said they planned out every minute for the visit back home like a railroad would plan a timetable.

We couldn't help wondering if Major George Fried's ears were burning red hot last Friday afternoon. Because they were talking about George in the floweriest of language.

Here's about the gist of what they said—"there was one fellow that was terribly missed when he left Kodiak. He did a whale of a job there. When he knew he was right he went to bat for the men every time. Sometimes he'd step on a few official toes but it didn't faze him a bit. Yes sir, the boys sure hated to see George leave."

SEPTEMBER 10, 1942

We've just had a ringside seat at one of life's little dramas. Mr. Rucker, The Star foreman who prefers to be known as "Ruck"—(he winces every time somebody discovers his given name is Ellsworth), is a proud grandfather.

Five months ago his daughter, Mrs. Keith Frost of Spirit Lake, Ia., came to make her home here with her parents. Her husband had gone into the army air corps. Keith has recently been in training at Midland Texas as a bombardier.

For the past six weeks it has been a race against time—the question being whether Keith would graduate in time to get home before the arrival of his first born child. The attending physician said he would wager his money that the Stork won the race.

Last Friday the great day came. A telephone call to the office brought "Ruck" to the phone.

Always poker-faced and working harder than ever to act blasé he calmly announced, "an eight and a half pound boy" and went back to his work.

"For land sake's go home and tell your wife," everybody yelled.

"Can't," he drawled, "I've got to pull this proof first."

Just about that same time came a telegram. It was from the just graduated Lt. Frost saying he had won the coveted appointment, handed one member of each class, and would be unable to get leave to come to Luverne.

———— ★ ★ ★ ————

Take a look at the girl on the front cover of the current issue of the Ladies Home Journal and you will see one of the companions of Bob Wildung, or rather Ensign Wildung, on a recent visit in New York.

The girl is Barbara Britton, star of the just issued movie "Wake Island" and she is the "adored" of one of Bob's close friends. Barbara went east, after making the movie, and so Bob and his friend escorted Barbara round the New York spots of interest, and were interested spectators at some of the broadcasts she made over chain radio programs.

Also appearing in the September 10 edition of the Star *was the following announcement under the headline,*

ROCK COUNTY HERALD IS SOLD TO McINTOSH

Purchase of the Rock County Herald by Alan C. McIntosh, publisher of the Rock County Star, was announced in a joint statement issued Wednesday by Mr. McIntosh and Mrs. A.O. Moreaux, representing the executors of the estate of the late A.O. Moreaux, former publisher of the Herald.

There is a gap in the newspaper archive from September 17, when the Rock County Star *became the* Rock County Star-Herald, *through the end of the year. It picks up again with the January 7, 1943, edition of the* Star-Herald.

Rock County
Continuing Rock County's Oldest Business Institution, THURSDAY, SEPTEMBER 2, 1943 —●— 12 Pages, 2 Sections

LUVERNE, ROCK COUNTY, MINNESOTA,

The Rock County Herald, Establis...

No. 49

...ty's Third War Loan Goal

...equired To Check ...riple-A Compliance

Measurements of Fields, Crop Practices Must be Reported To Committeeman

Rock county farmers participating in the 1943 AAA farm program will be required to check their own performance this year, according to Leonard A. Arp, county AAA chairman.

Shortage of labor, tires and gasoline, and the need to reduce expenses of the county association has made it necessary to eliminate the usual practice of county reporters visiting the farms in order to obtain information about the crops and production practices, Arp said.

"This year," he added, "it will be up to the farmer to determine the acreage of each crop grown and the amount of each production practice carried out on the farm. The responsibility depends wholly on the individual, who after he completes his report, will give it to his committeeman at a committee meeting to be announced later. These farm reports must be approved by the committeeman before any payments will be made.

"All farmers cooperating in the program will receive a letter from the AAA office in the near future designating time and place of the meeting in the township in which they reside. They will also receive a work sheet on which they are to fill in their various acreages and the crop practices that they have carried out during the year."

No special method has been set for measuring crop land, Arp declared. He suggested, however, that a simple method would be to check the measurements from the map or photograph of his farm which was used in other years.

...losed ...r Day

...banks and pub... be closed Mon... observance of ...holiday, it was ...week by the Lu... Commerce asso...

...Year-Olds ...in August

...ear-old Rock county ...stered with the selec... board during Au... announced this week. ...were Edwin Eugene ...uverne; Orval Grant ...ills; Joseph William ...agnolia; Burdell Dunref ...Beaver Creek; Donald ...Kruger, Magnolia; Thom... Graves, Sherman; Clar... ...bma, Edgerton; Gene W. ...Beaver Crek and Leroy ...Gonnerman, Luverne.

...he registrant was Clarence ...em, of Kenneth. Lockrem, ...was serving in the army at ...me of the first registration, ...not required to register a... ...time. However, when he was ...narged the past week, he was ...uired to register under the ...ective service act.

...he board also announced two ...norable discharges the past ...eek, Engvald Rote and Dale ...mith, both of Luverne.

...Russell Haakenson, Luverne, ...Lester Glaser, Luverne, Wayne ...Untiedt, Kananzi and Delmar ...Larson, Hills, will leave by bus ...at 8:40 Thursday, Sept. 9, to ...begin their duties with the army.

School to Convene In Beaver Creek Tues.

Pupils in the Beaver Creek public schools will enroll at 9 a. m. Tuesday, Sept. 7, Superintendent N. M. Hoyme states. All positions on the faculty are expected to be filled by that time. He also reported that there would again be bus service, and the busses would use approximately the same routes as were used a year ago.

NOTICE

...an rror in make-up, ...pears over

GRAND CHAMPIONS AT ROCK COUNTY FAIR

SHOWN above are five of the grand championship winners at the Rock County Fair. Lorene Mann, left, was the winner in the baby beef class with her Angus steer. Douglas Swenson had the best draft colt, and Carroll Winkler, extreme right, had the grand champion dairy calf. Kneeling in the front row on the left, is Allison Ordung, with the grand champion fat lamb. He also had the cham... Vernon Brandenburg, grand cham... man and Fred Wiggins, right, h... lon market poultry. Kenneth ... winning breeding poultry exhib... man, who had the grand chan... not present at the time the ph...

ROCK COUNTY STA...

Lorene Mann's Angus Steer ... All Beef Competition At Fa...

Lorene Mann's Angus steer won the coveted grand championship at the Rock County Fair this year in a field where quality outshone quantity. Number of entries in this division was smaller than usual, but the calves shown were all excellent animals.

Winning the reserve championship in this class was Paul Sandager. Verlyn Mann and Virgil Mann, were ranked next in line, and they together with the champion and reserve champion will exhibit their calves at the junior livestock show.

Best Beef Heifer

Marvin Laackmann had the champion beef heifer. Because of the fact that no stock was shown this year at the state fair, no trip was awarded. Reserve champion in this class was Rich... ard Welch.

The two Brandeburg brother... William and Vernon, had t... champion and reserve champi... respectively, in the market b... row class. William will exh... his pig at the junior livest... show.

Francis Crawford with ... Chester White won the ... pionship in the purebred ...

(Continued from Page ...

RURAL SCHOOLS BEGIN TUESDAY

Unless conditions change during the next few days, only three schools will have teacher vacancies in the rural system, according to County Superintendent of Schools Barrett. At the present time, 21 rural schools have decided not to reopen this year. The latest of these is district No. 69, two miles north of Hardwick. Pupils who normally would have attended school in that district will go to Hardwick this year.

Vacancies still exist in districts 10, 25 and 55, the superintendent stated, but every effort is being made to obtain teachers before Tuesday of next week when school will officially open throughout the county.

The roster of teachers as announced Tuesday is as follows:
1 Adeline Schwartz, Ellsworth; 3 Leona Kelly, Luverne; 4W Mrs. Edna Thorson, Luverne; 4E Mrs. Betty Hagemann, Luverne; 6 Edna Brooks, Magnolia; 7 Dorothy Doherty, Magnolia; 9 Mrs.

(Continued on page 6.)

State 4-H Officer

OPAL YACKLEY

As The Star-Herald was going to press, word was received from St. Paul stating that Miss Opal Yackley, county 4-H club member, ...honored by being ...the state

Maximum Price Set On Soft Drinks

...C AN... ...TOP...

A ...
Edith...
ed t...
Com...
dur...
to...
w...
se...
m...

WORTHINGTON C... SELLS PORTION...

1943

"He doesn't make any claim of bravery . . . or having done anything wonderful . . . he immediately made it plain that he wasn't in the first wave of Marines to hit the South Pacific island . . . but that he came long after."

—Al McIntosh

JANUARY 7, 1943

"You ought to start one of those 'rumor clinics' in the Star-Herald to run down and disprove rumors that are obviously untrue," said Ray Ronlund.

He was referring to the story circulated here that "all the boys on Guadalcanal had to eat for Christmas dinner was horse meat."

The loophole that proves the story nothing but a vicious rumor, obviously untrue, is that no letter from any boy in that area written on Christmas day could ever have been received here so soon.

JANUARY 14, 1943

"White Christmas" was a beautiful melody that would have been popular anytime—and "Praise the Lord and Pass the Ammunition" had an infectious swing to it . . . but still this war has yet to produce a song that will come anywhere close in universal popularity to those of World War I.

We were reminded of that at the Legion meeting Monday night when Bill Kemmis, the commander, pitched into the job of leading the singing. Now whether you can sing or not you join in when Bill takes command because he does the job with all the frenzied enthusiasm of a man bailing out a leaky boat in a hurricane.

But not once—during that period of community singing—did any man call for any of the new songs. You know what they asked for—"Smiles," "There's a Long Long Trail"—and all the others of that era.

———— ★ ★ ★ ————

There's an unusual sight to be seen daily down at the farm Dr. F. W. Bofenkamp has in the extreme southeast corner of the county. And to support the story Jullo Visker, who farms the place, has taken a picture in proof of his statements.

A deer feeds all day long in the pasture with the cattle. When the cattle go to the barn at night the young doe follows along. When the last cow enters the barn the doe clicks her heels, in a farewell salute so to speak, hurdles the fence and trots off. But she is right there, bright and early, every morning at the barn to await her bovine playmates.

———— ★ ★ ★ ————

And speaking of Dr. Bofenkamp—how many of you have ever extended an invitation to any of the soldier boys you see almost every day in Luverne to come to your home for dinner? The doctor, on the spur of the moment, invited a couple men because he thought of all days Christmas was loneliest to be away from home, tramping the streets of a strange town, thousands of miles from home.

Did the boys love it? A couple times the boys nearly "choked up" when the conversation veered to "home and mother" but they enjoyed every minute of the stay. One of the boys returned to Luverne, called again for a brief visit. He was so anxious to be "part of the family" that he kept suggesting things he could help do, like taking down the tree trimmings, washing the dishes. That gives you a measure of how lonely some of the boys are, behind their mask of indifference, and how much it would mean to them in the way of happiness if you would extend an invitation to them.

———— ★ ★ ★ ————

Trying to change Arm Carter's mind is as profitable as butting your head against a stone wall.

Arm walked in this week. "I want an airmail subscription to go to Kenneth Olson," he said. Everybody in the office told Arm that such a system was too expensive—that the postage might run as much as $8 a year.

"Doesn't make any difference," retorted Carter, "that's what he wants . . . and that's what he's going to get."

So—in Arm Carter's words—if Kenneth Olson, "somewhere in the Pacific," wants the Star-Herald so badly that is has to go airmail then that's what he's "going to get."

Kenneth is the navy man, you remember, who was wounded on that tragic Sunday in Pearl Harbor and who has seen continuous action ever since in the "hot spots" of trouble all over the Pacific—the naval battles that have made history. He'll have a real story to tell when he gets back.

Arm's eyes fairly sparkle when he talks about Kenneth . . . and you can see that he's proud as punch of the youngster's record.

(Aside to Kenneth—Here's a promise that one of the very first papers off the press every Wednesday night will be wrapped and stamped with your name and address . . . and we hope you enjoy it.)

JANUARY 21, 1943

Folks we don't envy are the members of the rationing boards. Giving uncomplainingly of their time and working without pay or glory they are doing their job because they regard it as a patriotic duty. If it wasn't for that you couldn't coax them into such a headache for all the tea in China.

In a neighboring city several workers cracked under the strain and were taken home in a hysterical condition. I doubt if folks realize that the board members didn't write the rules and regulations which they have taken a solemn oath to conscientiously and fairly administer. Nobody has ever said "thank you" but there have been plenty to heap on abuse.

For example—a letter came from a Mrs. L. B. We won't give her full name or address. It reads as follows:

Sir:

Was just wondering if I ever was going to get my coupon for my washing machine and iron. 1 gallon a month for my iron and 2 gallons a month for my washing machine. Here you guys sit & me scrubbing clothes for 4 on a board, when there are two kids under 2 years of age. Sure would like to see you fellows do it.

MRS. L. B.

P. S.—Had my order in before Christmas and haven't got my coupons yet where my sister has come along & got for her iron got here a long time ago. Don't have to think use are going to jep me out of it like with the canning sugar. Put in for 50 pounds and got two lbs. that's prety dam good. Didn't get the two lb Didn't nead 2 lb that bad and never got it.

(Operator's note to proofreaders—Don't blame me or start correcting this copy—it's set exactly "as was.")*

———— ★ ★ ★ ————

IN THE MAIL BAG

"In a few days," writes Capt. Ray Frick from Kodiak, "we will celebrate our second anniversary—that's a heck of a long time to be away from home and the ones you love."

Ray writes that outside of it "being lonesome and boring all is well, skating is at its best."

"My outfit," continues Ray, "(Worthington originally) is out

---

* Al McIntosh's orginal note

sweeping everything before them, a darn good hockey team. They trimmed Luverne 9-0 and they have scored 30 points to our opponents 2. They were equally good in all other sports and duties. A swell bunch of young men and they are eager to take a crack at our enemies, and if we are ever called on you can rest assured they will come thru with flying colors. We are aching for a change of scenery, Africa, Hawaii, or any place where we can carry the battle to the enemy.

"The war news sounds good, and many of the boys, one time members of our unit are now in Africa."

JANUARY 28, 1943

We've always twitted Irid with the accusation that a Norwegian could make a Scotchman look like a piker on amateur night when it came to thriftiness.

(Don't misunderstand us, we're not, in these days of rising publication costs, poking fun of any economies Irid can discover.)

But the thriftly little soul over reached himself last week and plopped us into a kettle of hot water.

When it came time last week to wrap up the single copies to be chunked in the mail sacks Irid spied a pile of old circulation expiration letters.

"No sense in letting that perfectly good paper go to waste," he probably mused, "I'll just use those to wrap the newspapers instead of cutting up any clean newsprint."

It was a great idea . . . and we never even knew about it . . . till a few letters started rolling in from bewildered subscribers, all of them like all other Star-Herald subscribers, paid in advance. The sum and substance of the letters, resulting from Irid's thrift move, was "how come I get a 'third' notice that my subscription is expiring when I am paid in advance."

After this Irid is going to cut up newsprint for his "single wraps."

————— ★ ★ ★ —————

Speaking of mailing of the Star-Heralds—we probably average at least a call a day asking "do the newspapers get thru to the boys overseas?" We say "yes—altho they may not come in sequence, they may get January papers before they get all of their December copies but eventually the mail goes thru. "(As a matter of fact we have had more trouble with the mailings going to one Oklahoma camp than we have had with all the other camps and overseas mailings combined.)

First to tell us about the fact that single copies sent to soldiers, unless they were bona fide subscriptions from newspaper offices, were forbidden was Irvin Staeffler. This information, also confirmed by Mrs. Frank Frakes, was officially brought to our attention by Gerrit DeVries of the postoffice staff.

From now on individual copies of newspapers will be accepted for dispatch "only where subscriptions are specifically requested in writing by the addressee or for subscriptions which are now in effect." Any boy now taking the Star-Herald need not send a request for it but any new subscribers with APO numbers must write his parents, who should bring his letter in to us, or he may direct his letter to us. Letters are kept in the Star-Herald office. Now each APO number subscription must have stamped on the wrapper "mailed in conformity with POD Order No. 19687." The ruling does not apply to navy, marine corps or coast guard personnel.

And don't ask us as one chap did, after the postoffice turned down his bundle of assorted papers and magazines for overseas mailing, to handle mail for you.

Few people understand what a terrible problem it is getting mail to the men in the service and why the mail goes "higglety-pigglety." Soldiers write back that they haven't received mail in "weeks" and then the home folks get upset. Then, the next day, the soldier is apt to get a bunch of 30 or 40 letters in one batch.

It is estimated that the army alone is now handling about 20,000,000 pieces of overseas mail a week. That is a huge volume of mail and it is competing with valuable cargo space, intended for munitions and supplies.

Most mail ships sail only in convoys and sometimes it takes weeks to assemble a convoy.

Poorly addressed mail retards delivery (and the APO number is most important of all) and it is estimated that 10 percent of all mail is incorrectly addressed.

The volume of army mail right now is THREE TIMES what it was at the close of World War I when twice as many men were overseas. If the volume of mail keeps pace with the growing size of the AEF, it is said that 25 11,000 ton liberty ships would be required to do nothing but carry mail.

Why is mail delayed? Remember it piles up at the ports of embarkation for probably as long as six to nine weeks, or your boy may have been transferred to a new post and he is always just one ahead of his mail. There is always a possibility that a ship carrying mail has been sunk, sometimes as much as 100,000 pounds of mail has gone down in just one ship sinking—that's a lot of letters and packages. Then the mail has to be censored.

Now that V mail is growing in popularity the mail problem will be lightened. That is where your letter is photographed on film, developed and printed on arrival. It is never lost because the original letter is not destroyed till the films arrive. A thousand ordinary letters weigh 22 pounds while 1,000 V mail letters weigh only four ounces. Quite a saving in shipping space.

The government realizes that nothing means so much to the man overseas as mail from "home" and is doing everything possible to see that the mail gets thru as safely and speedily as possible. Most of us don't appreciate the staggering problem presented by these mountains of mail at embarkation ports. That is why we felt a little explanation might be in order as to what might delay your mail after it leaves here.

———— ★ ★ ★ ————

One of the fondest memories of show business is that of George Cohan in "I'd Rather Be Right." Disregarding for a few minutes the lines of the play the elderly showman broke into some fast and furious "hoofing" and acrobatics just to prove good naturedly to the wildly applauding New York audience that the "old man was just as good as he used to be."

"Yankee Doodle Dandy," starting Sunday at the Palace, deals with the life of the showman who wrote the never to be forgotten "Over There." You won't want to miss it for it's a great show about a great man, a show that the whole family will enjoy.

FEBRUARY 4, 1943

Into the Star-Herald office this week came Ensign Robert Haakenson looking very fit (and we presume very fascinating to the feminine eye) in his resplendent new uniform.

He may have learned a lot about the navy during his intensive three months training but he certainly hasn't lost his sense of humor for he tells a good one on himself.

Graduation day—just an hour after he had received his coveted commission Bob had occasion to go over to one of the dormitories looking for an officer friend. As he entered the dorm the midshipmen, noting his rank, sprang to attention and Bob was highly delighted with all the goings-on. There was much snappy saluting and very nautical "carrys-on" from Robert. The midshipmen, needless to say, were greatly impressed. It developed that Bob's friend was absent so one midshipman courteously inquired "who shall I tell him called, sir?"

Absent mindedly the one hour old ensign replied "Midshipman Haakenson." Bob is still blushing because he imagines he can still hear the howls of laughter that followed him as he beat an abashed retreat out the door.

We have no illusions that he is due to become an admiral within a matter of months but it's understatement to say "he'll get along." (Understand we're not poking fun at this young man—because he personifies the high type of manhood that carries the navy to the heights of supreme glory it achieves. But you can't beat fun.)

His friends at Augustana college, where he was as busy in collegiate activities as a "one man band" knew he used to sit up late at night racking his fertile brain figuring out ways to coin a "fast nickel." We wouldn't have been surprised if he had figured out a way to install parking meters in Sioux Falls and then lease them back to the city.

A couple years ago Bob called up and said he wanted some homecoming football game booklets printed—and he wanted them in just about 24 hours. It was Wednesday night and we found he didn't have half the copy written, half the ads weren't sold so we tried to discourage him. We agreed to print them only if he showed up by 10 a.m. the next morning with his copy and ads complete and bring over 100 pounds of paper stock needed to print the job. We actually were counting on the fact that it was impossible. The back shop crew knew the job would be "rough" and they actually grinned with relief when 10 a.m. Thursday rolled around and no Haakenson.

But they didn't know the lad. At 10:15, out of a heavy cloudburst, appeared Bob and his partner, Gene Leland, lugging the 100 pound box of paper. Their car had quit in the rain and they had had to hitchhike in from Beaver Creek in the cloudburst. The back shop boys did their part . . . and Haakenson and Leland departed Friday, mentally rubbing their hands over the great profits they expected to make on the venture. They were still squabbling over whether to charge a nickel or a dime for the booklets.

Came the big night—Haakenson, Leland, the promoters, assisted by a dozen or so less visionary youths started selling the booklets—like the proverbial hotcakes.

Along strolled the dean—he was dumfounded that the students had gone into the program venture as a private profit making enterprise—so he confiscated them all. And to add further grief to the promoters he made them give away free all the programs.

(P. S. The college paid the printing bill but Haakenson was out his rosy dreams.)

No sir—you don't need to worry about Ensign Haakenson . . . he'll "carry the mail" wherever he goes.

———— ★ ★ ★ ————

Maybe we're mellowing with age but did anybody note that we got thru the eastern coal mines strike without writing a fire and brimstone editorial? While we mention that kind of editorial we really should have written one about the two Worthington young men who poured gasoline over a pup and set it afire. They thought it was very funny at the time when the dog, howling in anguish, ran away like a "ball of fire."

Or maybe we should write about the man who walked into a business establishment here (jingling a little extra cash as a result of conditions) and who said he'd "done so well" he wished "the war would last 10 years." On second thought, the mother of some boy in service, whose thoughts keep constantly turning in prayer for his safety, should write that editorial.

——— ★ ★ ★ ———

And speaking of prayer—we have nothing but contempt for the authors of the anonymous chain post card racket which is trying to frighten people into prayer. One such card, mailed at Minneapolis—and of course unsigned, was received by Betty Muilenburg. It is not understatement to say that Betty was greatly upset about it.

The card demands a prayer for the nation and that the recipient immediately write a similar prayer to "13 in 13 days."

"A lady once made fun of this and in 13 days her daughter went blind, don't let this prayer die in your home."

To test our own reaction we asked a local clergyman in whose opinions we place great reliance.

"A lot of superstition . . . it's too bad people are built that way," he said.

And then here's the way Rev. David J. Eastburn sized it up:

"Prayer should instill reverence in the heart of the person who is offering the prayer—the prayer should come from the heart.

"In this card the prayer is not as important as the incident that followed—namely the fact that someone was supposed to have gone blind—that established fear and not reverence as the motive for prayer.

"There is a psychological factor established in the mind of the person who receives the card—all their real and imaginary sins flash before their mind like a motion picture—and they become greatly upset."

Rev. Eastburn said it was regrettable that some people tried to put fear into the lives of people rather than love.

February 11, 1943

That isn't a Florida suntan that Frank Michael's been wearing lately—it's none other than an old fashioned "blush" of the firewagon red variety.

This dates back to the home guard meeting recently when Capt. E. J. Seiler, public relation officer for the Sioux Falls air base, was to be the guest of honor.

Like a fourth grade school teacher getting her pupils ready for a visit "from the superintendent" and as busy as a clucking mother hen, Capt. Michael had been giving his company a last minute "cram session" on the proper military due to the air base official. The command "attention" was to be the signal that the captain was arriving and every member of the company was to become a statue for the time being.

Ivan Hansen was right in the middle of a lecture on military etiquette when one of the watchers that Michael had posted shouted the warning that the GREAT MAN WAS ARRIVING.

"Tenshun," snapped the captain. Capt. Seiler walked in, was met with all due ceremony and escorted to the platform. Capt. Michael very ceremoniously pointed out a chair and invited Capt. Seiler to be seated.

This Capt. Seiler did—for one thousandth of a second . . . before the defective chair crashed to pieces precipitating him to the floor. It would have taken a military Emily Post to have satisfactorily glossed over that scene—Capt. Seiler, the guest of honor—sprawling on his back on the floor amidst the wreckage of the chair while Capt. Michael looked on in mortified horror.

FEBRUARY 18, 1943

There's no doubt that Ray Burg is on the job as a real air raid warden at Kenneth. And when Ray is in doubt he signals for a blackout.

A few weeks ago Julius Brown and "Shorty" Busch were phoning the county air raid wardens on a "white test." (Checking to see if the calls were going thru okay.) Burg wasn't quite sure what that "white test" signal meant so he gave the signal for a complete blackout at Kenneth.

Then he called back to county headquarters. "Say," he asked, "are we supposed to have a blackout."

Julius said "no—it's just a white test."

"Well," replied Burg, "we've been blacked out in Kenneth for 10 minutes."

Local officials agree that Burg has the right system—when there's any doubt just order a blackout and don't take chances.

———— ★ ★ ★ ————

Don't miss "Minnesota's Blitz Producer" in this week's Saturday Evening Post. It's as exciting as a mystery thriller, this account of the way J. B. Hawley Jr. "does things" for the navy in producing big gun mounts. Just to give you an example—when it came time for a big expansion of the plant Hawley was told that it would take 90 days alone to get the plans.

"Ninety," he roared, "I'll have it built and running in 60." And he did.

———— ★ ★ ★ ————

And for good, hilarious, entertainment, "Palm Beach Story," starting at the Palace Sunday, won't disappoint you.

MARCH 4, 1943

Probably one of the most unusual addresses we've seen for any army or navy man is the one that came in the other day for Bob Wildung. Here it is: Ensign Robert Wildung, Project Brass Hat, Fleet Post Office, San Francisco, Cal.

Ensign Wildung, who had been pretty sick with fever for a few days, is back at his regular job as disbursing officer for his post.

———— ★ ★ ★ ————

You can always figure on Luverne's blackouts providing at least one tiny "wisp" of news for this column.

We don't know what Mrs. Glenn Adams said but it might have been "Tain't funny McKay." And O. T. McKay probably tore his hair and yelled, afterwards, "why doesn't somebody tell me these things."

It all concerns the ambulance run that has to be made as part of the blackout test in which a simulated "casualty" is given first aid and then taken to the hospital.

Mrs. Adams was supposed to provide the "victim" and do the emergency first aid. None of the boys were willing to "play dead" because there was a basketball game. But Arline Hansen agreeably volunteered. So when the blackout signals rang the Red Cross aide and the victim started to get ready. Arline was wrapped in splints and yards and yards of bandage . . . then they waited for the ambulance and it wasn't pleasant—lying there wrapped up like an Egyptian mummy.

Officer McKay got the call to take the ambulance to such an' such an address, drove up, waved, grinned that cheery Scotch smile of his and trundled the ambulance back down town despite the vociferous protests of Mrs. Adams.

The attendants at the hospital were waiting to give lightning fast service to the "victim" who never appeared. "Mac" felt pretty bad about the whole affair, maintaining that was the first he had ever known that he was supposed to take anybody to the hospital.

MARCH 11, 1943

We happened to run across a file of correspondence in Ray Engan's office which you might find interesting. Other than pointing out that the attorney is Red Cross home service chairman for this county we will let the correspondence speak for itself:

Ft. Leavenworth, Kan.

To Ray Engan:

"Mrs. Earl Cortright reported sick in Luverne hospital. Home town is Kenneth. Does doctor state wife's condition demands soldier's presence. Rush reply Western Union."

—Ralph Philip, field director

To Field Director, American Red Cross, Ft. Leavenworth, Kan:

"Retel—Earl Cortright. Doctor Sherman reports baby boy born Dec. 26. Mother and son reported in satisfactoy condition. Shouldn't any proud father of a new baby boy have a furlough? On that basis furlough recommended."

—R. C. Engan, home service
chairman

Ft. Leavenworth, Kan.

To R. C. Engan:

"Retel—Earl Cortright—Duly proud excited parent starting 10 day furlough today."

—Ralph Philip, field director

And then came a letter to the local service chairman from J. O. Wiek, assistant field director of the Red Cross, which said:

"Your response to our Dec. 29 telegram concerning Earl Cortright was very prompt and pleasing. In fact, we have chuckled many times over your reply and submit that we have been looking for such a reply from someone all the past year. The question you raised was certainly very aptly put. We were more than pleased to reply in kind when we gave notice that the soldier was leaving on a 10 day furlough. We know that the quality of your service will not be diminished during this New Year which we hope brings many satisfying experiences to you."

Well, that explains how Earl Cortright obtained a furlough to see his young son. It is probably one of the happier experiences of the past year of the home service chairman—some of the requests have not been for such joyous events—but for serious illness or death of loved ones back home.

But in itself it highlights just one, just one, mind you, of the phases of the great, humanitarian work that the Red Cross is carrying on all around the globe today—at home, on the battle-front, serving to get messages out of prison camps or occupied countries. Never before in history did your Red Cross membership purchase so much in service to humanity as it does this year.

There is a Red Cross membership drive on right now—all the county banks are depositories for your contributions. Nobody needs to "sell" the Red Cross. We know, with your wonderful record for generosity, no more need be said.

March 18, 1943

May we explain why a number of the pictures appearing in the "Land, Sea and Air" column are of the half column or "thumb nail" size cut. From now on no new cuts will be made full column width. This results from an order of the engravers who are trying to conserve dwindling supplies of zinc—used in making newspaper cuts.

We are just as anxious as ever to run pictures of men in the service, for which there is no charge of course, but we are asking your cooperation because we will have to have the best pictures possible. With the smaller cut pictures of poor pictorial quality will not show up. Send us large snapshots taken close up, where the face isn't obscured by deep shadows.

———— ★ ★ ★ ————

One bit of red tape regarding subscriptions for service men overseas has been eliminated. Wes Winkler called our attention to a new postoffice regulation which says that the war department's ruling on newspapers has been revised. It will no longer be necessary for a soldier, overseas, to get a request for renewal okehed by his commanding officer before the subscription can be continued. The regulation still holds, tho, that no new subscriptions can be added for overseas service men until approval has been given by the commanding officer.

———— ★ ★ ★ ————

Help arm the soldiers from your town by saving tin cans. Tin is needed in all types of war equipment.

MARCH 25, 1943
"IT'S A SMALL WORLD AFTER ALL!"

When Corp. Russell Blinsmon, son of Mrs. Lena Blinsmon of Luverne, traveled more than 10,000 miles from home to land in India one of the very first persons he bumped into was Sgt. James Mitchell, radio operator on a bomber, also from Luverne.

Corp. Blinsmon left this country shortly after Jan. 1 and relatives were beginning to become deeply worried when nine weeks elapsed before word from him was received. His first letter, written Feb. 24, arrived here March 13. Blinsmon wrote that the trip to India wasn't "so bad" because two other Rock county young men, Arnie Aanenson and William Wiese, were on the same ship.

———— ★ ★ ★ ————

And also in the "it's a small world" category was the story told when he was home by Lt. (jg) Milton Olson. Olson, formerly in the TVA engineering department in Tennessee, went into the company commissary for lunch one day. He happened to sit down at a table with two men, one of them a slight acquaintance.

This chap said to Olson, "Ray here," pointing to his companion, "is a Minnesotan too . . . you fellows ought to get together."

"What's your home town?" asked Olson.

"Luverne," replied the stranger.

"Why, that's mine," replied Olson.

The "Ray" turned out to be none other than Ray Campbell, brother of Paul Campbell, who is with the legal department of TVA at Chatanooga, Tenn.

———— ★ ★ ★ ————

And speaking of the Campbell family—Mrs. Edward Ward of Rolfe, Ia. was in last week to say how much her husband fretted if the Star-Herald happened to be late. She blames it on the mail man there and says "There never was a mail carrier that carried the mail half as well as Paul Campbell . . . we wish we had him down there."

———— ★ ★ ★ ————

Leave it to "Bud" Sherman to cast gloom into the camp of those who love sweet corn.

"What good will sweet corn be this summer since they've rationed butter . . . sweet corn isn't right unless you've got plenty of butter."

But Max Voelz is still going right ahead with his sweet corn planting plans—butter rationing or not.

We'll make two predictions—just to see how far we miss it:

The Americans and British will have pushed the Axis out of Tunisia before May 12 and Italy will be out of the war by August 17.

April 1, 1943

To the man who inquired last week if those trucker's record books required by the ODT were in—the parcel post man brought them just three minutes after you had left.

———— ★ ★ ★ ————

It's too long a story to tell but Cliff Millard and Ivan Hansen have been "feuding" lately. Latest episode was Cliff's hanging a large sign, "Ivan Hansen—Notary Public" on the Hansen home Saturday night. The attorney didn't notice it till late Sunday. Then it came down in a hurry.

———— ★ ★ ★ ————

Irid, who has taken quite a bit of ribbing from farmers after his recent "steel bin" story offers the following in rebuttal:

Leave it to Commodity Credit Corporation to supply you with a news story every week.

Three weeks ago we had an article stating that corn stored in government steel bins could be bought by farmers, but the amount to each farmer would be limited to a 30 day supply. The next week, they changed their minds and decided that a seven day supply was all that a farmer could buy at one time, so we had a story on that. The next week, they changed it back to a 30 day supply, and this week, the local office received a wire from the state AAA office stating DON'T SELL STORED CORN AT ALL.

Leonard Arp explains that the changes from week to week are made to keep the corn moving into feeding channels at a fairly even rate, thereby preventing undue market fluctuations and also to prevent the commodity credit corn from competing with the regular commercial market.

———— ★ ★ ★ ————

One of E. A. Drake's ewes must have been reading the "food for freedom" publicity. The ewe had two lambs and then eight days later presented Drake with two more. He had a struggle to keep the first two alive and bottle fed them for a few days but they're all alive and healthy now.

———— ★ ★ ★ ————

Dr. C. H. Haggard indignantly denies that he is like the Scotchman who invited his wife out for dinner and then locked the door on her from the outside. But it is the truth that Mrs. Haggard did several more hours Red Cross work than she expected to recently.

It all started when Mrs. Haggard was the last to leave the Red Cross sewing rooms in the library basement. When she went to the door Mrs. Haggard found it locked. (Mrs. Main, thinking that everybody had gone, had locked the doors.) So there Mrs. Haggard had to stay until Mrs. Main reopened the library at 7:30 p.m. Because it was Saturday night and Doc usually eats with Lloyd Long, after the auction, Haggard never knew that his wife was "missing."

———— ★ ★ ★ ————

What is this younger generation coming to? The other night we saw Keith Connell and Dave Butler drinking the weirdest combination yet—a handful of salted peanuts poured into their Coca Cola bottles. And Willie Oltmans instead of taking his girl for a ride on his bicycle calmly climbed on the handlebars and let the girl do all the work.

———— ★ ★ ★ ————

The marines and soldiers fighting the Japs have appealed to the folks back home for knives, not "penknives" but "pigstickers."

Ed Hillebrand was exhibiting the one made by his father. Made out of saw steel, long, wicked and curved, and with a deer horn fitted for a handle, it should be highly prized by the jungle fighters. If any of you with mechanical ability, want to volunteer to make the type of knives needed the Star-Herald will pay all costs of seeing they get to their destination.

APRIL 8, 1943

Minnesota isn't going to let butter (the mainstay of this state's agricultural prosperity) be elbowed aside without a struggle—rationing or no rationing. One grocery store reported that state inspectors had ordered him to cease selling or displaying a featured "butter stretcher."

APRIL 15, 1943

How observing are you? We wonder how many noticed the picture of a Luverne man on that big two-color, wall poster sent out by the Treasury Department entitled "What Did You Do Today for Your Country" in the appeal. "Buy More War Bonds." The picture, and it was a good one too, was that of Major George Fried, stationed at Fort Snelling.

—— ★ ★ ★ ——

Mr. and Mrs. Normas Steine have proved the truth of that biblical quotation that runs something like this: "Cast thy bread upon the waters for thou shall find it after many days."

They have entertained soldiers from the Sioux Falls air base from time to time but one apparently was more appreciative of the hospitality. He wrote his mother who lives in Vermont about the Steine's kindness. The other day Mrs. Steine received a letter from the Vermont mother expressing her appreciation of the Luverne couple's hospitality. In her letter she admitted she didn't know much about Minnesota conditions but that there evidently was a real shortage of sugar, so "maybe a half-gallon of pure Vermont maple syrup will come in handy." Mr. and Mrs. Steine are now enjoying the finest maple syrup they've ever tasted in their lives.

Note: The article below also appeared in the April 15, 1943, edition of the Star-Herald.

WAR BONDS

(An Editorial)

This is an appeal to Rock county citizens to meet that $300,000 War Bond quota for the April drive.

It's not an editorial based on emotionalism, in connection with the daily sacrifices being made by men in the service, neither is it one dealing in facts and figures, as to why purchase of War Bonds will help drain off surplus, idle money and help prevent inflation.

It's just a plain, everyday, matter of fact appeal based on common sense.

We Read an advertisement the other day which has a headline which carried a jolt for the complacent—"They're Working Overtime in Tokyo, Too."

It points up, better than a column of words, the trap into which we Americans have complacently fallen—a feeling of cocksureness about victory. Instead of doing everything possible during every waking moment to insure victory some of us have alloed ourselves to waste too much time trying to guess the end of the conflict. Such an attitude is a pure and simple death trap . . . because there is no guarantee of victory in war.

The men at the front see the war too close to cherish any illusions that the road will be short . . . . or easy.

Such a statement isn't defeatism—it's realism. Let's just quote from an airmail letter received yesterday morning from one of Rock county's navy veterans who has been in the Pacific battle area for a long time.

"Al," he wrote, "this deal is a long, long ways from being over. Something should happen to make people realize that. They pick up the papers and see everything going our way. They just don't realize how vast and uncertain this whole war is. It is entirely possible that either or both coasts could be attacked. I wish I could talk and then I'd say plenty."

Now will you loan Uncle Sam some money to furnish this chap . . . and millions more like him . . . the money to buy the implements to fight with?

Buying bonds is the one thing we can do on the home front to help insure this victory . . . because after all those War Bonds are our Insurance Policies of Freedom.

Don't get the idea that because you're subscribing to War Bonds that you're "donating" to the government. You're just lending your dollars while others GIVE their lives. You're going to get your money back . . . with interest . . . while some of those men will never come back.

Buying bonds isn't an obligation but a privilege.

April 29, 1943

He used to be one of those light hearted, laughing youngsters that was always cutting didoes with his car (the kind of a kid you sometimes shook your fist at because of his highway antics.) And his car fairly groaned under the added weight of extra horns and the signs and lights made it look like a carnival midway.

It had probably been 10 months since I had seen him . . . but because he was a Pipestone lad I hadn't particularly been aware that he had been gone until he walked in the office wearing the dark green of a U. S. Marine Corps private.

"Hello," we said, "where did you come from."

And his low voiced, matter of fact, one word answer accounted for that drawn, haggard and prematurely aged appearance.

"Guadalcanal," he replied.

It was Private Virgil Meeker, well known here, who enlisted August 13, 1942.

He doesn't make any claim of bravery . . . or having done anything wonderful . . . he immediately made it plain that he wasn't in the first wave of Marines to hit the South Pacific island . . . but that he came long after.

He "caught it twice" but he thinks he is "lucky, very lucky" and his biggest worry, next to whether or not the doctors will reverse their decision and let him return to combat duty again, is how much gas the ration board is going to allow him for his car during leave.

The "first time" was when a Japanese night bomber dropped a load over their camp . . . on a nameless island. He and his four companions weren't in their fox holes but in a tent and the bomb concussion flopped them around like fish out of water. The concussion injured his lungs . . . but the climax came later when (he was a photographer's helper on a Liberator bomber) a Jap anti-aircraft shell hit their plane. Shell fragments severely wounded Meeker in the chest. Where, or how, he was taken for recovery shouldn't be said but the British are wonderful, and "particularly the New Zealanders."

"Those New Zealanders," he said, "I've never met finer people . . . they'll rob themselves to give you a good time."

———— ★ ★ ★ ————

Strange as it may seem, one of the best places to trust a secret is a newspaper office. The Tokyo "blitz" story was more or less generally known by newspapermen throughout the country for a long time.

The story was held back by the U. S. for propaganda purposes until the anniversary of General Doolittle's daring raid. All the press associations knew it and the Associated Press is still gnashing its teeth because the United Press man in North Africa was wily enough to "break" it through a friendly censor there. All over America newspaper offices in dozens of cities had "hold for release" stories that had been told reporters months before by participants in the raid.

MAY 6, 1943

We wonder if the members of the Palisade Lutheran church realize how particularly fortunate they are to have a dynamic, intensely human man for their pastor as Rev. E. W. Rossing.

It was a case of backward, turn backward, oh time in thy flight, make me a child again just for tonight . . . "I was Irid's son" at the annual Father and Son banquet held at that church last Friday night.

It was a refreshing experience—in that beautiful church, built on a windswept hill, overlooking the peaceful, clean, green, countryside for miles around.

There was a sincerity of feeling there that one finds missing in other churches too many times. And when it came time, after the dishes were being cleared away for the program, we defy any church anywhere to put on a better program.

There were a lot of names mentioned that night . . . because the Honor Roll upstairs in the church vestibule is a long and proud one. And on the church's service flag there is a solitary gold star that stands out with somber dignity among the cluster of blue stars—the star for Austin Rollag, who died fighting for his country at Guadalcanal. And from this congregation came Merle Larson, Rock county's ace flier who has won everlasting glory for himself in North Africa. A five-time ace today—yet one of the speakers remembered Merle as a boy who wasn't "big enough to play with the rest of us yet today he's fighting our battles."

And as Iver Henjum said, "boys in this church, like all American boys, know that it is possible that they could be elected President of the United States—where boys in dictator countries can look ahead to nothing more than 'just growing up.'"

It was good to visit this church—because you could feel and hear the resolute heart beat of an America because from farms and churches like these come the men and boys who make America great.

MAY 13, 1943

On March 25 the following appeared in Chaff, if you remember:

"The Americans and British will have pushed the Axis out of Tunisia before May 12."

And from "Analyzing the War News" by Glenn Babb in the Argus-Leader on May 10 appeared the following:

"The task of clearing the Tunisian springboard, preliminary to the invasion of Hitler's Europe is as good as done."

———— ★ ★ ★ ————

Little do we realize it now but the North African campaign of General Montgomery will go down in history as one of the greatest military campaigns in all history.

We should read all we possibly can about this man and this campaign because it will fill many a page in the history books a hundred years from now.

We like best the story of Montgomery, one of the last men to leave the beach at Dunquerque, who sat there on the beach coolly building sand castles. No he wasn't crazy—he was trying to inspire panicky men by demonstrating his utter contempt and lack of fear for the hell that was raining down on them in the form of bombs and shells.

And one of the finest pictures of all time, and I want to see it again, is "Desert Victory," which records the start of the big push to roll the Axis out of Egypt. A documentary film taken by the British, it cost many cameramen, killed, wounded and captured.

It's grim—but it's history, and you'll sit on the edge of the seat in breathless suspense.

The Palace plays it next week (remember the dates), Thursday, Friday and Saturday.

———— ★ ★ ★ ————

You can always count on a blackout (especially if it's a dull news week) to furnish at least one paragraph for this hodge podge column.

But we are sadly forced to report that one of our most distinguished air raid wardens was not at his post when the blackout took place.

Kay Aanenson was stopped by some vigilant air raid wardens south of Luverne as he dashed madly into town with his headlights stabbing through the inky blackness.

"Turn out those lights," they screamed.

"Can't," stuttered Kay, "have to get to my post."

"That's just too bad," they retorted, "park your car and run for it." And Kay did.

He stoutly denies that he was at his usual "headquarters" south of Luverne and claims he was visiting relatives. But nobody pretends to believe him.

MAY 20, 1943

The Government evidently just can't take kidding so the radio comedians are going to be up against it when it comes to making any further wisecracks about food rationing. The radio gags are irritating to thin skinned officials who are demanding a "freeze" on ration gags.

———— ★ ★ ★ ————

We'd say that Louis Jansma of Jasper would make an above average newspaperman for he knows what is news. Louis called to tell us that Raymond Boettcher returned home on leave just two years to the day from the time he left. Boettcher used to live north of Beaver Creek but his home is now southwest of Jasper.

In that two years in the navy the former Beaver Creek boy has packed in a lifetime of experiences. He is one of the survivors of the ill fated "Hornet," the big aircraft carrier that went down in the Pacific.

Boettcher, says Jansma, isn't too talkative about his experiences but he did say he didn't "like swimming in oil very well."

JUNE 3, 1943
HOW TIMES HAVE CHANGED!

It was but three years ago that an item about a girl driving a farm tractor was big enough news that the city dailies ran pictures of Anne Nelson, daughter of Mr. and Mrs. Pete Nelson, driving the tractor.

Now, on more than one farm, girls are doing a real "man's job" by helping in the fields. William Rogge says that four Hills girls are operating tractors this year, Dorothy Nelson, Frances Bakk, Joan Madison, Charlotte Larson. Any other nominations?

—— ★ ★ ★ ——

Don't miss "Casablanca" starting Saturday at the Palace—it's terrific.

—— ★ ★ ★ ——

Somebody is always disillusioning us. We can remember the rain makers who used to go round shooting off canons in the belief that cannonading caused heavy rainstorms. "T'ain't so," say the scientists, "that heavy bombings or shelling from cannon on battlefronts cause rain storms here."

"Terrific as the forces let loose in a heavy barrage or bombing raid may seem to us," writes L. A. Hawkins of the General Electric Science Forum, "they are utterly puny and ineffective compared with the forces which control the weather. It has been well said that we shall be able to control the weather only when we are able to stop a mass of air of 190,000,000,000 tons from going on its own way."

Perhaps the idea that battles caused rains originated with the fact an army usually gets into position during good weather while the roads are good so that by the time a battle begins a rain period would be due.

June 10, 1943

"RED OF THE A & P"

The four grim lead lines of the newspaper story seemed so tragically cold and bare.

"Staff Sergeant Richard E. Mueller, Dodge Center, Minn., today is reported missing with seven others following a crash of a medium bomber in the Atlantic near Columbia, S. C., Saturday. All are believed dead."

Four grim lines of newspaper type . . . that tell too much and yet so little. It dawned on me that we had, in newspaper parlance, very "little on" Staff Sergeant Mueller. We suppose he was 27 years old or thereabouts, that he went to grade school and then to high school . . . just like every other boy. Because here was a chap that was typically all American boy.

But after all you couldn't measure the boundless vitality or humanness of a chap like Mueller in mere words . . . and the cold facts so usually found in an obituary wouldn't do him justice. And he was one of the few fellows that left here for the service without our getting his picture before he left.

But for us, and thousands of other friends, none of the usual information, or even a picture, is needed to help us remember "Red of the A & P" . . . because that is the way he will be remembered here, not as Staff Sergeant Mueller.

———— ★ ★ ★ ————

With hair as vivid as a June carrot and a grin that had the power of a locomotive headlight this boy never walked down the street, or round the aisles of the store. He fairly danced or ran and you knew that here was a chap that was going places.

"Red" was the kind of a chap that you'd like your own boy to be . . . full of fire and a lot of fun . . . no sissy but he never did anybody any conscious hurt or mean thing . . . always having a lot of laughs and bubbling over with the sheer thrill of living.

We used to watch him and make fun of the weird breakfasts he'd eat, some of the worst gastronomical combinations we've ever witnessed. He'd get himself a piece of coffee cake, spread it thick with smelly cheese, munch it—great big bites—at a time and then wash it down with swallows from a pint bottle of milk—jitterbugging all the time behind the meat counter at the A & P store as he wolfed down the atrocious combination.

Red had a car . . . and a good one too . . . probably 70 per cent of his pay went to paying for, and maintaining, that car . . . and we used to watch him as he inspected it frequently at Rapp's garage. He was always jealously examining the finish for any unexpected scratches or dents. And no concert pianist ever listened to the tuning of his piano with more critical ear than did "Red" when the mechanics worked on the motor of his car.

"Red" did all right for himself in the army. He fought his way up the hard way. He'd write to his former employer, who really was more of a big brother to him than a boss. And invariably he would tell Floyd Lawson, "my work is tough but, oh boy, I love it."

I don't know just exactly what his job was . . . but Floyd said he understood that Mueller as Staff Sergeant Engineer was stationed right behind the pilot and the co-pilot. Nobody will ever know what happened . . . that grim telegram delivered to the family at Dodge Center held out no hope . . . but Mrs. Mueller is still hoping. She wouldn't be a mother if she wasn't.

But we'll gamble that even tho they were pitching straight down to the dark blue water that "Red" never once looked up but fought right up to the last second to find, and right, the trouble. And we'll never think any different but that if there was just a split second left, and a buddy was struggling to get free of the plunging plane, that Red, to use the old phrase of his "clerking days," called out "can I help you?"

JUNE 17, 1943

The two bombers which crashed in midair Sunday in S. D., with such a heavy loss of life are believed to be the same ones that were observed flying a tight formation over Luverne and Hardwick earlier in the day.

JUNE 24, 1943

If we ever had a favorite person this week there would be no argument about it—she is Mrs. Ray Weston. If The Star-Herald gets to you on time this week you can thank her.

We have been having what is referred to in newspaper circles as "linotype trouble" due to the sickness of one operator. Trying to run shorthanded on linotype operators is like trying to drive a car on three wheels—you make a lot of noise but you don't get anywhere very fast. "Five & Ten" Hillebrand has been gritting his teeth and doing his best—jumping from one linotype to the other like a one man band.

That's the background of the story why we like Mrs. Weston. She sent her husband in with a big bouquet of huge four-leaf clovers that she had picked. By pinning a four-leaf clover on everybody, and three on Hillebrand we may make it yet.

(Oprs. Note: "I ain't seen a four-leaf clover 'set' any type!")

And Major George Fried wandered in the office and we tentatively mumbled something about how nice it would be for George to "sit down for old time's sake and try his hand at the linotype keyboard." But the Major brushed our plaintive whimpers aside with the statement that about the best he could do nowadays would be a few "etaoin shrdlu's."

Oprs. Note again: "That's 'pie' to printers."

George is back from the deep, hot, blistering south. And if you ask him he wouldn't care, for all the money in the world, if he never heard "Carry Me Back to Old Virginny." If they ever get him there they will have to carry him—he'll never go back on his own free will.

He's going back to Fort Snelling and his old assignment and mighty glad of it. George tells how he was driving thru the camp and a bunch of soldiers working at an assignment happened to see the license plate on his car, screamed in ecstasy, "Minnesota, Minnesota." They were so excited they nearly kissed the car.

And to give credit where credit is due it was George that suggested that story we ran a few weeks ago about the high percentage of officers in the armed services that have come from Rock county.

And speaking of majors—there'll be a cocky, smart appearing, well-beloved (by his men) major pop into Luverne here Friday after an absence of over two and a half years—Major Marty Jensen. He's coming home after an agonizingly long delay and is expected to be assigned to duty in the states.

It hardly seems that long—but it probably seems like 20 years to him—that the train bearing Battery E men pulled out of the Luverne station.

In our mind's eye we can see him yet—as the cars flashed past—standing in the open door of the baggage car waving back as far as one could see the train. Marty has gone up the ladder fast, and he deserved it too, and he's going to get a real welcome when he gets back.

July 1, 1943

John L. Lewis has always been supremely contemptuous of what the people thought about his demands. But we wonder if he yet realizes that he may have started a three alarm fire of public anger. You should see what some of the men in service write us about Lewis and his mine strike. Sgt. Jim Mitchell of the air forces in China-Burma-India was the last to be heard from by air mail, so we'll let Jim sum it up for all the service men.

"In the first place you at home should put those miners in the army and give them a taste of what some of the boys go thru over here," he writes. "I am nothing in that line because if I got dead it would have to be from natural causes. There are plenty of them who have made "slit" trenches and boy IF THOSE MINERS ARE USED TO DIGGING THEY WOULD DIG AND DIG FAST FROM WHAT I HEAR AT TIMES. Perhaps they will come to when they realize what they are doing to their own sons and perhaps daughters, also. I know that I don't understand the full situation but I do understand the situation from a certain standpoint over here. It isn't very nice to hear that 100,000 miners walked out over the British Radio Station which must be good news to the enemy. I'm not telling anything that I don't hear right out in the open and over the air so if the censor cuts this out then I'd say that we need a new system of Censors."

(The censor evidently agreed because some of Jimmy's statements were underscored in the same ink with which the censor had deleted certain sentences about another subject.)

—— ★ ★ ★ ——

A close friend of the parents of those five Sullivan brothers, of Waterloo, Iowa, who were lost in a naval action in the Pacific is Mrs. Jim Kennedy.

———— ★ ★ ★ ————

Mike Ormseth of Canby was in the office the other day with his son, Marine Sgt. Orville Ormseth, who had just returned from Samoa.

"It was just about 26 years ago," recalled Mr. Ormseth "that we had to call Dr. Sherman away from a real nice party to come to our house one night. When, quite a bit later, he returned to the party they say that Doc said 'well, I just brought two soldier boys into the world.'"

Dr. Sherman didn't know how true his passing comment would turn out to be. One of the twins, Russell, is in a Jap prison camp, captured in the fall of Guam. The other, Raymond, is in the army but is still in this country.

———— ★ ★ ★ ————

No big corporation ever went about its business, with an eye to record keeping and labor saving devices, more enthusiastically than those two Victory Garden share croppers, Ray Koehn and Julius Brown.

They keep a record of everything, when they broke the soil for the first time, when the first tomato popped out, etc. To avoid stooping they strung wire fence for the peas so they can be easily picked.

But their latest is their method of shelling peas. They use the wringer on their electric washing machines and insert the broad end of the pod with the result that the peas squirt out on the other side like B.B. shot from an air rifle, unharmed. Whether the wives approve of dirtying up the wringers so that Julius and Ray can avoid tedious work we don't know.

JULY 8, 1943

Whoever would have thought that little Mrs. Mervin Funk would ever be called by herself, and proudly too, by the nickname "Rosie the Riveter."

She is also working on assembly work and blue print reading at Douglas Aircraft. Right now Marvel is working on the nose section of the wing on the new attack bomber, called the 9-26, that Douglas is building.

"Seems impossible," she writes, "that I'm really doing a small part toward building the first one. I like riveting and am getting such muscles in my right arm it almost looks deformed."

JULY 15, 1943

Major "Marty" Jensen had no more than landed in Luverne than he wired asking a 10-day extension of his leave. No reply and "Marty" said, "it will probably come after I leave." It did. The major left for Camp Davis, N. C., the 13th. The wire granting the extension came the 14th, a day too late as he said he wouldn't turn back if it didn't come before he reached Chicago.

—— ★ ★ ★ ——

From some of the stories we hear we could run something new each week on the various Victory Garden enterprises being conducted by some of our amateur gardeners.

We have sold our first "No Hunting" and "No Hunting Without Permission" signs of 1943 . . . to a Mr. Clifford Millard. (Who, they say, can really make life miserable for you with his perpetual teasing if he ever gets anything "on" you.)

It seems that the Pelstring and Millard gardens adjoin . . . but there is a great difference in the way operations are being conducted. On the one side it is all Mrs. Millard's responsibility for doing the muscle work, while Cliff is careful to keep in the shade. On the Pelstring side it is entirely different. Mrs. Pelstring is strictly and firmly forbidden to set foot in Ben's own little "Garden of Eden." Ben gets up as early as 7 a.m. in the morning (the first week 15 people fainted from shock at the surprising sight) to toil in his precious garden.

Ben had some decided theories about gardening (most of them bad—say the experts—such as mixing the beets and radishes together . . . probably hoping to come up with a "spiced pickle" plant . . . but both failed miserably.

Cliff has posted the "No Hunting" signs all round the Pelstring garden and even planted a scarecrow there. (And then has egged the neighbors on to compliment Ben on how much better dressed he is when working in the garden than during working hours.)

As far as gardens are concerned Millard is like the Lilies of the Field he "toils not" neither does "he spin" but nobody is having more fun out of the deal than he is.

JULY 22, 1943

Just a few "postmortems" on the scrap drive. If you had told a proud new father that his baby was homely you couldn't have seen a more crest fallen look than the one that appeared on Fred Herman's face. Fred's crew had towed a tireless old wreck of a car all the way from near Kenneth, Fred steering the clattering vehicle. And then Louie Cohen told the proud Fred that he "didn't know what to do with it." Walt Anderson and Pete Wiggins clattered down highway 75 towing an old binder, picked up near Jasper from Ben De Munck's place. Pete kept telling Walt to slow down in case one of the wheels came off but to no avail. The wheel did come off and the bull wheel of the binder plowed a furrow on the right of way, deep enough to lay sewer pipe in.

And down at the S. S. Birkeland farm one crew was told by Birkeland they could have anything they could salvage in a vacant house on an adjoining 80.

Brave Hugo Moeller and Ed Storaker climbed up a ladder to the second floor to be scared half out of their wits by a squirrel. All of a sudden Hugo saw "something" . . . so terrible he was afraid to even speak so he descended in a hurry. Ed turned round to say something and saw Hugo vanishing. "What's the matter," he asked. And then he saw "it"—a skunk who had already gone thru the motions of "Ready! Aim!" and was ready to "Fire!" Nobody will ever equal Ed's record in dropping down that ladder . . . and as far as they are concerned any junk in that house will stay there. And to top it off Lloyd Beatty's car in which they were riding caught on fire . . . and they all had to bail out and throw sand on the blaze.

The fire was caused by overheated brake shoes and they probably would have noticed it sooner except, in the words of one chap, "burning brakes and Ed's cigars smell just about the same."

———— ★ ★ ★ ————

And the Scrap Day closing of business broke a record of 41 years standing. It was the first time in that long stretch of time that Connells Drug store didn't open its doors.

———— ★ ★ ★ ————

Making mention this week of "flower freaks" were Aanen Skoland who reported a "Siamese twin" Regal lily and Mrs. Julius Arp who also discovered a "Siamese twin" dahlia.

———— ★ ★ ★ ————

Since we've mentioned two other druggists we think it's only right that Jay Treat "get his name in the paper." For about a month now Jay has been prodding us to write something about Mound state park. But the weather has been too hot for anybody to write any "burning" editorials even tho Jay says the condition of the roads there, and the "$5,000 building," are a disgrace. "Something should be done about it," has been his contention.

Well—he'll be happy to know that the U. S. army has "done something about it." A detachment has successfully captured Mound park and is holding it against all civilian invaders, who would like to picnic or fish there.

This will explain the soldiers in fatigue clothes, officers, MP's, army trucks, jeeps, peeps, etc., that have been seen in Luverne this week.

A squadron from the Sioux Falls army training school is located at the state park, north of Luverne, for actual field maneuvers.

Lt. Evans of the public relations office at the post, told us in a long distance conversation that the men will be here from 10 days to two weeks. There are "several hundred" he said.

They have their own field kitchens and are "tenting out." The men are being taught, as a phase of their technical training, in preparation for eventual overseas duty the actual combat conditions. They are learning the techique of "dispersement," the proper method of protecting themselves in the face of chemical gas attacks, the art of camouflage, etc.

You can't drive into Mound park any more as sentries are posted at the entrance. But you can drive along the north-south road and catch a glimpse of the men, if you wish. No use asking for admittance because the army has hung out the "no visitors" sign.

———— ★ ★ ★ ————

Add to your "it's a small world after all" collection the following items:

Having a reunion recently in New Guinea were two army men, Giles Busch, of the medical corps, and Leo Brandenburg, attendant on a hospital ship. And over in New Caledonia having a get together to talk over old times in Luverne were Marlowe Schneekloth (army) and Burton Knowlton (navy).

And in North Africa who did Lt. Merle Larson run into but an old school mate, Stanley Rollag (army air corps pilot) and Lloyd Ellefson (army air corps).

———— ★ ★ ★ ————

Mark August 12 down on your calendar as the date for the "shooting stars." About that date nearly 100 meteors an hour will be seen after midnight.

Meteors are commonly called shooting stars but are actually, according to the scientists, small bits of celestial dust which vanish in a flash of light when they encounter the friction of the earth's atmosphere.

———— ★ ★ ★ ————

Near completion is the Army Signal Corps' 2,000 mile telephone line, longest ever built, from Edmonton, Alberta, to Fairbanks, Alaska. Plan is to link the war department to the Alaskan fighting fronts by direct wire and the line will carry simultaneously vocal, telegraphic and radio messages. It has seven talking and 14 teletype channels and altho designed primarily for military use there is a good chance that it may be used to relay radio programs to the soldiers in Alaska.

July 29, 1943

Drawing a bigger Main street crowd of onlookers than a Memorial Day parade was the marching through town of the squadron of army men from Mound Park. The first indication that Luverne was to be "taken" was the appearance on three east-west streets of the vanguard of the advance—single soldiers well spaced out. And then came the main column swinging down Main street with their 70 pound packs on their backs. (It was a good thing that the temperature had dropped about 20 degrees Tuesday from previous scorching "highs" or the men would have been dropping like flies.

The men marched to the Country Club where they had their noon meal—and then they started the return hike, again with full equipment, to the Mound Park.

It's wonderful what a song can do, isn't it? Here they came headed west through Main street. They were slogging along this time. And then Lt. Wagner who was leading the march started off with a song, full of punch and marching rhythm. It wasn't two seconds till those bent over backs straightened up and the sun bronzed men lifted up their heads to shout the chorus of the familiar numbers of a quarter century ago.

The ambulance which trailed along behind the marching men didn't get much of a workout. But it may this week when the men march back the 30 miles to Sioux Falls.

———— ★ ★ ★ ————

"IT'S A SMALL WORLD"

Just one more little item about Lt. Merle Larson, the flier home from North Africa.

When he landed in New York he went to the Commodore hotel and put in a long distance call to North Carolina to tell his wife that he was back in this country.

The party who answered his call told the operator, "tell Lt. Larson that his wife is in New York and is at the Commodore hotel."

The flier couldn't believe it but he put in a call for her room and found it was true—but she was out. He left word to have the operator leave a message for Mrs. Larson that her husband "was calling."

When she received that word she said, "that's impossible . . . he can't be calling from North Africa." But she found out in a few minutes that dreams do come true after all—that fate had brought them to the same city—on the same day—and to the very same hotel.

AUGUST 5, 1943

Those Red Cross letters from the "old country" are still coming through . . . some containing tragic news . . . others with "no news" which comes under the heading of "good news."

Mrs. Severt Thompson, who lives near Luverne, received a Red Cross letter which was written over eight months ago in Norway. It told of the death of her parents, one on October 30 and the other on Oct. 31. Her parents were 69 and 71 years old and when Mrs. Thompson visited in Norway about seven years ago she told them she would be back, if everything was all right, to help them celebrate their golden wedding anniversary. That anniversary, by coincidence, would have been observed July 18, just 10 days before Mrs. Thompson received the sad letter from Norway.

But it was good news for Mr. and Mrs. Sigvart Helle in their letter from Norway which came thru at the same time. There was every indication that everybody was still alive.

———— ★ ★ ★ ————

Of all the army papers, from the standpoint of rugged surprises and editorial "vitamins," the Kodiak Bear tops the list. One of the frequent contributors is Pfc. Arnold Klindt, an Edgerton boy who left here with Battery E. His latest gem, which appears below, concerns another Rock county boy, Pfc. Herman Huisman.

FIRST-TIME FATHER

Pfc. Herman Huisman is a mother. Huisman was taking a little stroll on the sands of the famous White Way beach with his mind probably way back in the Land of Ten Thousand Lakes, when he noticed a furry object on the sand. His curiosity aroused, he approached it with the stealth of a cat, reached down to pick it up and found himself the guardian of a baby seal. Returning home with the baby seal in his arms, he exhibited it to his pals like a first-time father.

After a little dilly-dallying the seal was finally christened Oscar. Since that time Oscar has taken permanent residence with Huisman and is more or less the outfit mascot. He isn't a bit bashful when hungry and can make plenty of noise for a kid his size. The boys have all taken a liking to Oscar and give him the care they would give their own child. Since Herman was the one who made the discovery he is now the caretaker, pen-cleaner and mother, and we do mean mother.

Pfc. Arnold Klindt.

AUGUST 12, 1943

Hoff of "Hawf and Hawf" of the St. Paul Dispatch devoted a paragraph in his column the other day to some people well known here. Hoff tells of Mrs. Russ Wiggins dropping in at the Dispatch office with pictures of Russ, former owner of the Rock County Star and later managing editor of the Dispatch. He is now a captain and in North Africa. Their son, Bill, is now "P. T. Boating in the South Pacific." And Mrs. Wiggins related how Perry Dotson, returning with his ship through the Panama canal after some months in the South Pacific, met a mail ship. There were five sacks of mail for Perry's boat. In the five sacks were four letters for the crew—the rest of the mail was nothing but Pioneer Press Dispatch papers for Perry which had been chasing him for half a year.

AUGUST 26, 1943

Ordinarily—when it's a girl's birthday she can confidently expect that a telegram will say "Happy Birthday, Many Happy Returns of the Day." But that wasn't the type of telegram, by one of fate's grim twists, that was received Saturday on her birthday by Mrs. Lois Kroeger Weldon.

Instead it was one of those dreaded messages from the war department—the kind that read "we regret to inform you," telling of the death of her husband, Technical Sergeant Bertrum Weldon, in North Africa.

It's hard to write much about Sergeant Weldon, he was one of those fellows we knew and liked and yet really didn't know very well. One of the first to go from here he hadn't worked at Lampert Lumber Co. very long, but long enough to win a lot of friends in his own quiet way.

By some freak of nicknames he was called "Sandy" but he was coal black haired and handsome and he had an easy grace in the way he worked and lived that you couldn't help admire. He seemed to do everything the "easy" way and it wasn't hard to imagine the deadly precision with which he would handle his gun turret job on the big bomber or hard to understand why he had been decorated for his accomplishments in "missions" over Europe from English bases.

"Sandy" had had it plenty tough in air battles but it never seemed to get his nerves or dull his sense of humor. Letters home told more about his accomplishments in buying, repairing and re-selling motorcycles and other business escapades than he did about his part in the war.

Somewhere in our picture file downstairs is a picture taken at one of the dances down at the armory. We can distinctly remember it because up in the foreground stands "Sandy," gay, debonair, you can tell that he was having the time of his life. And that is the way he lived—probably making ten times the number of friends in his short span of life than most of us will ever make in a lifetime.

───── ★ ★ ★ ─────

Now that Aviation Cadet Bryce Connell is home we might as well relay the straight story as to why he was given a year's discharge from the Navy. And curiously enough it wasn't the injury caused by his parachute jump that put him "out" but a minor incident which almost seems like an anti-climax.

Bryce and his instructor were on a check flight, with the instructor at the controls, flying upside down. Bryce noticed sparks streaming back, notified the instructor and got ready to jump because there were auxiliary wing tanks, and already the wings were on fire.

Bryce stepped out and asked the instructor if he was ready but the officer shook his head saying he thought he could land the ship. They only had 1,000 feet altitude by then. Bryce got down nearly all right but could not "roll" as he had been taught because by then he was on the edge of a cliff, his foot got caught between two stones and with the parachute tugging at him he received a nasty ankle injury.

The instructor managed to get the ship down all right, then rolled onto a plowed strip, the ship nosed over, he evidently was knocked unconscious because he made no move to get out and burned to death.

Bryce recovered fairly well from that ankle injury but later he jumped from a ten foot wall on the obstacle course breaking the ankle.

———— ★ ★ ★ ————

Tuesday night's blackout was a success, marred only by a few scattered incidents. According to the story told us the most agonizing wait for the lights to come on again was experienced by the participants in a big poker game. I guess they really "sweat it out" wondering what kind of a "hand" the other fellow had . . . and if they still had all their chips.

SEPTEMBER 2, 1943

It was coincidence that last week in writing about the tragic death of Sergeant Bertrum "Sandy" Weldon in North Africa we referred to his love of motorcycles, how he liked to buy, repair and resell them.

"Sandy," the gunner who had been thru three major aerial campaigns—the invasion of North Africa, the Tunisian campaign and the battle of Sicily, wasn't killed in combat as first believed, he met death riding his beloved motorcycle.

A participant in over 30 raids Sgt. Weldon had over 100 combat hours to his credit and it is said that there is a possibility he will be given a posthumous military award.

———— ★ ★ ★ ————

For the benefit of the boys who are overseas we should report that Dick Wildung was the standout star in the All Star football game in Chicago last week. The All American tackle left Tuesday for Northwestern to enter the Navy's V-7 class starting there early in September.

———— ★ ★ ★ ————

Still no word from Ed Swenson . . . and still no picture of his "Ferdinand the Bull." But we can tell you that it wasn't quite a "photo finish" when George Ralfs tangled with a bull at Forrest's Dairy Wednesday morning. George was racing for the fence, with the bull right behind him, snorting rage for all things human. George almost made it thru the fence in time but the bull "helped" him the last three feet of the way. No serious injury was discovered by the attending doctor but it was said George would be "terribly stiff and sore" Thursday.

SEPTEMBER 9, 1943

It's a small world after all, as we so often like to say. One of the U. S. Navy men to receive one of the packages sent out by the local Red Cross chapter was James Key, a brother of Mrs. Ed Kolbert. So you never can tell who you're helping when you "put your shoulder to the wheel." The rumor is that Clarence La Due has just about concluded a deal for the sale of his dairy and property. The Hills Crescent is coming back to life after a few months' suspension. George Schuleter of Canistota, S. D. had leased the Crescent from Roy Hanson. And everybody wishes him well. Don't miss "Five Graves to Cairo" starting at the Palace . . . it's one of the better entertainment bits of the year. We didn't have as good luck with the prediction made seven months ago on Italy as we did on the North African surrender. We had predicted, if you remember, complete surrender by August 17th. Here's a postscript on the "Thone incident." Sheriff Roberts drives up, sticks his head out of the window, grins and says, "just for the sake of the record better say that the local authorities did notify Sioux Falls police that Clarence's car had been recovered." And Snoose Steine recalls that the same thing happened to Clarence's father in the same town. It seems the elder Thone had just made a thumping big sale of cattle but he hadn't bothered to dress up or shave. The police happened to see him stepping into a new Cadillac and they couldn't believe it was his . . . so they held him for investigation, despite the fact he had a pocketful of big bills and a huge commission firm check.

———— ★ ★ ★ ————

Of the hundreds of letters that come to this office from service men there was a weird coincidence about four letters. They came regularly from four men, from four scattered points on the globe . . . and yet they always arrived on the same day. If you found an air mail letter from one in your morning mail you would know for sure that there would be letters from the other three. It never failed until just recently.

The men were: Jimmy Mitchell, with the army air corps in India; Jimmy Connell and Ken Olson from "somewhere in the southwest Pacific" and Jess Frakes of the SeaBees.

Yesterday we only received one letter . . . and that was from Jimmy Mitchell. He's just been released from the hospital and he sent a gift of an exquisite ivory letter opener, carved with almost unbelievable delicacy in an elephant pattern. Connell is "late" with his letter. Olson can be excused . . . we know that he has volunteered for a special and dangerous mission and is unable to write. And Jess Frakes is "home."

———— ★ ★ ★ ————

All of us use the phrase "after the war" so much it almost becomes meaningless. The harassed business man uses it when he refers to labor worries and rationing and red tape headaches. The motorist uses it when he thinks of new tires, a new model car and the right to drive as fast and far as he pleases. But for all of us, altho the words aren't often spoken, it means the day "when the boys come home." It means, if you had witnessed a portion of a little drama as we did this week, the ecstatic happiness and the wild gladness of thousands of family reunions.

The other morning an unshaven weary, uniformed man, with a string of gayly colored ribbons on his breast, slipped off the morning train here and was driven to his home. Instead of going in the front way he went around to the back, un-noticed. Probably he just wanted to feast his eyes on "home," the place he'd probably wondered a hundred times, as he cursed the tropical heat, if he'd ever see again. His children were watching at the front, their noses almost boring holes in the window panes as they watched the street for a sign of "daddy." Nobody needs to describe their shrieks of joy when he walked in from the back door to surprise them.

If you could have seen them later, hanging on to his hands for dear life as tho they could hold him home forever, you couldn't have helped getting a bit misty eyed yourself.

It was Jess Frakes we're speaking of, "carrot top" himself, the chap who used to start so many arguments at the morning coffee shop sessions and who we used to tease so unmercifully when he was breaking in his "new teeth."

Jess knows what it is to undergo a torpedo attack on ship, to be shelled and bombed on an island and to hear the Jap radio announce that they (the Americans on that particular spot) had been "wiped out." The boys used to laugh at that one.

Jess is a bit vague about where he was but when he says Captain Joe Foss used to eat at their mess quite often you can get an idea where he was working.

What's the point of all this editorial rambling . . . why single out one man when there are so many from this county? All we wanted to do was picture for a brief second what "home" and "after the war" means . . . as if you didn't know. For this man and for a thousand more . . . that is what it means for them . . . and their families.

You can speed their return . . . quicker . . . and safer . . . "tomorrow" if you'll just buy War Bonds today. Need we say another word?

SEPTEMBER 16, 1943

If there is some man overseas that you would like to send The Star-Herald to as a Christmas gift the postoffice department has relaxed its regulations for a limited time so that it would not be necessary for you to obtain a written request from the soldier for the subscription. This waiving of the postal rules applies only to the period between Sept. 15 and October 15 so any Christmas gift subscriptions must be received before that time at our office.

———— ★ ★ ★ ————

Cleanliness is next to godliness they say but you can carry it too far, says Don Storaker. Company D went over to Jackson Sunday for field maneuvers. One objective of the home guard commandos was to ford a rather deep creek. "Follow me" yelled the commanding officer, tip-toeing his way across a precarious plank to make his crossing. Don wasn't so lucky and plopped in up to his neck. Thoroly soaked he was taken to town, dried off, and given a dry uniform.

The best improvement in many a year here was performed recently by the Rock Island railroad in connection with the depot which looked like a picture taken from a "haunted house" album. They've painted the place all fresh and bright till you would hardly know it.

———— ★ ★ ★ ————

Earl Cameron says we missed a good story about the last "blackout." He says that when the warning signals were given by the Hills fire siren that people thruout the countryside jumped into their cars and hurried to Hills to help put out the fire with the net result being just the opposite of the intended blackout.

———— ★ ★ ★ ————

We'd like to know who in the world it was in Luverne that was so nice to Sgt. John H. Richardson, now at Williston, Florida. Even tho the letter is a bit long for Chaff the sergeant says so many nice things about Luverne folks that we're going to reprint his letter in full. It appears below:

"Dear Sir:- As I know of no other way to express my thoughts to the people in Luverne, and the people adjoining Luverne, I wish to do so thru your paper.

Luverne is a fine town. The people are swell, I made many friends, not only among the younger set; but also among their elders. I only wish that I too could be one of them. Each and every person that I met, showed me every courtesy and respect that I could expect from my own mother and father. It seems that they realize that we are at war, and they were trying their best to keep up the morale of the boys who visited Luverne and the surrounding county.

I visited several of your homes and churches, and was welcomed far beyond my expectations, but I soon found out that, if a soldier will only be himself; he will be made at home in any home in your county.

Words can't express my feeling toward you people; nor can my actions. Your younger generation is very fine to know, I can proudly relate to my people back home of the happiness and good times that I have had while in their company.

I only hope that the soldiers of Sioux Falls will not over ride your welcome mat that lies in every home.

And when this war is over, I hope that it will be possible for me to return again and visit the people and the town of Luverne.

I would like very much to hear from my friends, and I will make the promise that I will answer any and all letters that I receive.

And now my parting words, next to home, I will pick LUVERNE, MINN.

> SINCERELY,
>
> SGT. JOHN H. RICHARDSON,
> 99TH BOMBARDMENT GROUP
> MONTBROOK AIR BASE
> WILLISTON, FLA."

———— ★ ★ ★ ————

George Fosdick, Minneapolis film salesman, was showing Mrs. Herman Jochims a wicked looking work of art which had been made by his son, Robert, who now is in North Africa. The soldier had made a dagger from parts of captured enemy equipment. The blade was from a German bayonet, the handle pieces had been taken from a German plane propellor, a three toned color effect had been achieved on the handle by using pieces of German plastic glass taken from a captured plane and parts of the recoil mechanism of a machine gun.

———— ★ ★ ★ ————

Have you noticed? A lot of the people who are so confidently predicting the war will be over with Germany by Christmas are the same ones who bet on Landon against Roosevelt in '36.

SEPTEMBER 23, 1943

If you've been wondering who was piloting the Flying Fortress that blasted Luverne several times Monday with the mighty roar of its motors it was Lt. Darwin Nelson.

"Oh," said his mother, Mrs. G. W. Nelson, "I'm still weak" when she was asked if it was a thrill to see Darwin flying the ship.

She had an idea who was piloting the ship when the Fortress zoomed low over their farm south of Luverne. He later called from Grand Island, Neb., to tell his mother that it was he flying the ship. Where he had come from . . . and where he is going is a military secret . . . but it's not hard to guess.

———— ★ ★ ★ ————

People who day dream over their present jobs about the "dream wages" being paid in big city defense plants might profit by listening to Lawrence Foight. Stopping just long enough, as he worked on a Krug truck, to say "hello" Lawrence said, "you can put it in your book that $25 or $30 in Luverne is more money than $100 a week in Detroit, about all you have to show for the big wages is the fun of handling it for a minute." Lawrence ought to know . . . he's been there for a year.

———— ★ ★ ★ ————

If you're interested they report the total number of fainting "casualties" at the "Dust to Dust" show last Thursday as eight, and not all women.

———— ★ ★ ★ ————

You'll get your money's worth out of "Crash Dive" starting today at the Palace.

———— ★ ★ ★ ————

It's a crazy season . . . Morris Jensen brings in apple blossoms, which were in full bloom on a tree at Adam King's place. They think that a recent hail storm is the cause of the tree starting to bloom again.

———— ★ ★ ★ ————

And speaking of oddities Mrs. Charles Meints brought in a collection of freak shaped potatoes and cucumbers, "bullfrogs, P-38 fighter planes" and other strong resemblances.

———— ★ ★ ★ ————

The following item is from Paul Smith's Lyon County Leader at Rock Rapids, Ia.

"We've all heard about the streets of gold that are supposed to be in Heaven. We're beginning to hear rumors that Luverne is planning that same kind of paving—with Rock Rapids folks caught "off base" footing the bill."

All we can say is: "Tut! Tut! Mr. Smith, nothing of the kind. Luverne isn't planning any paving, gold or otherwise. We think that maybe a few Rock Rapids folks need their eyes tested.

Their "astigmatism" has evidently caused them to think that Luverne's "Welcome" sign reads "The Sky's the Limit."

———— ★ ★ ★ ————

Did you see the picture of Gov. Stassen taken with Minnesotans "somewhere in the South Pacific" which appeared in the daily papers?

If you had looked closely you would have seen Burton Knowlton and Warren Moi.

SEPTEMBER 30, 1943

One boy came home on leave, the first time in three and a half years, and another boy left to join the navy—that's the way things happen at the Peter DeBoer home at Ellsworth.

And if any family in Minnesota can beat their record we want to hear about it. When they hang out a service flag at that house there are seven stars on it now. And the father, not to be outdone, joined up and worked on the Alaskan highway.

Jake DeBoer, home on leave for the first time in that three and a half year period, was escorted into the office Tuesday night by his uncle, Harm Smook. (If you remember the Smook family . . . and Mrs.DeBoer was a Smook—there were six boys in the service in World War I.) Jake's a tight lipped fellow and he is not going to have any ships sunk by any of his idle talk . . . and we respect him.

Anyway—here's the line up for the DeBoer family: Harm, with the army at Kodiak; John, machinist first class in the navy, thought to be in the submarine service; Jake, navy; Hilko, army, in Camp Butner in North Carolina; Henry, with the army at Kodiak; Peter, with the army air corps at Miami, Fla.; and Otto, who could hardly wait until he was 17 so he could enlist. Otto left Sunday for Camp Farragut, Idaho. And the father, Peter DeBoer, Sr., worked for a number of months on the Alaskan highway.

OCTOBER 7, 1943

Mort Skewes once remarked that Bob Haakenson had such a talent for making friends that you could drop him off on a lonely island and within a month the natives would elect him president.

He hasn't gone that far yet but the Naval ensign recently wrote home about meeting Capt. Randolph S. Churchill, son of the British prime minister. The younger Churchill was returning from Italy to North Africa aboard the ship to which Haakenson is assigned.

"Captain Churchill definitely resembles his father," Bob wrote his parents, "his features are a little sharper, and he is likely a bit larger. He has blond, fine, hair that blows about a good deal. He seems to have quite a nervous temperament, plays a lot of two deck solitaire with great expenditure of energy. He insisted on a ride and "driving lesson" in one of our amphibious craft while shelling was going on. Richard Llewellyn, author of "How Green Was My Valley" was supposed to have been with him on the beach."

Ensign Haakenson couldn't say much about the invasion. "Suffice it to say it was plenty hot," he added.

OCTOBER 14, 1943

Rock countians can puff out their chests a bit for reaching their War Bond drive quota. At last reports their neighbors in Nobles and Pipestone counties were still working trying to meet their goal.

OCTOBER 21, 1943

Altho critical Bible students will hasten to put me straight I still think even tho there is no similarity in the subject matter, that the words in Luke, 15-24, are in themselves fittingly descriptive.

They read: "for this my son was dead, and is alive again, he was lost and is found."

Those were the words uttered by the father of the prodigal son but probably were not far from the fervent rejoicing uttered up this week at the H. O. Hansen home. There's great rejoicing in that household for their son, Lt. Lloyd Hansen, who was feared dead is reported alive and safe in a German prison camp.

The analogy, as I said, ended with the words for Lt. Lloyd Hansen is no prodigal son. Rather he could be well called the Indestructible Man or the Man with Nine Lives . . . for like a cat he seemingly, and literally, lands on his feet.

It was only a couple weeks ago that H. O. Hansen was in this office trying to appear matter of fact over the fact that his son was once again reported "missing in action."

Now word comes thru the Red Cross to the bombardier's wife that he was captured by the Germans after the bomber, on which he was a member of the crew, was shot down in flames.

His capture followed by exactly two months another crash—one which ended in the English channel after their bomber had been shot down. All the crew members were rescued from that one. Lt. Hansen had one other close call—when the tail of a plane was completely shot off but the pilot managed to make a landing in England.

———— ★ ★ ★ ————

Floyd Lawson, even more critical than usual, complains that there isn't anything in Chaff (who doesn't) except items about freak vegetables. Floyd blithely waves aside our offer to let him write the column for a change. Just to keep him in his usual even tempered (mostly bad) mood we should report this week that Herman Jarchow brought a carrot which had 11 separate carrots, and that Mrs. Mike Wiggins picked a pan full of peas Wednesday from her garden, the second crop of the season.

———— ★ ★ ★ ————

As exciting as fiction is "The Wild Flight of Norway's Gold" which appears in this week's issue of Liberty. It tells how the undaunted Norwegians outwitted the Nazis and managed to smuggle out Norway's treasure of 60 tons of gold, worth $100,000,000. Air mail service gets even more unbelievably swift. Mrs. Frank Frakes of Magnolia received a letter from her son, Marion, in Australia. It was mailed at 4:30 p.m. October 8 and reached her on October 12, at 1 p.m. The "Reck Club" high school student recreation center opens Friday night.

October 28, 1943
One of the outstanding dramas of the year is "The Watch On the Rhine" which starts at the Palace Sunday.

November 4, 1943
"Hardwick women aren't the only ones who can paint houses in these days of manpower shortages," said Mrs. John Connell. It seems that she and her husband decided if a farm building was to be painted they would have to do it themselves—which they did. That is one time we surely missed a good picture, Mrs. Connell at the top of an 18-foot ladder painting away a mile a minute.

NOVEMBER 11, 1943

If you read that article in the October 23rd issue of the Saturday Evening Post, "Burma Bomber" we should tell you that the Gordon Berg of Eugene, Oregon, mentioned as "the collector of sweater girls" is a grandson of Mrs. Fredrika Berg and a nephew of Mrs. Oliver Aanenson, both of Luverne.

NOVEMBER 25, 1943

Probably Mr. and Mrs. Jerry DeBoer, route 1, Luverne, have never heard that new song, "I'll Be Home For Christmas" but they know all the thrill implied by the song's lyrics.

They've received the following telegram from their son, Peter: "Dear Mother, Dad, I am fine and I am back in the USA. May be home in 30 days."

Peter has been overseas for two years and the last two months he spent in an Australian hospital recovering from malaria contracted in New Guinea where he was stationed, as a medical detachment member, for seven months.

If you've never seen radiant happiness written all over a mother's face you should have seen Mrs. DeBoer.

DECEMBER 9, 1943

If ever anybody deserved special mention for faithfulness to a vital home front project, to which she devoted many long hours of painstaking work, that woman is Mrs. Max Zack. When they got around to totalling up the hours spent making surgical dressings for the Red Cross Mrs. C. L. Sherman discovered that Mrs. Zack had given 389 hours of her time to this cause since September, 1942.

DECEMBER 16, 1943
"ONE OF OUR BOMBERS IS MISSING!"

How often we've heard that phrase used over the radio and we've thought how that ominous sentence must strike cold terror in the hearts of every mother and father who is wondering where "he" is tonight.

The grim import of that laconic summation of an aerial raid struck home this week when Mr. and Mrs. George Nelson received one of those dreaded messages Sunday morning from the Adjutant General's office which read:

"The secretary of war desires me to express his deep regrets that your son, Second Lieutenant Darwin G. Nelson, has been reported missing in action since December 1 in the European area. If further details or other information are received, you will be promptly notified."

I think in times like these it would be so much easier to be a newsman on a city daily where news of this type doesn't have so often such a deep personal meaning—it's when you know these gay hearted, laughing, youngsters and their families that your heart really aches when you have to record in cold, black, type, that they are "missing in action."

We think that Darwin Nelson is (and we deliberately are using the present tense because we have a strong premonition that somehow this big strapping youngster made it down to earth all right) one of the most vivid personalities we've ever encountered.

Polite . . . and then some . . . about every tenth word was "sir" and it wasn't just poll parrot politeness . . . no southern "colonel" could have been half as gracious in manner. And he has a grin on him that has about as powerful a radiance as a locomotive headlight. And with that big frame of his, you didn't have to guess twice that he was a Flying Fortress pilot . . . for he looked every inch of it.

If you remember . . . it was just a bit over two months ago that he gave Luverne a roof rattling salute as he power dived his big Fort over the business district in an ear drum blasting "hail and farewell" as he flew over enroute for "over there."

We've often thought what he was thinking of as he circled several times low over the family farm south of town, the home and the buildings that he knew so well. And his final gesture as he waved goodbye to "the folks" was to do a little bombing on a small scale as he dropped clothing and belongings that he could not take with him.

Last week we carried a story from the Eighth AAF Bomber Command public relations office. (Altho no name was signed to the story we think Sgt. Henry Davis, formerly editor of the Herald, probably wrote it.)

In that story Darwin was quoted as describing his first flight over Gelsenkirchen in Germany's Ruhr valley as "easy."

But things began to get tougher. In a letter received a week ago Tuesday by his parents, written November 26, just after he had returned from his fourth raid Darwin reported he was safe and sound. He wrote: "I guess God was with us because it was a miracle we got thru without a scratch."

As we said before . . . we're hanging onto a strong hunch that Darwin is safe and sound—who knows he may be having a reunion right now with George Pederson and Lloyd Hansen.

———— ★ ★ ★ ————

It shouldn't happen again!

Of all the forlorn sights we remember of last Christmas the worst was that of the soldiers from the Sioux Falls air base who came here to spend the holiday away from the camp.

If they were hoping for something brighter and more cheerful than an army post they didn't find it, or only a few of them did. Most of the restaurants were closed and they had a hard time finding enough to eat. They strolled up and down the streets, aimlessly, looking in the store windows. We remember some of them walking thru the residential district . . . and if you think I'm kidding you're crazy when I say that they were wistfully looking in the windows of Luverne homes, the lights of the Christmas trees and the Christmas window candles . . . envying the happiness of those who were inside.

Have you ever spent Christmas away from home? Christmas of all days. If you haven't, then you have not hit the depths of heart-sickness. Christmas, away from home, unless somebody helps do something about it, can be the most doomed, lonely day in the year.

All right . . . let's get down to business.

Comes an appeal from Paul Myers, secretary of the Sioux Falls chamber of commerce and an ex-soldier from Luverne. Sure they're going to give them a swell dinner at the post and they are going to give the boys from Christmas Eve until morning of the day after Christmas off. But Christmas without being in somebody's home isn't much like Christmas.

So—why don't you sit down now and drop Myers a letter or send word to Hugo Moeller in Luverne and he'll pass it on, and say "sure . . . I'll take one or two boys for over Christmas and we'll try to show them a nice, homey time."

Maybe, Somebody, Some place else . . . will be nice to your boy. Who knows? Send your name to either Paul Myers or Hugo Moeller and indicate how many boys you want.

——— ★ ★ ★ ———

This following string of paragraphs is especially addressed to our Rock county boys who are "away" this Christmas. There's no law against your reading it—but proceed at your own risk.

Dear Gang:

There's a saying that "shoemaker's children go barefoot" and it looks as if the printer will be without Christmas cards. That's about the way it will wind up if McIntosh doesn't get busy soon. If he follows his usual habits of procrastinating until the last minute his cards, if any, won't be on the press until Christmas Eve. So— just to be sure—if you want to get any personal greetings from us—we better write a Christmas letter right now.

And—considering all the weird names and places this copy of the Star-Herald will wind up in—and how far it will have to travel in—and outside—this country—it should have been written a month ago. But you know this "put offer."

Who'd have thought four years ago that you'd be reading this—in all the states of the union, maybe in Africa, India, Iceland, England, Alaska, New Guinea, Australia, Caledonia, Hawaii, New Zealand . . . and a score of other places with funny names. It's a million to one bet you never dreamed you'd wind up where you are.

Well . . . we're just about ready for Christmas in Rock county. Up until late Monday it didn't look much like Christmas, more like a drab, early November day. And then, like the poem which starts "the snow had begun in the gloaming and busily all the night" the soft, white flakes fell so silently, swirling in white clouds almost blotting out the street lights at night. But it didn't last very long, just enough to throw a little mantle of white in patches over the dark, bare, dirty looking ground. The fields aren't covered and the countryside is one rolling expanse of black and brown patches.

Tuesday morning the snapping cold came. All those buffalo coats and coon skin coats that you'd have sworn had vanished with the buffalo and Indians blossomed out again. Gabe Gysland was in town with an old timer of a fur cap and coat outfit that was a dandy. And John Connell was in proudly patting his fur lined cloth coat. Years and years, ago, more than he'll admit, he paid $25 for it and quite a few years back he handed over $40 to have a new "shell" made for it. And he still wouldn't sell it for $100. Feels mighty good on a 10 below morning.

The usual crowd was not visible hanging around the post at the G & B corner . . . they'd all moved inside to soak up all the heat . . . and the windows were fairly steaming from the mass of humanity clustered around for the tall tale contest.

Wednesday morning the smoke from the chimneys was hanging like white plumes in the clear, quiet, frosty air.

The garages were doing a roaring business Tuesday morning with the tow cars yanking in the stalled cars. It was such a headache for the garages that most of them were running about six hours behind schedule . . . and wouldn't be a bit offended if you went "some place else." The 6:30 a.m. Omaha passenger staggered into the depot at 9 a.m. Tuesday. (The world's greatest fiction writer was the chap that wrote the time table for this branch of the system.)

There's quite a lot of flu here [. . .] plenty of people with flushed cheeks and feverish eyes and you know they've "got it."

You know for a couple years now Hugh Fay has had the ticklish and unenviable job of helping pass on who is—and who isn't—"essential" in the eyes of selective service. Well . . . Fay found out the other day that he wasn't "essential." Both Hugh and his helper, John Bailey, were flat on their backs with the flu. Looked like the lumber yard would close up for sure. But Dorothy Koens, the book-keeper, and Billy Fay, 14, ran the yard until the "tough guys" could get back on their feet again.

Sheriff Roberts has been battling the flu but is still staying on his feet . . . but it's cost him a few pounds. (It's an ill wind that doesn't blow some good.) Ben Pelstring fell, while hunting, and suffered a badly sprained ankle in a 34-foot fall. His son, Sam, lies across the hall, sick with the flu . . . and Mrs. Pelstring is running from one room to the other with her two babies yelling for "service." She took it as long as she could then said "all nurses get at least three hours off" and left them to do some shopping.

Mr. and Mrs. Chuck Rober's little girl has pneumonia and Mr. and Mrs. Tony Suurmeyer, are breathing easier now . . . but they were pretty worried for a while about their baby that had near pneumonia.

Speaking of cold weather this is what the fuel dealers have long dreaded . . . they were just squeezing past before but the cold snap now makes it critical. (Don't forget to drop John L. Lewis a Christmas card to "thank" him for his fine, patriotic, help in creating a fuel shortage which may turn out to be a national disaster.)

Bill Goodale was thinking Monday about the "good old days" when coal dealers used to have to offer "easy payment budget" plans of trying to sell coal in the summer time. Now the dealers are driving the railroad men and the coal companies crazy trying to find out when their cars of coal will be arriving.

Looks like Sid Hammer was pretty smart moving to a city steam heated apartment. Sid said he "got tired of seeing his wife shovel coal" but I guess he saw this crisis blowing up.

Santa Claus is coming to Luverne. Town isn't going to have the old holiday atmosphere outwardly. (But it will at heart.) No special lighting or festooning or decorations round the lamp posts. There aren't any supplies available and if there were there isn't any surplus manpower to put them up. Santa is going to be here 3 days. But there's such a shortage of candy and nuts and apples are so high priced (and a lot of that candy, by the way, comes from Mexico) that the youngsters are going to have to be satisfied with free movies at the Pix.

The boys got to speculating the other day about who really looks "most like Santa Claus" . . . or would if he wore the traditional red suit. Some favored Bill Preston but Tick could never sit still that long. One fellow said Dan McCormick would be ideal. Others favored George Johnston and Ed Kolbert had the "girth" but too much height.

School won't be out quite as early this year because of the late start. Just happened to notice this noon . . . the little tots in the grade school had all the windows of the schoolhouse filled with cut outs of Christmas bells, trees and wreaths. Right cute. And

Christmas was made for the little tots anyway.

They're starting with the Christmas programs in the schools and churches.

They're beginning to sing "Silent Night, Holy Night." We know how lonely you'll feel when you hear it far away—and there are a lot of people here who are going to be mighty blue here on Christmas—with you away. Some of you are going to have it rougher than others—because some of you have only been in a couple weeks or so—and this will be your first Christmas away from home in your whole life.

But there isn't much that can be done about it—except what you're doing. Because—in fellows like you lives the only hope of the world of seeing "White Christmas" again reigning triumphant where peace and good will are uppermost instead of hate, evil and greed.

There's some prayers, a whole lot of them being said here for you fellows. They're not eloquent prayers like a minister "works up" for his Sunday congregation but they're just as fervent and just as earnest and sincere—even tho some of the parents may fumble a bit as they get down on their knees at night there isn't any fumbling as for what is in their hearts.

After all—Christmas isn't a "place." Christmas is "in your heart." Everybody's thinking of you—and hoping for the day when you will all get back safe and sound again to pick up where you left off.

So . . . for now . . . "Merry Christmas and Happy New Year."

—A. C. Mc.

DECEMBER 23, 1943

Once in a while dreams do come true and it was "I'll Be Home for Christmas" for Floyd Strassburg, pharmacist's mate, 2nd class. With his chest beribboned like a rainbow he walked into our office the other day wearing an ear to ear grin as he announced that he wouldn't trade a single acre of Rock county land for all the southwest Pacific.

The son of Mr. and Mrs. Julius Strassburg of Hardwick, he is now enjoying a 30-day leave, to which he is well entitled. Last Christmas he spent in Hawaii—and he has seen plenty action between those two dates.

The ribbon of which he is most proud is the presidential citation ribbon which bears a star indicating a second award of the same kind. The first citation was given his unit, the first air group to land on the Russell Islands. The star was awarded for exceptional duty during a bombing raid on Guadalcanal. We understand that, disregarding his own safety, he rushed out to give aid to the wounded during the worst period of the raid.

On his Pacific duty ribbon there are two stars, indicating two major battles and his third ribbon is the American Theater of War ribbon, indicating duty outside the continental United States but not in the war zone.

Strassburg, 28, can wear either navy or marine uniforms. In the navy he is attached to the marine air corps as a ground crew member. His squadron was the famous "Hellhawks" and, beaming all over, he declared, "We've a record to be proud of, 104 Jap planes knocked down to the 8 we lost."

The Corsairs used by the squadron are the best planes in the air today, he says. During the past year he spent four months on Guadalcanal, two short hitches on the New Hebrides, a little time in Hawaii and some time on the Russell Islands.

In the Russell Islands campaign the raiders made the first landing, picking off Jap installations, then the gallant Seabees dashed in to build an airfield which, as soon as was usable, was taken over by the crew of which he was a member to service planes.

The Russells, said the Hardwick boy, are the "paradise of the Pacific," lush with green grass and foliage, few mosquitos and a nice climate. Natives are small, very black, intelligent and speak good English and say they "love" the Americans.

Just because Guadalcanal is held by Americans doesn't mean that life is easy and that the Japs let the islands alone. During his four months he underwent 50 bombings raids and the Japs hit something every time. Strassburg says "don't under estimate the Jap bombardiers."

He took care of eight Jap prisoners for a while, two of them graduates of the University of California. Nearly always sullen and uncommunicative they would speak at times.

"One little Jap," said Strassburg, "told me 'you may have taken Guadalcanal but you'll never take back Hawaii or California' and he actually believed it."

In all the time he was gone, and although he asked every place he went he never saw any "home county" men altho he met men from Pipestone and Worthington.

He expects 6 months of duty in this country after he reports back to San Diego for orders and when he is shipped out again he hopes it isn't the southwest Pacific.

———— ★ ★ ★ ————

And another Rock countian back in the states for Christmas is 1st. Sgt. John Goeske who called to announce he was home from Italy on a 30-day furlough. He'll spend Christmas in Riverside, Cal., with his family. Overseas a year he served in two African battles, the invasion of Sicily and the invasion of Italy. John sailed from Italy Nov. 16.

———— ★ ★ ★ ————

Rev. H. C. Knock stopped us to "nominate" for the "cheapest and meanest man in the county" the chap who slashed down two of those nice evergreen trees near Beaver Creek.

———— ★ ★ ★ ————

I never can remember that old line about "sauce for the goose" etc., etc., but it would seem to apply here.

The last day of school before the holidays things were pretty free and easy at school. But when he heard two girls, seated together, tittering boisterously, Coach Hal Meyer, who had that particular study period, slipped around to the back of the room. Walking up from the back of the room he discovered the cause of the merriment—the girls had smuggled in a copy of Esquire in which they were finding great entertainment.

That was going too far decided Meyer so he confiscated Esquire and marched up to the front of the room with it. Then (behind the security of a high desk top) he sat and read Esquire himself the rest of the study period.

———— ★ ★ ★ ————

We have, right or wrong, a stand-in rule here at the Star-Herald of "no poetry." (Because of space limitations—and if you print one poem you have to print them all.)

But we're going to break that rule—JUST ONCE—because a chap in the South Pacific wants to "toast" the folks back home. And if that isn't a good reason show us a better one.

Here's the letter we received:

Dear Editor:

"I am sending in a little poem which I would appreciate very much if you would publish in the Rock County Star-Herald as a toast to all my friends and relatives as practically all of them take your paper.

"I am down here in the South Pacific a long way from home and it is impossible for me to send a card to them all. I thought this would be a good way to let them know I am still from good old Rock county. Here is the poem or toast.

A CHRISTMAS TOAST

A little sailor
    would like to boast
A little poem
A little toast
A little wish
For Christmas Day
A Happy Year
Not Far Away.
A little cake
A little—(here his handwriting
    was illegible)
A little car
A little spin
A little love
A little fun
A little sleep
When all is done
A little memory
    to stay with thee
At Christmas tide
In forty-Three.

"And so I remain just one of the many who read the Rock County Star-Herald."

Vernon C. Hansen AM 2/c.

(Complete address withheld because of the censorship code.)

———— ★ ★ ★ ————

It's true there's no financial comfort in a fire but Bill Tomlinson and his corn shelling crew decided they might as well get some physical comfort out of the blaze in their outfit—so long as it was burning anyway. So everybody at the Oscar Roos farm, where they were shelling corn, crowded round the fire and warmed their hands

———— ★ ★ ★ ————

Just one more paragraph to write and then we're "all thru" and can go into our regular press day routine.

The printers have long ago learned to put up with it—as just one more of the hardships they have to put up with here. Of no help whatsoever to the production of the paper they have learned to tolerate us.

From now until the forms are on the press we'll pace the aisles of the back shop, ringing our hands in despair as we watch the racing hands of the clock (like an expectant father at a hospital) wondering how in the world we'll ever "make the train." We'll peer over the shoulders of the men who are really accomplishing something, offering useless suggestions, asking about every 90 seconds "how are you doing" and just generally getting in everybody's way.

Until we can breathe that blessed sigh of relief when the mail sacks are on board the train there won't be much holiday spirit in our hearts.

Oh, yes . . . we started to say we had one more paragraph to write . . . this is it. The Star-Herald wishes you and yours, wherever you are, the most Merry Christmas and Happy New Year.

May your Christmas be bright with hope and joy and love . . . and may your New Year be one filled with bountiful blessings and much happiness. So . . . on behalf of myself, Irid, Georgia, Alice, "Ruck," Max, Dow, Ruth and Charlie let us say . . . as simply but as sincerely as we can . . . "Merry Christmas."

DECEMBER 30, 1943

A telegram one day and a long distance call the next, from a point still closer to Rock county, gives Mr. and Mrs. H. O. Hansen the idea that their son, Cpl. Herbert Hansen may be home for New Year's after all.

He'll have a lot to tell because a lot has happened since he went away. He was in one convoy that got a terrible "working over" from German subs and his ship had to limp back to an unnamed eastern port. He was in Ireland in the winter of 1942 and left in January for Africa, going thru the African campaign. Then he went to Italy. Herbert is a member of the medical corps. His parents received a telegram from West Virginia saying that he had arrived back in this country, the next day he called from Chicago.

Rock County
Continuing Rock County's Oldest Business Institution, The Rock County Herald, Established in
The Rock County Herald, Established in
OFFICIAL COUNTY AND C

LUVERNE, MINNESOTA, THURSDAY, JUNE 8, 1944

No. 36

The Invasion With Bonds Is 5th W

Honor Roll
Registratio
Here Satu

Announcement
may register the
in service at the H
on Main street,
noon and evening
made this week
post here. Dona
cost of the hono
also be accepted
Permission w
F.W. by the co
day night to en
the vacant lot,
city hall.
Speaking for
charge of the
ty honor rol
'I install said
ister that ma
board of it a
Rock county
means we h
rect list an
miss anyon
"This is
we need
everyone,
names, w
board."
Those
in their
to regis
he adde
the ent
week.
it as a
and go
side t
have

a Ot
y Men
Mon.

Majority of
ngent; Two
Physicals

ordered for in-
county on Mon-
go into army gen-
e local selective
t this week.
Luverne; Orville
er Creek; Orval
Falls; and Warren

o will go into the
hard Sevatson, Hills;
meling, Luverne, and
ell, Luverne.
rs" called for navy
arren Eitrelm, Garret-
aymond Hansen, Hard-
nteer.
ty will also be credited
nd Lemmerman, father.
o into the navy from the
ard. Lemmerman form-
at in the local high school.
ng the same day for pre-
physical examinations at
will be Vernon Branden-
d Jack J. Heinz, both of

Jasper Pilot Home After Making
28 Missions Over Enemy Targets

Lt. Kenneth M. Haugen Over
Berlin Five Times, Knows
What Fear Means

Having completed 28 missions
over enemy occupied Europe,
part of the time as co-pilot of a
B-17 Flying Fortress, and later
checking out as first pilot, 1st
Lt. Kenneth M. Haugen, son of
Mr. and Mrs. Tom Haugen, of
Jasper, admits he is not sorry
that he is missing the big push.
Lt. Haugen knows what it is
to feel the sting of battle, for he
has come home from a mission
many times with his plane full
of holes made by enemy flak. He
is proud, though, to state that
"not one member of our crew
ever received the Purple Heart".
The purple heart is awarded for
wounds received in action.

Has DFC and Air Medal

The young Flying Fortress
pilot recently arrived home from
England, having served in that
theater of war since November
of last year. He is wearing the
Distinguished Flyin' Cross, the
Air Medal with three Oak Leaf
Clusters, and the European
Theater of Operations ribbon.
He is enjoying a leave with his
parents, and with his wife and
14-months-old daughter, Joan
Kay. He will leave here to report at a rest area on June 27.
Lt. Haugen entered the army
air forces in September 1942, and
was commissioned at Blackland
Army Air Field, Waco, Texas, in
July, 1943. After he completed
his Phase training at the Rapid
City Army Air base, he left for
overseas duty, arriving in England November 2 of last year.
"First thing you get when you
reach your base," Lt. Haugen
stated, "is a 'flak' lecture. All the
old timers meet the new boys
and tell them about their experiences with flak and fighters.
They'll tell you the truth, but
in most cases, it's painted a little bit to make it sound as bad
as possible. When they're done,
you're scared as hell but not
as scared as you are after you
come back from your first mission and really learn what flak
and fighter opposition really is.

More Frightened on Second

"You start on your second mission more frightened than you
were on your first, but after you
get back from that one, it seems
as if you can take it. Truthfully,
though, I don't think there is
anyone in the whole air force
who isn't just scared all the
time. There may be certain
degrees of fright, but everyone
I've ever talked to feels the
same way about it that I do, it
seems".

That Lt. Haugen had plenty
to worry about on all his missions
was evidenced by his statement
that he encountered anti-aircraft
(Continued on Page Four.)

ROCK COUNTY STAR-HERALD PHOTO

LT. KENNETH M. HAUGEN, son of Mr. and Mrs. Tom Haugen, of
Jasper, has returned home from England where he completed 28 bombing missions over Germany and enemy held territory. He served as co-
pilot and also as first pilot of the Flying Fortress, "Pochahontas," so
named because the original first pilot's name was John Smith. Lt. Haugen
is now on leave and will report on June 27 for a new assignment.

ls Man Is
ommander Of
istrict Legion

A Rock county man, Earl A. Stev-
ns, of Hills, was elected commander of the Second District of
the Minnesota American Legion at
their annual convention held Sunday at Worthington. He had previously served as vice commander.
The district comprises 11 counties
in southwestern Minnesota.
Other Legion officers elected
were: Robert Bird, Fairmont, first
vice-commander; Frank Koep, Lake-
field, second vice-commander; A.
H. Getty, Worthington, third vice-
commander, and A. W. Stewert,
Worthington, Chaplain.
Delegates chosen to attend the
national convention to be held in
Chicago were Mr. Stevens, Hans
Becken, Hanska, and C. River,
Mankato.

Auxiliary Officers

Mrs. Leigh Winter, Redwood Falls,
was elected president of the women's auxiliary of the Second District. Other officers named were:

CAR USE STAMPS
ON SALE JUNE 10

Every owner of a motor vehicle which is used upon the highways is required to secure a new
$5.00 use tax stamp and affix it
to his vehicle on or before July
1, according to Arthur D. Rey-
nolds, collector of internal revenue. Stamps will be placed on
sale in all post offices on Saturday, June 10. They will be ser-
ially numbered, will be gummed
on the face, and will have provision on the back for entry of
the make, model, serial number
and state license number of the
vehicle.

SON OF FORMER ROCK
COUNTY COUPLE KILLED

Mrs. Ed Donth, Magnolia, received word that her nephew,
Pvt. Curtis Nagel, 20, had been
killed April 28th in England. No
as to how the young man
were received.

Famed Red Cross
Leader To Give
Address Here

An unusual opportunity to hear
one of the most outstanding personalities of the American Red
Cross will be afforded Rock
Countians Friday evening, June
16.
Carl "Dutch" Meyers, former
Minnesotan who is now held representative for the American Red
Cross, will come here from St.
Louis to address the annual meeting of the Rock county Red Cross
chapter.
The meeting will be held at
p.m., June 16th, in the cour
room at the court house. Att
ance is not limited to Red C
members but is open to the
lic.
Meyers received wides
publicity several years ag
ported missing in Burma,
been stationed at Lashio
foot of the Burma road, he
up later bringing a car
women and children to
had led out of Lashio

SWIMMING POOL MAY
OPEN ON SATURDAY

1944

"We sat by the radio for over an hour listening to the breath taking announcements of eye witness observers of the assault. And then we went back to bed—to lie there for a long time, wide eyed in the darkness— thinking 'what Rock county boys are landing on French soil tonight?'"

—Al McIntosh

JANUARY 6, 1944

Remember the tragedy of that London dance hall that was wrecked, and so many Americans lost their lives, when it was hit by a bomb dropped by a Nazi plane that had slipped thru the city's air defenses? Nick Jepson just happened to remark the other night that his son, Cpl. Junior Jepson, had been in the hall that night . . . and had left only 10 minutes before the bomb hit. And speaking of England . . . Lt. Ray Cragoe, co-pilot on a Fortress, is now flying combat missions over Europe.

———— ★ ★ ★ ————

We should mention that we received a Christmas present! (Now what makes this news was not that anybody would be sending a present to a newspaperman but the fact that there was no clue to the identity of the sender.)

Our chubby little fingers eagerly tore thru the layers of gay tissue wrappings, fairly ripping off the gay ribbons and seals. But it was all anti-climax.

Somebody had taken a big photograph folder and had inserted a picture of President Roosevelt. Then they had pasted the caption "Still President!"

It's taken quite a lot of quiet detective work but we finally unearthed the guilty party—none other than Bill Merrick. But who'd have thought Bill, who feeds his political prejudices daily on the administration hating Chicago Tribune, would ever do a thing like that.

JANUARY 13, 1944

We regret to say that the rumor that Mr. and Mrs. George Nelson have had a letter from their son, Lt. Darwin Nelson, reported recently "missing in action," is untrue. No word of any kind has been received.

———— ★ ★ ★ ————

Time goes so fast that it seems like only last week that Ensign Neal Blinkman was home. But how these boys do get round these days.

Chris Blinkman was beaming all over Monday—he and Mrs. Blinkman had received their first letter in a month from Neal.

His ship sailed from an un-named east coast port Dec. 5. Since then he has been in Scotland, and made quite a tour of our "home country," visited England and has also been in North Africa. He hadn't yet caught up with his ship, to which he had been assigned, and it was necessary to make a 1,300 mile plane trip to catch his ship.

And—walking down the streets of London on Christmas day, who should Neal bump into but Lt. Helen Long, daughter of Mr. and Mrs. Lloyd Long, who is in the army nursing corps.

———— ★ ★ ★ ————

If we should have such poor judgment as to even hint that somebody in Canton, S. D., is a dog thief we know that Andy Johnson, editor of the Canton News would immediately give vent to screams of outraged civic pride.

So we won't say it but we should report that everybody now is very happy at the D. J. Ahrendt home in Jasper. If you'll remember the black labrador dog . . . the personal pet of Sgt. Duane Ahrendt, now a paratrooper in Italy, disappeared when his father, D. J. Ahrendt, was visiting Christmas day at the home of his mother, Mrs. Dora Ahrendt, in Luverne.

It seems that a Canton man, who had friends in Jasper, happened to notice a black labrador dog, with a Jasper dog license, was aimlessly wandering the streets there. The Canton man notified Jasper friends who knew of the Ahrendt loss. To say that there was a very happy reunion at Canton, of dog and Ahrendt, is gross understatement.

JANUARY 20, 1944

Here's the best news of the week!

There's real joy at the George Nelson home this week. Because there is new hope that their son, Lt. Darwin G. Nelson, may be alive. "Missing in action" since a flight over Europe December 1, the parents of the Flying Fortress pilot have had a long period of agonizing waiting.

Tuesday they received a telegram from the Foreign Broadcast Intelligence Service of the Federal Communications Commission which read as follows:

"The name of Second Lieutenant Darwin Nelson has been mentioned in an enemy broadcast as a prisoner of war in German hands. The purpose of such broadcasts is to gain listeners for the enemy propaganda which they contain but the army is checking accuracy of this information and will advise you as soon as possible."

This division of the FCC maintains 24-hour a day listening posts where highly trained operators sit at their posts listening to every broadcast from every enemy radio station possible. Not only do they try to pick up clues as to conditions in enemy countries but they also relay on to parents significant and important items such as in the Nelson case.

——— ★ ★ ★ ———

So near and yet so far!

Sgt. James Mitchell has been "sweating it out" in India. More than once in his many letters to us from that land of heat, disease, filth and hardship half a world away Jimmy has expressed a doubt if he would ever see this county again.

He finally made it —coming back from half way 'round the world but still he wasn't able to get home. He called his folks Saturday night from Minneapolis to say that he was "back" but couldn't make the 250 miles to home as he was ordered to Great Falls, Montana.

JANUARY 27, 1944

If from time to time you think the Star-Herald has been seemingly indifferent in interviewing some service men returning from a combat zone and only run a brief paragraph when you knew the fellow had a story columns long to tell we should explain.

Censorship is tightening up, particularly for navy men. We just happened to learn of the orders that had been handed one naval officer home this week. He is absolutely forbidden to have his newspaper photograph taken—or to even "talk" with newspaper reporters. It isn't that we don't want to run a longer story—it's a case of where the chap might get in a bad jam if much more popped in print than the brief fact that he had been home.

——— ★ ★ ★ ———

Dana Baer, our volunteer bus meeter, nearly got himself kissed the other day. An Ortonville sailor stepped off the bus Monday to stretch his cramped legs, and found a telegram catching up with him here that authorized ten extra days' leave. Jumping up and down with glee he just about planted a kiss on Dana, whiskers and all.

———— ★ ★ ★ ————

After 13 years in the navy, Chief Commissary Steward John Leech can say that he has met more than one person from his home community. Now serving with the fleet, he wrote his sister, Mrs. Gerald Wiggins, this week that he had met Darrel Noble, of Adrian, on his ship, after they had been at sea on the same vessel for two months.

Noble happened to locate Leech after he had come across the latter's copy of The Star-Herald, which he had left in the reading room of the ship. Recognizing the newspaper, he immediately set about looking for its owner, and since finding him, they have had many good chats about home, Leech states. He had met only one man from southwestern Minnesota previous to his meeting Noble. He was Leo Brandenburg, Luverne, whom he saw some time ago.

FEBRUARY 3, 1944

We had a moment's concern when we saw County Clerk Soutar headed for our office door with a rifle slung over his shoulder. But we couldn't remember of any reason for Charlie getting hostile and drew a sigh of relief. It was a Japanese rifle and bullets, that Charlie was bringing us to put on display in The Star-Herald window. The captured equipment was sent home from the South Pacific by Cpl. Robert Ruud of Hills.

In a letter Cpl. Ruud said, "the rifle is fairly accurate but like everything else it is inferior to our equipment."

FEBRUARY 10, 1944

When Marlin Hudson, 18-year-old son of Lt. and Mrs. Ed Hudson, left for Fort Snelling Monday for induction into the army we're just wondering if it didn't establish a new "first" for Rock county in World War II.

We may be wrong. (If so we'll surely hear about it.)

But we think the Hudson family is the only one where both a father and son are serving in the armed forces.

Marlin's dad, Lt. Ed Hudson, is now at Camp Haan, Cal., where he is assigned to a prisoner of war camp.

———— ★ ★ ★ ————

And speaking of the unusual there will be a ceremony at the V.F.W. meeting Thursday night that will be something out of the ordinary.

This will be when Earl Tunstall gives the "obligations" to his sons, Cpl. Marmon and Cpl. Marbert Tunstall, at the meeting.

Earl was the first commander of the Rock county VFW post and Marmon and Marbert, just back from 2 1/2 years in Kodiak, will be the first World War II veterans to join the local post. To make it a complete family affair Mrs. Tunstall and Maxine, the daughter, will also be present as members of the VFW auxiliary. So far as we know this is the only complete VFW family in the state.

———— ★ ★ ★ ————

Arm Carter's eyes were sparkling this week—with reason. For "Kenny" was home. As if you didn't know, from the way Arm has talked about this boy for whom he has such a deep love even tho there is no relationship. "Kenny" is Chief Petty Officer Kenneth Olson.

Olson was one of our regular correspondents from spots all over the Pacific. And to talk about him without writing a "bang up" story is hard to do. But naval regulations and censorship rules still have to be observed.

He's got a double decker string of ribbons, and there are plenty of stars nestling in those ribbons too, but he does not give them any more concern than the average soldier gives his "year of service" ribbon. Because this slim, dark haired, wiry youngster is thinking of only one thing, have a little fun back in the "states" and then get back to help win the war.

If you'll remember he was wounded that fateful Sunday at Pearl Harbor, December 7, 1941, but he bounced right back at the Japs. In fact his record will show a citation for sticking at his post of duty for 48 hours without rest helping bring order out of chaos.

We can't tell you, because of regulations, where he has been or what he has seen. But put it this way—start with Guadalcanal and then name most of the major Pacific sea battles, the major ones, that you can think of. And you won't be far wrong if you'd say that he'd seen most of them. It probably isn't out of line to say that he's seen as much, if not more, action than any other Rock county youth.

Scared—sure he's been scared, and by his own admission, plenty of times. But you don't win that coveted rating of his, and the hard way too, unless you have a cool head when cool heads count.

Doggonit . . . talking about a chap like Olson and being hog tied by censorship is like writing about a three alarm blaze and saying only "there was a fire."

———— ★ ★ ★ ————

Pfc. Lloyd Lorange has been away from home a long time and has traveled over 10,000 miles but he had never seen a "home town boy" till just the other day. In the amphibious engineers on New Guinea Lloyd was given a 15-day furlough. He wanted to spend it in Sidney, Australia, so he went to a nearby air base to see if he could "thumb a ride." Who did he see there but Sgt. Giles Busch, who is in the medical corps attached to the air corps. Giles was the first Rock county man Lloyd had seen since the day he left the army induction center.

FEBRUARY 17, 1944

There will be a special radio program on Friday, March 3, from the Sioux Falls army air base. Mrs. Lloyd S. Hansen will make the trip from her home at New Richland, Minn., to receive the Air Medal and 2 Oak Leaf clusters earned by her husband, Lt. Lloyd Hansen.

As you know, Lloyd, the son of Mr. and Mrs. H. O. Hansen of Kanaranzi, is now a prisoner of war in Germany, having been shot down in a Fortress raid over the continent.

———— ★ ★ ★ ————

Add this to your list of "war hardships." That beauty salon for dogs, where the elite of the canine world can get shampoos and "hair dos" in New York, has closed due to the "manpower situation." It's about time.

———— ★ ★ ★ ————

Just another item about "The Voice." The Columbia broadcasting network has issued strict orders to all programs that the script writers must "lay off" making nasty cracks about Sinatra. Good indication that the midwest hasn't gone "off its nut" about this flat note specialist is that Herman will play his starring picture, "Higher and Higher" at the Pix. And did the booking agents scream over that.

Speaking of broadcasting there are great days "soon to come for radio listeners." The new radio company, "The American Network" is getting set for business. This will be a FM (frequency modulation) affair which will reproduce voices and music in the full, glorious, natural tones, the highest note of the violin, the lowest notes of the drum. You'll only tune the receiver once, the volume won't fade or swell and there'll be no static or interference. Manufacturers expect to sell 5,000,000 FM sets in the first postwar year and 20,000,000 in the second year.

FEBRUARY 24, 1944

Just one little item about Chief Petty Officer Ken Olson who returned again to Luverne last week after making the trip from the west coast to Kansas City by plane.

It sounds ridiculous—this chap who has been in the navy during the "thick of it" had one thing on his mind when he got back—to find out if there was any pheasant hunting. You'd have thought he'd heard enough gunfire and done enough Jap hunting so that pheasant shooting would be a bore by contrast.

"It's fun to shoot Japs," he explained, "but you can't eat them."

Kenny was delighted to find that South Dakota was still "open" but the shell problem was the big worry. So for that reason we nominated Walt Anderson as the GOOD SAMARITAN OF THE WEEK.

Hearing about the navy man's dilemma Walt took one of his last remaining boxes of shells, that he had hoarded for his hunting (which he loves next to "wife and sons") and handed them over to Olson. So now everybody's happy—nice going Walter.

———— ★ ★ ★ ————

Trip your friends up by asking them how long the "Star Spangled Banner" has been our national anthem. The answers you will get will amaze you. As a matter of fact it has been our national anthem for only 13 years, believe it or not. Official action wasn't taken until 1931 by President Hoover and the Seventy-First Congress. Everybody knows that Francis Scott Key wrote the words but how many know that the tune was written in London a decade before the American Revolution.

MARCH 2, 1944

We're not going to use any "mighty appeal" or flowery words about the most important subject of the coming week—the Red Cross drive. You Rock countians have done such a magnificent job in all phrases of war work and your generosity stands out as a shining example for the rest of the state that an extended appeal isn't necessary.

You know the Red Cross and the great work that it is performing today. Your money will make the continuance of this humanitarian work possible. Need we say more? We know, because you're the kind of people that you are, that nothing more need be said.

——— ★ ★ ★ ———

The middle aged man, his shoulders bent just a bit more that morning under a crashing blow of sudden grief, came out of the Western Union office, clutching a yellow piece of paper, and walked over to where we were talking on the sidewalk with Les McClure.

"I was just coming down to your place but maybe you'd care to look at this now if you want to," and he handed over the telegram with shaking fingers.

It was one of those "we regret to inform you" type of messages, the kind that hundreds of Rock county parents live in terror of, day and night.

We copied down the text of the official telegram. What could we say? Absolutely nothing. For words at a time like that are so futile. Nothing, no matter how much you mean it, can ease the heartache the slightest bit.

He tried to be so casual, to choke back any word that might reveal the depth of his emotion.

But I thought then—"I wish that some of those people who like to say so patronizingly 'you folks out here in the midwest don't have the slightest idea there is a war on' could have looked at the tear reddened eyes of Herman Wiese, Sr., that morning.

If they had—they never would utter such a slander again.

———— ★ ★ ★ ————

Of all the lucky breaks any Rock county man in service has had yet, being stationed only 30 miles from home, we think 2nd Lt. Erwin Brown has hit the all time jackpot.

Lt. Brown and his wife arrived Wednesday to spend 10 days with his parents, Mr. and Mrs. Julius Brown, before Erwin takes up his duties as meteorologist at the Sioux Falls air base.

Graduating Monday from the meteorologists school at the University of Chicago where he received his commission, Erwin was asked to designate his choice as to where he wanted to be stationed. So he put it down this way: Sioux Falls, first choice; Sioux City, second choice; anywhere else, third choice. Three meteorologists picked Sioux Falls as No. 1 choice but by a stroke of luck Erwin was given the assignment. This means that his parents will see more of him than they have during the past five years, as he has been attending school and working.

———— ★ ★ ★ ————

Jack Benny is cutting adrift this spring from his Grape Nuts program in favor of Pall Mall cigarets as his radio sponsor, at a $25,000 per broadcast salary.

March 9, 1944

When Russ Haakenson used to work at the creamery he wore glasses. When Pvt. Russ Haakenson came home on furlough he wasn't wearing glasses. It seems that the army hasn't improved his vision any but that after doing four months of Military Police duty in the Union depot at Kansas City Russ decided he didn't need glasses as much as he thought. It seems he had one scuffle with a drunk (his only incident) and after he broke those glasses he decided "to heck with it."

It was interesting work, watching crowds of 80,000 people a day hustling and bustling to the scores of trains that roll into that busy place but Russ is glad he is being transferred to the new assignment in Omaha, in which he will deal with business machines.

He doesn't think the dislike of M.P.'s is as intense as it was in the first World War. "That's what the old timers say," Russ said. Very little trouble is experienced but one night it looked as if there would be a real free for all. There was a group of soldiers returning from overseas who took exception to a request made by one of the M. P.'s. Only some cool heads saved the day, and a general riot was averted.

MARCH 16, 1944

If you want a "Jap haircut and a shave" you may be able to get it one of these days. Master Sergeant Boy Cowan, son of Mr. and Mrs. A. B. Cowan, is sending home a captured Jap razor and pair of clippers to his father.

──── ★ ★ ★ ────

Despite the sleet and cold our bird lovers report that robins were seen here last Thursday and Saturday and that they were followed by martin scouts and a few blue jays.

MARCH 23, 1944

Simple things are best . . . we never can quite catch up with John Gabrielson who is home on another leave. This good natured blond always seems to draw navy assignments that put him in the "hottest" places. Just back from Tarawa . . . and the rest of those bloody engagements in the South Pacific John was reported as having a lot of fun helping at the farm . . . and also sorting out baby chicks at the Rock County Hatchery.

──── ★ ★ ★ ────

It's been a long, long time and so much has happened since they went away. Little did any of the several thousand people who watched that train steam out of the Omaha depot here that morning dream that it would be so long before the men of Battery E would be back.

Yet . . . a few months stretched into a year, then two years, then three years. Some of the boys got back on furlough and the rumors would fly around that "everybody was going to get a furlough soon." Some of the fellows sought escape from that dreary Aleutian island by transferring into the air corps, others were transferred.

The rumors started flying again a few months ago . . . the report was out that all the trunks had been shipped back to the states and that the men would soon follow.

Now—at long last—it looks as if the rumor was really the truth. Long distance calls have been coming into Luverne this week. One chap said "all the men of the 215th are now back in the states." And they probably are. Some of them have been sent to El Paso, Texas, others are in Seattle, some in other camps. But it shouldn't be long until they all should be home. Should be an excuse for a real celebration here.

In mind's eye we can still clearly see the picture of that leave taking . . . there were a lot of tear stained faces in that crowd that morning and there were a lot of red eyed young girls moping at their jobs the rest of the day. War still seemed terribly far off but the leave taking was still a grim fore runner of the sad goodbyes that have been said so many times since.

When the men were transferred to Kodiak everybody was pretty much in the dark as to what and where Kodiak was. Bud Sherman wandered in about that time with an Alaskan magazine and there was an article in there extolling the beauties and delights of Kodiak as a hunter's paradise and a beautiful spot. So we jotted down, for Chaff, some of the facts listed in that article . . . we thought the mothers would be so happy to know in what a nice spot their sons had landed. Oh, brother. We are still quivering from some of the letters that resulted from that description. Some of the things the men said about Kodiak shouldn't have been written on anything else but asbestos paper.

But at that—it could have been worse. One of the legends that has grown up in the past two years is that for a while it was a toss up as to whether the 215th was to go to the Philippines or to Kodiak. The final decision was in favor of Kodiak. You can imagine what would have happened if it had been the other way— Rock county men would have been in that tragic "death march" following the surrender to the Japs.

Of the Battery E officers who stood in the door of the baggage car waving goodbye, till the train went round the curve, that winter day in 1940 the group has been scattered wide and far. Lt. Col. A. A. Anderson is no longer with them, but at Camp Callan, San Diego, Cal. We probably will get our neck wrung for printing street gossip but the story is that "Andy" should be home in the near future for good. (It will be one way to get a letter from the colonel . . . print a rumor.) Major Fried is now one of the "top men" at Snelling. Major Marty Jensen is now at El Paso, Texas, at Fort Bliss. Lt. Clarence Jensen was on Attu but he is now back in the states. Major Ray Frick went to the Worthington "outfit" but he's back in the states and should be heading home on leave. And that's just about the way it goes. It was a hard, long, dreary three years. And the men were in what was expected to be one of the "hottest spots" in the entire Pacific campaign. They knew, those first few desperate months, what it is to stand grimly at a post knowing that you are under gunned, under equipped, under manned with no air strength to speak of—knowing that your job was to fight a suicidal delaying action. Happily, it didn't work out that way . . . but those were the facts that they gallantly accepted.

MARCH 30, 1944

Been complaining lately, about life's hardships have you?

Maybe you'd like to trade places with some of the boys—for instance Sgt. John Wahlert, just back from Italy. One night not very far from Cassino, shell concussions knocked Wahlert out of his fox hole three times, tossing him from 10 to 15 feet each time. But he was so exhausted he'd crawl back to the hole, usually filled with four inches of ice water, and drop off to sleep despite the continuous roar of artillery fire.

His gun crew had 11 planes to their credit, mostly Focke Wolfes and ME 109's.

And the same day we talked to Chief Petty Officer R. W. Skeen, a brother of Mrs. George Pitts, who is back after nearly two years in the Pacific with the SeaBees.

"One night on this island," said Skeen, "a bomb lit just five feet from my foxhole, killing three men in the next foxhole, and turning mine 'upside-down'."

Chief Skeen said that his outfit had arrived at one island to undergo the longest continuous air raid on record, three hours and 50 minutes. Thirteen American planes were destroyed but he proudly boasts that the SeaBee crew had the damaged runway back in operation within an hour and fifteen minutes.

Skeen was "in" on the Rickenbacker rescue. For three days the patrol plane from their island base had flown over the Rickenbacker life raft—finally spotting it on the fourth day. One plane was left to circle around the position of the raft while the other patrol plane came in to the base. It was dark by then and Skeen and his crew rigged up four huge floodlights in tree tops so that the patrol plane could taxi out again without hitting the reef. The plane met the other plane and they effected the rescue, taxiing in 40 miles to the base because they were unable to take off with the heavy load. P. T. boats were sent to rescue the other two life rafts of the Rickenbacker party.

The flier has been taking quite a "beating" from organized labor as a result of his denunciation of strikes in wartime. But what he has said is nothing to the scathing rebuke given by Skeen.

"He's right," said the SeaBee officer, "men quit their jobs to go overseas to fight a war, work sixteen hours a day, go thru bombings and hell for less than a fourth of the wages paid back home, and pray for materials which we couldn't get because somebody at home was on strike."

Back from the Pacific March 1 he spent two weeks in Shoemaker hospital, California, for "nerves." But he looks good now and takes pride in the fact that his battalion was the longest outfit "out," went without any training to speak of, their equipment was sunk but they got in six months hard work until their equipment finally arrived.

———— ★ ★ ★ ————

If you have been lagging a bit on those war bond purchases read the following eloquent letter from a captured Fortress pilot. From where he sits in a German prison camp he still thinks that buying War Bonds is still the best investment in freedom anybody, at home or a prisoner of the enemy, still can have.

The following letter, postmarked 18-12-43-0-11, was received March 22 by Mr. and Mrs. George Nelson.

Dear Mother, Dad and Ken,

"At last I can write you and tell you I am well and alive and uninjured at all. We all got out all right. THE RED CROSS FEEDS US VERY WELL HERE—FROM NOW ON GIVE TO THEM. Do not write to me here—I just wanted to write and tell you I am all right. Smitty (his co-pilot) is here with me . . . I'll be able to write more at our final camp. THE RED CROSS FEEDS AND CLOTHES US WELL—THAT'S ALL THAT KEEPS US GOING—CONTRIBUTE WELL. AND YOU CAN CONVERT MY MONEY IN THE BANK TO WAR BONDS. Don't worry about me—I'll be all right. Tell everyone 'hello' and don't write till you hear from me again. You should see my lovely red beard. I'll be back there soon, and please don't worry—I'll be all right."

All my love,
Darwin

APRIL 6, 1944

Already the men from Kodiak, who certainly have led nothing less than the most rugged existence for nearly three years, are beginning to wear a haggard, wan, appearance.

That well worn cliché that society editors like to use about "a giddy whirl of social events" is beginning to undermine their otherwise perfect health.

"Who said this town was dead?" said one of the youngsters with a sigh of exhaustion.

And the worst is yet to come—what with family dinners, family reunions, visits at the "girl friend's" house, a Rotary luncheon, the American Legion inviting them to the meeting, the VFW doing the same, the Civic and Commerce Association staging a dance in their honor next Wednesday night, a belated mass charivari at Hardwick for all the married men of the battery—they certainly are facing a packed social calendar.

We make so much of Battery E's return—for two reasons. Not only because the community is whole heartedly welcoming back these men who have been so long away but because their return is symbolic of that happy day, that all parents dream and pray about, when all the boys, scattered so widely around the world, will return for good.

Three years waiting for the parents wasn't nearly as tough as the three hours they waited last Friday for the first contingent to arrive by the afternoon Omaha passenger train.

Wouldn't you know that the engine would decide to stage a display of temperament that particular day? At the time the train was due here it still hadn't staggered into Rushmore. When it wheezed in here the train crew was discouraged for fear they couldn't whip up the "iron horse" to make it the rest of the way to Sioux Falls and it was half an hour after the conductor called "all aboard" before they managed to get the balky "critter" out of the station.

There were some joyful reunions at the depot . . . the kind you don't like to watch too closely because they are too intimate in their happiness. And there were some pretty long faces, too, on the parents of the boys who had not yet arrived.

Because some of the Battery E men did not arrive home last week for some reason or other, we've been busy all week trying to find out who is and who isn't here. With the help of one of the men we were able to compile the following list of those who are here. These men left with the battery, and are either still members of that organization, or have transferred to some other unit. Anyway, they all served in Alaska, and returned to the states last month. If we have omitted someone, or have given someone the wrong rank, it is wholly unintentional.

S/Sgt. Max Schlader, Sgt. Maynard Qualley, S/Sgt. Bernard Eberlein, T-4 Maynard Davis, Sgt. Martin Kvaas, Sgt. Geo. Carsrud, Sgt. Vernon Fremstad, S-Sgt. Howard Haakenson, Sgt. Leon Opsata, Sgt. Willard Schwartz, T/3 Russell Gunderson, S-Sgt. Alvin Ringen, 1st. Sgt. Karl Heiden, Pfc. Herman Huisman, Pfc. Jacob Schellhaas, Pfc. Henry DeBoer, Pfc. Matt Bendt, Cpl. Dale Earl, Cpl. Lowell Obele, T/5 Wallace Haakenson, Sgt. Gerald Tatge, Sgt. Floyd Zwart, Cpl. Lester Ripley, Pfc. John Appel, Pfc. Lyle Horrigan, Cpl. Don Obele, Sgt. William Ryan, Cpl. Harold Haibeck, Pfc. Vernon Stelling, T/5 Harm DeBoer, Sgt. Robert Barrett, Pfc. Clarence Stubbe, Cpl. Lloyd Fleshner, Pfc. Kelmer

Remme, Sgt. Frank Cooksley, Cpl. Robert Gibbons, Pfc. Gordon Jepson, Pfc. Orville Thompson, Pfc. Harry Schadwinkel, Pfc. Sigurd Thu, Pfc. Charles Meyer, Pfc. Herbert Oehlerts, T/5 Les Erickson, T-5 George Fabel, Sgt. Edward Rauk, Cpl. Herman Studsdahl, Sgt. Quentin Lynch, Pfc. Peter Funck, Pfc. Lyle Youngsma, Cpl. Robert Gray, Tech. Sgt. Lennen R. Naley, 1st Lt. John Jensen, Capt. Paul Hagemeier.

We'd like to run pictures of all who are home, but we'd like to get as many in groups as we can. We took one group picture following Monday's Rotary meeting, and any one not in that is asked to stop at The Star-Herald office Thursday afternoon at either 2, 3 or 4 o'clock, Friday afternoon at 4 o'clock, or Saturday afternoon at 2 or 3 o'clock. Be sure to come right on the hour, as the pictures will be taken at each of the above hours of those who are here at that time.

We don't like musical comedy type pictures and I don't know which is the greatest form of torture—to have to sit and squirm thru a "musical" or get up and have to walk past Herman who fixes you with a "hurt" stare of the "you don't like my picture" type.

But—if you like singing and dancing and pretty girls then maybe "Cover Girl" is your "dish." We "caught" a bit of it at a preview. Plot was very familiar but the picture is done in the most gorgeous technicolor in history.

April 20, 1944

This business of writing Chaff is something like riding a merry - go - round . . . once you get started you can't quit. We'll admit Chaff is never very interesting, about all you can say for it is that it's "clean." And this is one of those exceedingly dull weeks when we give fervent thanks that there are personalities like Kay (Ha! Ha! Ha!) Aanenson on the loose to write about so we can fill up space.

(Editor's note to compositor—that opening paragraph ought to fill up at least a couple inches space so don't set it "tight")

What we started out to say is that the whole town is chuckling this week at the signs that blossomed mysteriously Sunday morning on the windows of Kay's hair cutting emporium, The Gyp Joint.

For those who didn't see the signs (put there by little men who should have been in church) here is the gist of what they said:

"JUSTICE OF THE PEACE AND MATRIMONIAL BUREAU. Rates: men under 50, $10; men over 50, $5; men in uniform 50 cents; men over 85, free. After midnight, add 10 cents an hour. **Reliable, sympathetic, gentle.** Fifty Eight Years experience. No time for hair cutting." (And the wags repainted the name from Kay's Gyp Joint to "Hitch Joint.")

That 58 years' experience started a terrible argument raging . . . "just how old is Kay anyway." He's as skittish about telling his age as any woman over 22. It's admitted that our jitter bugging justice of the peace barber looks 34, and acts like 17 . . . but the question is, "how old is Kay."

Bill Goodale says Kay is older than he is, and Bill is 57. One woman, who says she "knows" declares that Kay is within a few months of her age . . . and she is 60. (But for reasons of TACT we won't divulge her admission.) "Mac" MacDonald says he knows positively that Kay is "away over 60." Who knows . . . Kay might even be a prospect for our "Diamond Club."

As to the identity of the sign painters all we know is that Ray Ronlund, early Sunday morning, saw Doc Getman, Shorty Busch and Cliff Simon carrying stepladders, brushes and yellow paint cans back to Nelson's store.

———— ★ ★ ★ ————

And Major Ray Frick says Battery E is "no more." It's been changed to Battery A . . . and if you want to write anybody formerly with the outfit when they go back to Fort Bliss from here, says Ray, this will be how the address will read:

Name————————; A. Battery, 599th A.A.A.; A. W., Fort Bliss, Texas.

———— ★ ★ ★ ————

They say there are two old ladies that haven't been getting out much lately that didn't get to the Civic and Commerce Association's "Good Neighbor Party" a week ago. Just about everybody else was there. You can get any figure you want as to the crowd estimate. Some insist that there were at least 3,000 people there during the evening.

At any rate Hugo Moeller and Henry Wuertz were frantic about 9 p.m. They called up in the most plaintive voice saying "what will we do with all these people." It seems they had hoped maybe 900 or so would turn out but they ordered enough buns, weiners and coffee to take care of 1,500, just to be on "the safe side." And then a crowd almost double that amount, and all as hungry as locusts, descended on the lunch tables.

For a while it seemed as if they wouldn't be able to get the Omaha passenger train in to the depot, cars had been parked across the tracks, on the platform blocking the baggage and passenger entrances. Outside of the fact that the public address system used by the orchestra was terrible, everything else was wonderful, according to the verdict of those that attended.

Comment by Mrs. Mike Hemmer, Luverne, seemed to be the sentiment of practically all who attended the party. Said Mrs. Hemmer, "I think the 'Good Neighbor Party' was a swell idea, and everyone I have talked to said the same thing. I think the Civic and Commerce association is to be congratulated for this generous gesture. I'm sure everyone who was there appreciated it."

APRIL 27, 1944

Why is it that we always seem to make typographical bobbles when it concerns Magnolia people. We are just beginning to get back to normal, and the ruddy blush is barely leaving our cheeks, after the boner a few misplaced lines happened when we referred to Glenn Alcox and his garage "equipped for four children in September."

And then on April 6, mentioning Pvt. Russell Wilder we made another. It should have read that he "recently enjoyed a 7-day furlough." But Frank Ferguson's keen eyes spotted the fact that it read "decently enjoyed a 7-day furlough" and added this comment, "Say, Mac, was Cpl. Wilder an exception?" Oh me!

MAY 4, 1944

I suppose we should make a report to the boys that are away just what the score is "back home" in Rock county. If we were writing a letter it would probably go like this:

Dear Gang:

Well—life goes on in Rock county but the faces get longer and longer every day on Main street. They say you never get "something for nothing" and the farmers are beginning to believe that's right. Because we certainly are paying thru the nose now for the California winter we had.

One of these days we'll probably bust around the weather corner and have blazing summer heat all at once, without ever having had any spring.

This last series of heavy rains really fixed things. Even with several days of hot weather it will still be quite a spell before much farm work can be done. Art Rogness, of Hills, is typical of several hundred farmers in the county.

"There's one field," he said, " that I haven't been able to even get into yet. This keeping the cattle in the barn is making it tough on the feed supply too."

Rock river is rising and you can hear the roar of the rushing of the current but it really isn't on the rampage yet. But it kind of spoiled the fishing for the rod and reel boys on the opening day of the fishing season, Monday.

The rains have made the lawns a brilliant emerald green and they're really beautiful to behold. And speaking of the spring season you would have had a chuckle Monday night, thinking of your own "tiny tot" days watching the parents out with their youngsters hanging May baskets on the doors of their friends.

It's been a mighty quiet week. Either the censor has been busy or you have quit writing because we have only about a third of the usual amount of news about you men in service for this week's Star-Herald.

There'll be some excitement, tho, the day of the school election. There'll be some competition this year and they're thinking about calling up the cops to the school house to help handle the crowd. Last year they only had 64 votes cast but some are predicting there'll be nearly 400 or more votes this year.

The highway patrol is busy pinching speeders and the rumor is they have one eye specially "peeled" for one young man who has been keeping the speedometer above 80.

You won't see "Brownie"—one of Luverne's famous canine characters any more. The dog that used to ride on the fire truck to every fire had to be put out of his misery. And there were real tears on Snoose Steine's face when he came walking back, carrying the shovel, after digging Brownie's grave.

Things happen so fast in the newspaper business at Pipestone that you get dizzy trying to keep up. The first change was made last year when the Pipestone Leader went from a twice a week paper to a Thursday paper. The next thing happened early in January when Fred Smith of the Pipestone Leader sold out to Ralph Hay, of Hoopston, Ill. Hay had the paper only two weeks and then Smith took it back because of Hay's announced ill health.

Then the Pipestone Star went from a twice a week paper to a Tuesday only edition.

Now the rumor is that the Pipestone Star interests have purchased the Pipestone Leader and that the merged publication will be known as the Pipestone Star-Leader.

Bluest girl in town this week was Mrs. James Argetsinger (The former Phyllis Brooks if you didn't remember.) She planned for some time to go to see her husband, Corp. James Argetsinger, who was stationed in the east. But you can't go ahead with plans like that when there is such a thing as scarlet fever. After her daughter had recovered and the quarantine signs were taken down Phyllis made new plans to go as her husband wired that he would have a four day pass. She got on the bus Tuesday. After she left there came a call from her husband saying "don't come—I'm being shipped out." So Ed Brooks had to get busy and see that Phyllis was headed off, at Sioux Falls, from making the long trip east.

There aren't many G.I.'s from Sioux Falls around any more. There were only about eight buying tickets at the train last Monday morning to go back to camp. And there used to be fifty or sixty, sometimes a hundred or more, in town over a weekend.

They really had quite a time at the Drost-Petersen wedding last week at the State Line Presbyterian church. When the ring-bearer decided to go on "strike" the flower girl thought for a minute she didn't want to participate either.

It all started when Darrell Boyenga, 4, the ringbearer was due to start his march down the aisle. Evidently Darrell is going to be a bachelor because he made evident right there what he thought of weddings. About that time Pryllis Petersen, the flower girl, decided she didn't want to march either—but she yielded to persuasion. The bride, Esther Drost, couldn't delay any longer and she started for the altar. Frantic signalling resulted in a woman in the church getting the hint. Dale Kuper was hurriedly drafted into service and he grabbed the ring and hustled down the aisle in great shape.

That wasn't all either. Esther thought she smelled smoke and thought her right arm felt "hot." She took one horrified look and discovered that she was on fire. Her long veil had brushed against one of the burning candles nearby and in another split second, save for the quick help of one of the men, she would have been blazing like a torch.

And speaking of Churches:

The high wind Tuesday night toppled a brick or two, loosened by the years, from the top of the Methodist church. So Dr. Eastburn decided that the chimney or whatever you call it better be leveled before somebody got hurt. Ant that is when somebody nearly did get a brick bounced on his noggin. When Jack McKay started clambering down Harm Smook walked over, without saying anything, to hold the ladder. Not knowing that Smook was below McKay bounced down a couple more loose bricks. Smook was white as the proverbial sheet when the bricks started bouncing round his head.

The county's getting "wilder" all the time. Art Schmidt phoned in last Friday to say that he had sighted two deer on his farm east of Luverne. They came from the east and disappeared into the wooded area near the river, northeast of the city park.

Well—that's very little news to write but it gives you a sketchy idea of about how life is "back home." In the meantime . . . best of luck.

Al.

MAY 11, 1944

Here's a personal prediction—based on information from one of the best sources we know—the war in Europe will end in the same month that it did in World War I—November.

———— ★ ★ ★ ————

And speaking of juvenile delinquency Superintendent of Schools Barrett referred to the "woodshed" as one of the greatest institutions that ever helped "build character" in America. Incidentally—Barrett's talk was one of the best of any kind made in Luverne for many a month. He should be asked to give it again—this time to a bigger audience.

———— ★ ★ ★ ————

You're very silly if you keep your gasoline ration coupons in the glove compartment of your car. Some boys, real young ones too, were sighted prowling cars the night of the golden wedding celebration of Mr. and Mrs. James P. Kennedy. Those who investigated first thought nothing had been taken . . . but it later developed ration coupons had been stolen.

———— ★ ★ ★ ————

How many noticed that picture in the Argus-Leader Tuesday night which showed Major Geo. Fried swearing in a group of Indian young men at Fort Snelling?

MAY 18, 1944

The Tuesday afternoon train's whistle echoed mournfully as it vanished round the curve. The little group of friends, who had assembled to meet it moved from the hot sun in front of the depot to the shaded platform at the west end.

There they stood in respectful silence. The navy lieutenant stood in the summer heat, holding his cap and brief case under one arm as he wiped his brow with his handkerchief, by the side of the waiting funeral coach.

A man wheeled up the baggage truck. Heads were reverently uncovered. Six husky men, some of them dressed in rough work clothes with perspiration staining huge dark blotches on their shirts, moved up and grasped the handles of the heavy casket and gently lifted it into the waiting coach. Every creed and several nationalities were represented in that group. But nobody then was asking his neighbor "what are you." They were friends—no more—no less.

They tenderly closed the doors of the coach and moved aside. One of those men unashamedly wiped his eyes with his shirt sleeve and turned quickly away. A woman who had been in the group of friends, broke away quickly and walked to her car, her eyes swollen with tears. The funeral coach's tires crunched in the cinders as it drove away.

Ensign "Bill" McCardell had "come home."

———— ★ ★ ★ ————

If you have at some time or other been a Boy Scout here is your chance to do your "good turn." They've reorganized the Boy Scouts here. You know what a uniform means to a youngster, everything in the world when he's at Scout age. But you can't get them during these wartime shortage days. If you have one—or any Scout apparel—or if any member of your family has been a Scout—why don't you call Dr. David J. Eastburn about what you'd like to give or sell.

———— ★ ★ ★ ————

Remember the false Armistice "flash" that rocked the world back in 1918? The radio networks are in a dither for fear they may bobble and broadcast a false "invasion" flash. Back and forth across the Atlantic the radio executives talk by phone each day to set up broadcasts, make reports, etc. For some time the correspondents have been using an intricate system of verbal codes to get around the censors. The cues are ordinary, every day, words so not to get the censors wise and the radio executives are jumping jittery for fear one of their correspondents may inadvertently use in conversation, unwittingly, one of the code words which might be taken as the "invasion" flash signal.

———— ★ ★ ★ ————

Staffs of daily newspapers all over the country are on "alert" in case the invasion breaks . . . key executives don't stir very far from a telephone day or night. The belief is that the long awaited flash will come sometime after 11 p.m. but before 5 a.m.

MAY 25, 1944

We just happened to notice that it was just two years ago to the day that we published a letter from Tommy Campbell, then a student at Worthington Junior College. Tommy was bitterly critical of some phases of a patriotic observance. He said it was probably due to the "indifference of the citizens of Luverne."

A lot has happened since then. Tommy is now a flight officer "somewhere in England," a glider pilot waiting to spearhead the long awaited invasion. His high quality of patriotism takes on a new meaning.

Outwardly things haven't changed here. The lilacs are out in full bloom, making the air heavy with their rich fragrance. Tulips are one big splash of color round the homes and the lawns. The countryside was never greener . . . at night there are a million or more stars winking in the summer sky . . . with a couple of million bull frogs parked along the edges of the bank full ditches croaking a mighty chorus.

But things are different. Rock county never did go in for the synthetic, "hip, hip, hurrah" type of "patriotism." It was always something deeper and finer than that. There no longer is any of the "indifference" here that Tommy had a right to criticize. When Rock county mothers go out next Tuesday morning to put up the Flag they won't do it in a perfunctory manner . . . there'll be loving reverence in the way they handle the folds of Old Glory and there will be prayers in their hearts. The old days when civilians were slow to bare their heads as the colors passed by are gone.

There's a new "note" at home. Because Memorial Day means something this year. There are newly saddened hearts in Luverne. Some are mourning at new graves and others mourn for those for whom there is no grave—here. Mrs. Lloyd Petersen was in the office the other day, holding a Purple Heart award and trying to wink back the tears that she couldn't stop. Her husband, missing in action, since August 21 over Italy, is now officially listed as killed in action. With incidents like that, how could anyone be indifferent?

There's a new note of patriotism, of reverence as Memorial Day approaches. It now means something more than a chance to get away on a picnic.

We should have written a Memorial Day editorial. But, we had the disturbed feeling that everything we tried to say had been said a thousand times before—and a lot better. And then, Wednesday, came a letter from Burton O. Knowlton, now in the southwest Pacific, which carries a patriotic message, better than anything we could write.

"You know, Al," he wrote, "the more I see of this world the more I realize what a wonderful country the United States is. I feel sorry for people who are living way out here and will never know the opportunity of living in so great a country. If I was to travel the world over I know I would never be satisfied in any place but America. Several New Zealand people told me that they had never met a people that were as proud of their country as the Americans are. You don't realize this fully though until you are away. And then it really hits you."

There's the theme for Memorial Day . . . let's have the same love of reverence for our country as the boy who is serving its cause many thousands of miles away.

———— ★ ★ ★ ————

We've seen "This Is The Army" twice, in Minneapolis and in Sioux City, and we're going to see it for the third time when it starts Thursday at the Pix. Don't miss it—it's great entertainment. Leaves you feeling good all over.

———— ★ ★ ★ ————

Frank Willers, former Luverne man who now is one of the midwest truck "magnates" was one of the unsuspecting stooges picked from the audience to dance with one of the chorus girls of the Sons of Fun show at Sioux Falls Monday night. And he did a right smart job, too.

———— ★ ★ ★ ————

We walked into Ray Engan's office the other day to find the comfortably plump barrister (look who's talking) sitting at his desk, holding his head in his hands. It was another case of the old saying of Bobbie Burns, "the best laid plans of mice and men gang aft aglay." Jimmy Horne knows what that means but if you don't understand Scotch dialect it means that the best laid plans usually get, to put it in vulgar slang, "balled up."

Anyway—Ray was holding a telegram which stated that Julian Sletten, who was slated to give the Memorial Day address here, had undergone an emergency operation. "I knew everything was going too smooth," moaned Ray.

So Father P. E. Matthews steps in as pinch hitter for the Memorial Day oratory on short notice. We think it's just as well.

He won't have as much time to prepare the address as did Sletten, but what he'll say will come from the heart and will have a deep meaning for Americans All.

JUNE 1, 1944

This little tale might properly be entitled "Footloose Papa Nearly Gets Inducted into the Army."

You, no doubt, know that Bill Cameron recently went to Fort Snelling to enlist in the army reserve (ASTRP) having just passed his 17th birthday.

Going along for the ride was his dad, Earl, who both from size and disposition resembles nothing more than a banty rooster.

Earl decided to also go out to the Fort and pay a visit to Major George Fried, the "Mr. Big" of Snelling executive affairs.

But restless and full of zip Earl couldn't sit still for long and disregarding George's suggestion to stay at his office, the Luverne man started wandering round the Fort. The first thing he knew he was picked up and shoved into line. The 51-year-old man was hopping around so peppy that the sergeant thought he was a stray from some group. Sure enough—they checked all the lists—found a name Cameron on a special list from Rock county and they "knew" they had their man. So they insisted that Earl butt in line. In another two minutes they would have had him completely stripped and "on his way thru" but Major Fried just happened to start looking for Earl about that time.

Earl, pale and trembling, just a bit when pulled out of line by Fried, still thinking what a close call he had had.

"I admonished him it would be best in the future if he sort of confined himself to my office," Major Fried wrote us.

"But Earl still chafed for excitement. He disappeared and about an hour later I finally found him again—this time surrounded by a big group of boys. I'll quote excerpt from a letter I received from him, explaining in detail what happened to him.

"I had some fun while at Snelling. I was at the canteen and struck up an acquaintance with a sergeant. A bunch of inductees from Rugby, N. D., (my old home state) were there. Most of them were bellyaching. I had the sergeant go out and then come in again and announce that I had passed the physical 100%. Boy, that laid them out, when I told them I was 51 years old and had been drafted. 'Boys' I said, 'this is the happiest day of my life.' I bet things are buzzing at Rugby, N. D., when they tell that an old man 51 years old was drafted."

Major Fried said that Earl had not told him what happened at the canteen but since getting his letter he checked on the story and found it was true—every word of it.

"What Earl doesn't know," Fried wrote, "is that his little act boosted the morale of those North Dakota boys. One of those boys remarked, 'Boy, this war must be getting pretty tough when they take guys like that. What the ——— have we got to squawk about?' "

——— ★ ★ ★ ———

With the starting deadline nearing for the War Bond drive don't ever get the idea that the men overseas aren't watching closely to see how the folks at home back them up.

"Rock county," writes Pfc. Alvin S. Huiskes from an island somewhere in the Pacific, "has really got a big bond quota to make this time.

"Oh well, just leave it up to good old Rock county. They will make it. If everyone was like the people up there it wouldn't be bad."

With a reminder like that we must not fail in the bond drive. All patience of service men overseas is just about exhausted with the strikers back home, if you can judge from what Huiskes says. "What burns us boys up," he added, "is all these strikes going on all the time. That's what really hurts our morale over here. But I guess there's nothing we can do about it here."

There's a reason why Billy Brooks was beaming all over like a lighted Christmas tree this week—he'd been accepted by the U.S. Marine Corps.

That doesn't sound like anything to start jumping up and down about until you know the story back of this youngster. He was rejected last year after his physical examination for the army and was classified as 4-F. Billy was completely "whipped." If you ever saw a kid that was eating his heart out to get into a war then he was the one. He went and had an operation—and then kept pestering the draft board here for another physical examination. He got it—and passed. That's why he's so happy this week.

We can imagine if he ever gets one of those "dress blues" outfits of the corps what a heartbreaker he'd be. Billy is going to make a doggone good marine tho, as well as look good in a uniform. One of the nicest kids you'll ever meet, polite and quiet as a church mouse, you don't want to write him off as a softie.

Gerhardt Ahrendt tells the story on Bill about the time a plug ugly, not nearly as drunk as he was letting on, started abusing Bill at the filling station where the youngster was working. The kid took it all, with mild remonstrances, like a sheet of blotting paper until—the drunk made the mistake of making a "pass" at Bill. They say his left flicked out like a snake's tongue, not over a foot or so—and the next the drunk knew he was flat on the pavement staring at the stars. His two companions came piling out of the car to avenge their pal's "honor." Billy started backing away—to get a little room—with the men taunting him as "afraid to fight" coward. When they charged him it was, says Ahrendt, a case of "wham-bang" just two blows being struck, all by Bill. The two birds were flat on the sidewalk. The curly headed blonde youngster politely helped them all into the car and requested them to come back again when they were feeling "better."

———— ★ ★ ★ ————

Paul Soutar thinks he's established a "first" in tomato production for this year. He has a tomato already, about the size of a quarter, from a planting he made about three weeks ago. Anybody to dispute him for the title?

June 8, 1944

When we sleepily stumbled down the hall to answer the clamorously ringing telephone we made a mental note that it was shortly before 3 a.m. We picked up the receiver, thinking it was Sheriff Roberts calling to say that there had been an accident. Instead it was Mrs. Lloyd Long, playing the feminine counterpart role of Paul Revere, saying "get up, Al, and listen to the radio, the invasion has started."

Altho we had written in this column several weeks ago that the news would break between midnight and 5 a.m. we still couldn't believe that the long awaited "D" Day had arrived. We sat by the radio for over an hour listening to the breath taking announcements of eye witness observers of the assault. And then we went back to bed—to lie there for a long time, wide eyed in the darkness—thinking "what Rock county boys are landing on French soil tonight?" "Please Lord, may this not be another Dieppe."

And so the invasion news came to Luverne, quietly. There were no whistles, no sirens. People got up and automatically turned on their radios to get the biggest news in all the world's military history.

There were no demonstrations—not much was said. The coffee shops were filled almost to standing room as the 10 o'clock news approached. Argus-Leader "extras" were grabbed up like hotcakes and eagerly scanned. There were sober faces on the men as they listened to the news but there was a smile of exultation when they heard that the Allied forces had penetrated ten miles inland. One mother dropped in the coffee shop. She shook her head and pushed the cup of coffee, which had been placed in front of her, aside. "I just want to listen to the radio," she said. Her boy, by all the odds, was "there." One didn't have to be psychic to know what was in her mind—or her heart. The prayer that she was uttering right then as she listened to the announcer was multiplied a thousand times and in Rock county countless times during the day.

This is no time for any premature rejoicing or cockiness because the coming weeks are going to bring grim news. This struggle is far from over—it has only started—and if anyone thinks that a gain of ten miles means that the next three hundred are going to go as fast or easy he is only an ostrich.

———— ★ ★ ★ ————

There's a War Bond Drive starting next Tuesday. Rock county has a big job cut out for it. But Ned Brown, county chairman, is gambling on the patriotism of you Rock countians. Ned is starting the campaign where the last one left off—without a single meeting of any of the workers.

"I don't feel like calling a county meeting of the workers," he said, "that's asking an awful lot right now when most everybody is busy with their farm work, asking them to take off four hours to come to a meeting."

Here is the way Ned looks at it—the workers have been thru four previous campaigns—they know their job and what has to be done. There is nothing new he can tell them that they don't already know. Why should he impose further on these volunteer bond salesmen by taking their time for an organization meeting when they will have to give so much time during the drive.

With a man having so much faith in the people of Rock county we can't afford to let them down. Just remember this— some of those boys who are battling ahead in France will never "get back" but you'll get every dollar you invest "back" and with interest too. It's "better to buy bonds than to wear them."

———— ★ ★ ★ ————

And another thing—the Red Cross has received a terrific quota for surgical dressings. These are needed—and will be needed. Let not any woman in Rock county think that she isn't needed in this effort. Your help may save a boy's life. Need we say more?

———— ★ ★ ★ ————

Probably the most chagrined person in town, to turn to the lighter side of life, was Ed Kolbert. He dropped off to sleep at midnight in his overstuffed chair. It was 3 a.m. when he woke up and stumbled off to bed, not thinking to turn the radio on for the possibility of any invasion news.

———— ★ ★ ★ ————

During his visit to Luverne Lt. Haugen captured the admiration of everyone he met with his charm and modesty. He was about as unconcerned, coming back after his 28 missions over Europe and his DFC decoration, as if he'd been out behind the barn pitching hay all day.

Asked Monday by Major R. Ross, head chaplain at the Sioux Falls air base, what he thought about religion, Lt. Haugen made it plain that there aren't any atheists in the air as well as "the foxholes."

"You haven't time to do much praying or thinking about religion when you're on your bombing run over a target, you're too busy watching out for flak and fighters, while you're trying to drop your bombs.

"But religion is something everyone has when he's making the run home after a mission. You know in your heart, whether you ever went in for church or that sort of thing, that somebody big was taking care of you and had his arms around you. Of course I was brought up in church to believe in religion but I know a lot of fellows who never went in for 'believing' before who are Christians now."

JUNE 15, 1944

Sgt. John Goeske got a Christmas card the other day nearly seven months after it was mailed. A certain Luverne man (who we promised Chaff readers a month ago that we wouldn't use his name for a whole year) mailed the card to John in November. John was in Italy at the time of the mailing but had left for the States by the time the card arrived. From Italy it was started on its way back, going thru Sicily, North Africa, across the Atlantic, to Norfolk, Va., then to Riverside, Cal., then back to Fort Bliss where it caught up with him nearly a half year late. Three or four thicknesses of paper had been pasted on the front of the letter, a new one going on every time there was no longer any room on the front for an address. Just goes to show you what efforts Uncle Sam takes with service men's mail.

JUNE 22, 1944

It was at Rotary Monday when the club entertained two visiting soldier guests. One is on his way to combat—the older man is stepping out.

We couldn't help watching the youth. Many a time we'd admired his gay impudent manner on the basketball court as he would trick some opponent into letting him slip thru the defense in order to make a basket.

To us his fine, sensitive face with the steady, deep eyes personified the American boy who is fighting, and winning, this war. You can tell to look at him that he won't like war—he'll find no joy in killing—but he'll tackle it as his job. Like thousands of other young chaps who came of age too late his heart was broken at first when he was washed out in the middle of his pilot training course. To be told then that he was to be a flexible gunner seemed like nothing at all to him those first few dismal weeks. Now he's proud of his job—and doing it the best way he knows how.

As he spoke briefly to the club he looked straight at the older man, who wore the insignia of another service branch, and said, "begging your pardon but the air force is the best branch of the service, sir!" That is what is known as morale.

The youth was Keith Connell. The older man was Lt. Col. A. A. Anderson.

———— ★ ★ ★ ————

"Andy" Anderson is home—getting ready to take off the uniform that he has worn for three and a half years. And then it will be "civvies" and no more snappy salutes from soldiers on the streets.

Unlike some who will return and will have to buy complete new wardrobes he isn't badly off as his clothes will all fit. He weighs 186 now, four pounds less than when he left.

Even tho he thinks that he is better able to adjust himself than the younger chap, Anderson admits that it's difficult.

"It's a kind of a funny feeling," he said, "I'm not really at ease. It's going to take quite some time for these young fellows to get back to civilian life and the swing of things. They're going to have to learn to take things in stride."

He's glad to get back home.

"There isn't a better place than Rock county and I've driven over a . . . lot of country. Don't forget that every one of the boys that are away from here are dreaming of the day when they will get the war over and get back to Rock county."

Now on the inactive status list Anderson is still subject to call but at 57 there is little likelihood of that.

He's going to take it easy for a few days, maybe do a little fishing along with some visiting, before he makes any plans.

"I plan to go back in the banking business," he said.

———— ★ ★ ★ ————

Mrs. Andrew Brekke, Beaver Creek, reports that her son, Cpl. Elmer D. Rollag thinks enough of war bonds that he has bought his 12th $50 bond. He's been with the army engineers in the southwest Pacific two years and of that time 16 months was spent on Guadalcanal.

Kind of puts a lot of people to shame doesn't it?—considering that a corporal doesn't make any "defense wages."

JULY 6, 1944

There are only two naval chaplains for the Dutch government who hold the rank of Commander, one on each coast. The man who holds this distinction for the west coast assignment is a former Rock county man, Commander Edward E. Fikse. The son of Mr. and Mrs. Evert Fikse of Steen he was formerly a pastor in California having been called to organize churches in the Central Valley district of California.

When war broke out and Dutch sailors were then heartsick men who knew that their home ports were under Nazi control but who were grimly resolved to keep on fighting Rev. Fikse answered a call from his own heart. He went to the seaports to voluntarily minister to these sailors on Dutch vessels. He was given the rank of Naval Chaplain in the Netherlands Royal Navy on the Pacific Coast. He was later raised to the rank of Commander.

——— ★ ★ ★ ———

We've had a couple letters from boys out in the South Pacific asking for more of those columns describing how life "goes on" back in Rock county. Just to oblige we'll tell them how the Fourth of July was spent "back home."

Dear Gang:

Well—this is being written the evening of the Fourth of July. It's been the longest, quietest Fourth that Rock county has spent in many a decade.

We said "longest." The business men decided to close not only for the Fourth but the preceding day and if you'd seen everybody wandering around like lost souls you didn't need to talk to them to know that they were swearing under their breath "never again." Sunday-Monday and Tuesday in a row with nothing to do was just too much.

We said "quietest." We only heard one firecracker pop all day long. And we didn't hear the explosions from any home made bombs either.

People spent the day in a mighty quiet way. First of all they hung out the flag either at their home or their place of business. (You never saw so many flags being displayed in Luverne.) Then about noon they headed for Luverne's park down by the river under the big trees.

If you could have parked another car at the park you would have been infringing on the sardine can patent . . . every last foot of parking space was taken. We don't need to mention that every single table was in use—and it's a good thing that the city had those tables built extra strong for they were veritably groaning beneath the load of heavy picnic baskets. After everybody from "dad" down to "junior" had stuffed themselves into a stage of near coma everybody flopped on the grass, like a bunch of Mexicans to take a siesta.

But the youngsters didn't quit eating—they kept busy on ice cream and pop all afternoon long. (If the Luverne doctors didn't do a roaring business all night long answering tummy ache calls then the younger generation is hardier than we think.) We noticed about 4 p.m. one youngster who had built himself a fire in a tin can. He was toasting a weenie, which he held on a stick, with one hand, while he drank a bottle of pop with the other.

After everybody had revived a bit they turned to a little bit of exercise. The young folks drifted over to the swimming pool which was packed. Some of the others, with their elders, were busy in a soft ball game. The old timers drifted over to the horse shoe pitching headquarters and you could hear the familiar "clink" of the shoes hitting the steel peg as far away as the highway.

Trying to get some privacy a group of young couples drifted over to the south edge of the park to whisper "sweet nothings" to each other.

Late in the afternoon the families nibbled a bit at the remaining bits of food (and there was plenty), packed up the babies and placed them in the car and headed for home.

Things in Rock county look good altho the corn is way late, but the last week or so of hot, humid, weather has boosted it along so you can almost see it grow by the hour. Some of the farmers didn't pay any attention to the double holiday. A good number of them spent the Fourth working. We saw others in town getting their tractors fixed.

The highways and streets have a lot of khaki on them—G.I.'s from Sioux Falls over here trying to get away from the thousands roaming the streets in Sioux Falls. They have a pretty subtle way of getting rides without actually giving the "give me a ride" sign. They get out on the street, almost in the middle of it, and you have to swing wide to miss them. Makes you feel kind of guilty driving home for dinner and passing them up. You feel like getting out and explaining that you're not going to Sioux Falls. Carl Wiese was driving his truck back from Sioux Falls the other day headed for Luverne. He passed a whole string of them and then stopped. Twenty-two grateful soldiers hopped aboard and got a quick ride to Luverne.

You wouldn't have thought there was gas rationing judging by the cars you saw the Fourth. Rock county hasn't been hit by any curtailment of supply altho one of the bulk men is supposed to have said that he will only get 50 per cent of his normal requirement in July.

Another dealer said he had been promised a normal supply so you can't tell much about it.

We were watching Lt. Ray Cragoe the other night sitting in a filling station. From where we sat he looked bored and restless and we asked him about it.

The boy, who has seen plenty of action and lived a couple lifetimes in the past six months, said he had dreamed desperate dreams of being "home." Yet when he got here the home town seemed different. Probably things are terribly quiet for the fellow who comes back but the truth of the matter is that the fellow who comes back misses seeing all of you chaps who belong here.

We said it was a long, quiet day. There wasn't any excitement—no speeches, no parades, no band music. Everybody spent the day quietly—but they were all thinking of you—and hoping and praying that this would be the last Fourth of July you'd spend away from home.

Well—that's about the story as to how things are going back home.

> Best regards,
> Al

July 20, 1944

Somehow the gossip "grape vine" had heard that there was a telegram coming thru after 6 p.m. last Friday for Mr. and Mrs. Ray Lester of Magnolia. Ray Lester heard about it and his heart was heavy.

He started walking down the street—on the way he met "Scotty" Dewar, the depot agent.

"Which one is it?" asked Lester—because there were four boys to worry about in that family. After being told he went sorrowfully home to break the news to his wife.

It must be a hard job handling those death messages. Dewar had known Kermit since babyhood—it was more than he could do to carry that message to the home—he took and left it in the Lester box at the post office. And the family understood why.

And it was a gracious gesture that was made at the dance in Magnolia last night. When the crowd heard the news—the dance was halted immediately out of respect to the memory of the fighting marine.

———— ★ ★ ★ ————

Let's hope that the Andrew Larson family will have as happy an experience as that one last week in Farmington. A boy from there had been reported "missing in action." Two hours after the message had been delivered the boy walked in the door of his home. It isn't hard to imagine the joy that prevailed there.

Capt. Merle Larson, Rock county's first "ace" and one of that small but gallant band of P-38 fliers who flew night and day in the early phase of the North African campaign to hold the "aerial fort," is now reported missing.

His brother, Alvin, of Omaha has the strong feeling that Merle will turn up all right. Why not? He's been lucky before. Larson was shot down one time in North Africa and after a lot of hitchhiking he finally made his way back to headquarters—to see his name posted with the notation, "missing in action."

JULY 27, 1944

Three years and a half is a long time in anybody's book, but it seems even longer ago than that when we went down to the depot to take our first picture of a Rock county man going into service.

It was cold and bleak and snow was on the ground that 28th day of January, 1941. Ed Schmidtgall was a novelty, like a newly arrived panda in some zoo, because he was going into "service." War still seemed so terribly far removed from this country and he was only going for a "year's training."

He was our first service man's picture—and like the man who fondly remembers the first nickel he ever earned—we remember the occasion most distinctly. Arnold Qualley, then draft board clerk and now with the SeaBees in the Pacific, was down to bid official farewell and if we aren't mistaken, Hugh Fay was there, too.

(For the sake of the record, Schmidtgall was the second, not the first, Rock county man to leave. The first was Donald Sovereign, who left Nov. 22, 1940. Schmidtgall, altho he didn't have a low number either, volunteered Dec. 9, 1940, and was cleared thru the draft board here on Jan. 28, 1940. That was way back in the days when the county draft quota might run from one to three men per month.)

Well—Ed was in the office the other day—only it's Cpl. Edwin R. Schmidtgall now and he's just back from 23 months of foreign service.

(He was released once in 1940 because he was over age at 28, but when the war started he was recalled.)

He used to be Ernest Juhl's "hired man" and he still is as unemotionally philosophical about his part in the war as if he had just gotten thru shocking 160 acres of grain.

He didn't have any complaints about Italy, the mud, the cold, bitter fighting or the filth. He'd just grin and say, "it was pretty rugged," and for him that covered everything.

Schmidtgall was in Africa a long time but never got into any action.

A tank gunner on an M-4 tank he said about all he did for a while was repair tanks. Every time new tanks came some other outfit grabbed them and Ed's outfit got the old ones. He missed out on the Sicilian campaign and docked at Salerno just after it had been cleaned out.

Finally, tho, they got "into it" and had a few "skirmishes" in Italy. He doesn't know how many pieces of enemy equipment his tank smashed up but he proudly asserts his tank was still in there fighting the last he had heard.

Schmidtgall served in Italy with the French, whom he described as the fightingest fools who scrapped like "cats and dogs when they met the Germans—and they didn't give a hang about anything."

Well—that's all Cpl. Schmidtgall had to say—he wasn't wearing any campaign ribbons on his chest and he didn't think he had done a great deal in the war. He said goodbye and went out the door.

If it hadn't been for Ernest Juhl we would never have known that this "hired man from Rock county" had been decorated with the Silver Star for devotion to duty at the risk of his own life. It seems that the corporal, in the face of withering enemy gun fire, exposed himself to the enemy in order to make repairs to a jammed gun. By so doing he was able to get the gun into action again and his bravery saved the tank and its crew from certain destruction by the enemy.

But if you'd ask him he'd day he hadn't been "such a much." He now goes to a southern camp for reassignment after his 21-day furlough. His parents live near Selby, S.D.

He was our "first" service man as far as pictures were concerned, so we hope you don't mind our reminiscing a bit about him to such a length.

———— ★ ★ ★ ————

It wasn't any surprise to Hardwick folks when S/Sgt. John Goettsch, son of Mrs. Tena Goettsch, received the air medal. An aerial gunner, now stationed in the southwest Pacific, Sgt. Goettsch, says Irv Grunklee, is one of the best shots ever known around Hardwick, a chap who loved to hunt and shoot better than anything else in life.

AUGUST 10, 1944

Monday to our desk came the August issue of the International Teamster with an article by Daniel J. Tobin, the international president of the trucker's union.

This sentence caught our eye in Tobin's article telling about the union grievance.

"I do not like to throttle our government now and hold it up at the point of a gun to gain certain conditions for truck drivers. I would rather have our people suffer slight injustices rather than hinder our war effort, where the lives of millions of our people and the freedom of the nation is endangered."

(His pious words didn't mean a thing—his members went out on strike before the magazine was hardly off the presses—tying up vital deliveries all over the midwest.)

Here's more from Tobin:

"We will endeavor to get what we believe is reasonably ours, what is just, what we think belongs to us, but we will obtain it through just and peaceful means from tribunals set up by our government, and not by stabbing our fellow members in Africa and Australia in the back or by throttling our government in its darkest hour of danger."

(But his union broke its promise they didn't wait until the president had passed on their case before they took action. And in the words of their own president they're "throttling" our government in its darkest hour of danger.)

The Minneapolis spokesman for the union justified the walkout by saying, "our men got tired waiting for their wage increase."

(There are nearly 1100 Rock county men that right now are "tired" too—not of their wages, which are inadequate, but of war. They're "tired" too of fighting filth and fiendish enemies, of jungles, and malaria, of the hedgerows of France behind which lurk enemy snipers. They're "tired" too of the noise and smell of death. And I imagine that some of the Rock county boys wounded in the invasion are "tired" too of hospitals and pain.—But the strikers were "tired" of waiting for their wage increase.)

Over the Pacific and over Europe Rock county fliers fly daily sorties trying to smash the Nazi lines of communication knowing that if they can knock out locomotives and trucks the enemy's ability to fight can be paralyzed.

(But over here—our transportation system is paralyzed too—not from strafing from enemy fliers—but by the action of some chaps who were "tired" of waiting for their wage increases.)

AUGUST 24, 1944

Well informed newspapermen declare that Hitler will probably resort to the use of poison gas within two weeks . . . they also say that the "robot bomb" situation is still a long ways from being told. A newspaperman comes up with an interesting explanation of why Hitler has so long spared the life of Franz Von Papen, his tricky ambassador. It seems Von Papen was one of the three men directorium named by the former Chancellor Hindenburg—that Von Papen threatened publication of the will and as a result managed to make a "deal" with Hitler.

AUGUST 31, 1944

It would have served him right if his wife had thought the scratching in the window screen early Sunday morning was done by a prowler and had fired a shotgun blast thru the window. But that was the way Jess Frakes (we should say Chief Petty Officer) announced his unexpected return to his family the other morning from Camp Parks, Calif.

Jess says there are two Oakland, Calif., couples who will always be gratefully remembered by Rock county service men. They are Mr. and Mrs. Almer Olsen and Mr. and Mrs. Ernest Olsen and they both have apartments in the same building. Jess says it would be hard to say how many Rock county men they have befriended, giving them wonderful meals, a good bed, driving them to trains, etc. They go out of their way to look up former friends from here that are in nearby camps.

We should mention another Petty Officer that was in the office this week . . . It's Albert Johnson, brother of Mrs. Grant Curry.

A frequent comment of returning service men is "lots of times I never thought I'd ever see Luverne again." But Johnson can say that . . . double. It's been five years since he's had a chance to get back to Rock county . . . and when he talks about it seemed good to get back "home" he kind of choked up . . . as much as a taciturn fellow like Johnson could get.

In the navy eight years, lacking two months, Johnson had about as many ribbons and stars as we've seen in a long time, five bronze stars on his Asiatic-Pacific service badge. He's been aboard a battleship that has been in all the major Pacific engagements with the exception of Pearl Harbor.

"When I got home," said Johnson, "the folks seemed to think that I should have had more than 18 days leave. I said that most of the fellows are just plenty glad to get back at all . . . to say nothing about getting a leave."

It's the people back home that are the optimists . . . not the men who are fighting the battles. It still is rough going. Johnson said the battles are getting tougher than easier . . . and that his last battle was the roughest of all.

"I hate to think of 'em," he said, "they make a lump come to my throat." (That is as far as we can take you along this line without violating censorship rules.)

Johnson arrived Sunday and expects to leave Monday or Tuesday of next week. In his five years since he has been "home" he has little time off to speak of. He had a few days liberty early this year and used it to visit his mother and brother on the west coast that time. He'll see everybody this trip except one sister.

SEPTEMBER 7, 1944

"Women are wonderful!" sighed Neil Roberts.

We wondered what on earth had prompted such a romantic outburst on the burley sheriff's part. It seems as if it weren't for women he wouldn't be able to solve half of his cases.

I guess that if it weren't for women Neil wouldn't have had such good luck recently. For instance—the Illinois man just returned for alleged forgeries here met his downfall because he couldn't resist writing to his girl in Illinois. A woman happened to see the address and remember the name of the town so the "law" knew right where to look.

And—here's the story behind the recent pick up here of a soldier from Jackson county who had been A. W. O. L. for three months. The soldier who had been hiding out couldn't resist sending word to his wife who was working at Worthington to meet him here. The Jackson sheriff got a tip to that effect so he came over here and he and Roberts met the bus. They spotted the woman getting off the bus and followed her west a block on Main street. Suddenly, "out of nowhere," seemingly, appeared a man in overalls. The meeting place had been prearranged for it was the A. W. O. L. chap . . . the husband of the woman. The two sheriffs pounced on him and it wasn't long till he was in army custody.

---- ★ ★ ★ ----

Considerable discussion has been had in Luverne as to "what to do" when V Day finally comes. And the day isn't far off.

We happened to turn an old newspaper file Monday to the issue of 25 years ago which told of the celebration then. It can be summed up in the writer's words, "for hours a veritable bedlam prevailed."

Word had first reached here at 2:10 a.m. of the Armistice signing but the news was withheld for several hours. Dr. C. O. Wright, as mayor, had arranged for the fire whistles to blow and fire bells to ring and the fire truck dashed thru the streets with siren screaming. From then on in pandemonium reigned all day.

We're just wondering what it will be like this time. We think it will be a far soberer occasion. Sure—there'll be wild, unbounded, fierce joy in everyone's heart that the war in Europe against a terrible foe is finally over.

But—we think a lot of people will remember that it's different this time . . . that it's still a case of "two down and one yet to go" and that about half of Rock county's men are fighting in the Pacific theater of war.

The most dangerous thing that could happen would be for everyone to adopt the "it's all over" complex and lapse into an easy going attitude. That would be breaking faith with the men who realize that there is bitter fighting and dying still ahead in the Pacific. We must not let down one ounce until total victory is won.

Incidentally—one of the sanest forecasters in the business had this to prophesy Monday . . . that there will be rapid disintegration and collapse inside Germany . . . that Himmler, Goering and Goebbels are likely to try to flee to Argentina or Japan, that Hitler will be killed. He believes it possible that there may never be a formal surrender . . . because everything will come "unstrung" loosely rather than an abrupt climax. He believes that there may be no armistice at all as an excuse for one big celebration. And there may not be one actual "V Day."

And as a reminder . . . that there are plenty of heartaches yet ahead . . . and that we should solemnly remember the sacrifices that have been made, we are printing a letter received by Mr. and Mrs. Ray Lester from the buddy and corporal of their son, Pfc. Kermit Lester, who fell at Saipan. It is a sorrowful letter to receive but there is one satisfaction . . . Kermit never knew what hit him . . . and he made the Japs pay dearly . . . the next morning it was discovered that 200 dead Japs were piled up in front of the machine gun he and his companion manned. The letter follows:

Dear Mrs. Lester,

"I don't know how to start this and I am hoping it gets to you thru the address Lester gave me. You see I don't want to reopen a wound but I had to write. Ever since your son got out of boot camp he has been in my squad.

"I guess he has spoken of me as I have of him when I write. We were always together and he was like a brother and more to me and the rest of the boys.

"I can't tell you how I felt when it happened and I can't now. I fixed him the best I could the next morning and got his watch off his arm . . . that is what I want to ask you . . . and find out if this will reach you. I was taken off the island a few weeks ago and this is the first time I have a chance to write you.

"If you will write me I will send you his watch if you wish.

"I don't know what to tell you. I do want you to know that he did not know what hit him. It was quick and I am glad of that—as I know you will be. You can and always should be very proud of him. He was always in there—the night it came it was our first night on the beach. There was about eight hundred Japs trying to come thru our company.

"Lester and Walters were both killed on the machine gun but there was about two hundred Japs in front of their gun. I was proud of all my squad and I always will be. There is only one left . . . but he and I will always remember the BEST BOYS I have ever known and hope to know. I don't think I will be able to fight again. I hope I am on my way home. I was shook up by a shell in the last run but I am okeh now.

"Well . . . I hope I didn't say too much or too little. I will put my home address below as I have no address in here at the time being.

"It is no use to say I am sorry . . . it is more than that."

Cpl. George Amburn,
Galveston, Texas

There isn't much comment anybody can make to the above is there? Anybody who moans about "sacrifices" here on the home front should be made to memorize that letter.

SEPTEMBER 14, 1944

Lt. John Stavenger, bomber pilot now in England, has decided it's a mighty small world after all. He hadn't hardly landed before he bumped into Lt. Howard James of Luverne.

Then—he leisurely settled back to read an English magazine. He looked at one big picture of a wrecked plane in the magazine. The picture carried the caption:

"THE MAN WHO WAS LOST RETURNS TO BASE"

And beneath it were a few lines telling of how the pilot of this particular P-47 Thunderbolt had been seen by the squadron commander blazing "like a comet" after flak had hit him after an attack on Nazi tanks.

The write up concluded, "but he brought it home, tho the undercarriage collapsed on landing."

The pilot in question was none other than Lt. Quentin Aanenson of Luverne.

His family here knew nothing of the incident altho they did know that Quentin had been in a rest camp.

And the picture showed the Luverne youngster walking away from the wrecked plane, which came in on the proverbial "wing and a prayer," as blithely unconcerned as if he'd just bought a nickel's worth of candy.

———— ★ ★ ★ ————

A day after we had written the above lines came a letter from Aanenson telling of the "incident."

"I was shot down by flak August 3rd," wrote the Luverne boy.

"My little ship was ablaze so I started to bail out over German lines. Just as I was cutting all switches the fire died out so I decided to try to reach our lines. My luck held out and I managed to crash land on our landing strip. I wasn't hurt much, just bruised up a little. The next morning I was sent to England for a rest.

"Later I found out that my parachute had been damaged so if I had jumped, I'd probably still be bouncing. Never a dull moment."

The youthful pilot said "those German gunners can shoot the wings off a fly at 30,000 feet."

He has received the air medal with two oak leaf clusters and his group has been recommended for presidential citation.

Lieutenant Aanenson was in the leading squadron of the 3,000 planes that swept over Normandy about three weeks after "D" day in an attempt to smash all German lines.

———— ★ ★ ★ ————

The story is that the Americans are all ready for the cracking of the much vaunted Nazi Siegfried line. If the report is true the American ordance experts have devised special artillery for the grand assault. It is said that this artillery was tested at the Aberdeen proving ground where sections of the Siegfried line had been reproduced in massive concrete and steel to the very last detail . . . and the American artillery proved brutally effective.

———— ★ ★ ★ ————

Several gentlemen who are addicted to "looking on the wine when it is red" have been telling some fantastic stories down town about "haunted houses" and of seeing "wild animals" peering out of a house window on North Freeman street.

Their friends on hearing these tales have shaken their heads in dismay as much to say, "poor chap's mind is slipping."

But now on good authority, none other than that of Rev. E. G. Meierbachtol, can we say that the story is true.

Rev. Meierbachtol says that a fox has been seen peeking out of the window of that house Stanton "Stub" Hinkly is remodeling on North Freeman. The fox roams thru the house and peers at passersby from many a window.

We haven't checked but we'd bet a nickel that the fox is the one adopted recently by the Richard Torrison family.

SEPTEMBER 21, 1944

The selective service contingent that left last week got to say their farewells twice in one day but the postponement of their leaving was a rather trying experience for everybody—the prospective army men, their families, local draft board officials, and Ike Johnson, bus depot agent.

The men said their goodbyes as the 8:30 bus pulled in and started to get on board. The driver already had a load and said he knew nothing of any selective service contingent to be taken to Windom. The driver, Ike, Mrs. Nora Campbell all got busy on the long distance phone. Something had slipped, between state head-quarters and the bus line, and the special bus that should have been here had never come. A bus showed up at 12:30 p.m. finally from Windom to pick them up.

When the delegation were taking their routine physicals again one examining doctor took a look at Bill Nath's feet and asked "have you ever been here before?" Bill said "yes." The doctor took another look, scratched a big red cross all over his chart and waved him on his way home.

——— ★ ★ ★ ———

Case Van Engelenhoven was hunched at a desk at the elevator this week, one ear glued to the radio and one eye cocked at a map of Holland . . . it seems the American parachute invasion of Holland at Nymegen was taking place just five miles from where his parents, brothers and sisters live.

——— ★ ★ ★ ———

And the death of Pvt. Russell Wilder in France should be a sobering reminder for all of us that grim and tragic days lie ahead.

The war may end by October 7 as some expect but whether it does or not there will be many a saddened home like the one in Magnolia this week. If you remember the first World War between the time the German high command told the Kaiser late in August all was lost and the signing of the Armistice we suffered 90 per cent of our total casualties of that war.

The days of kisses and cheering for the Americans are over. No longer are they going to be welcomed by flowers, fruit and kisses. They are to the point now where they come not as liberators of a captive country but as invaders of the land of the enemy. The casualties are going to be many . . . we can have no reason for relaxing when the men across know that the toughest going lies ahead.

———— ★ ★ ★ ————

Lt. Dave Butler "wowed 'em" at the Rotary dinner Monday night. Called on by "Bud" Sherman to say a few words young Dave, whose dry wit is of the Will Rogers variety, went on to say how much he was enjoying his leave . . . which came to him thru the courtesy of "our Commander in Chief." A few eyebrows raised in wonder as to why Dave was getting so formal in referring to his getting a leave but he smoothly went on to add: "Dad said if I didn't get in a plug for Roosevelt I couldn't have the car tonight."

———— ★ ★ ★ ————

We're not going to have the front office windows at the Star-Herald washed (yes—we do too have them washed from time to time) until we take the present display out. There are so many finger and nose prints made every day that window washing would be a losing battle. Causing the interest are two captured German machine guns, one of the heavier field type and the other a typical "tommy gun" type. They were sent back by Lt. (j.g.) Bob Haakenson as a gift to Ensign Warren Schoon. Leave it to that amazing entrepreneur Haakenson to acquire a couple of guns like that and get them back. He'll probably be shipping some robot bombs next. And Fred Herman yielded to that suppressed desire that burns in the heart of every youngster "young and old" and climbed into the window to play with the guns . . . aiming the "tommy gun" at all the apartment windows across the street.

———— ★ ★ ★ ————

You don't realize how big a part maps play in the invasion plans until you learn that the invasion of France required the printing of over 70,000,000 maps. All told they weighed as much as 83 Pullman cars. Small wonder there's a paper shortage.

———— ★ ★ ★ ————

There's an amazing amount of frankness creeping into our advertising lately. First it was Preston advertising that his office was "anywhere on Main street." Now it's Bill Merrick who at the bottom of his ad says that his office is in the Luverne National bank building but that most of the time he can be found in the coffee shop.

SEPTEMBER 28, 1944

The men in the Pacific are going to feel bitter if they think the home folks celebrate V Day with a "school's out for good—let her rip" riotous type of celebration.

You get that impression from a letter written by Lt. F. A. Dubbe in which he enclosed an editorial from the Honolulu Advertiser. Fred underscored the following lines:

"Here in Honolulu there will be no such celebration.

"The day of the Nazi surrender may mean that the war is won and over so far as the British, French, Russians and Mainland Americans are concerned, but it has nothing to do with the grim, deadly, tremendous war that is being waged by us against Japan in the Pacific and in Asia. We are still in the thick of it, our young men are fighting as desperately and dying as hard as any soldier in Europe, and it is a far longer and more difficult road to Tokyo than it is today to Berlin."

"If you can convey this same thought in your area the war would surely end sooner," concludes the flier.

———— ★ ★ ★ ————

We wish we could have been over at Kenneth the other night and see the rousing "hero's" welcome they gave one of the home town boys. It must have been a great sight.

S/Sgt. Russell Mork, son of Mr. and Mrs. G. H. Mork, returned home from overseas and the town really turned out . . . the band and crowds of old friends. Russell shook hands till he was limp all over.

This chap who has been a crew engineer on a B-26 probably has flown more missions (and we know if we're wrong you'll correct us) than any other boy . . . 67 missions in all or two more to his credit than was necessary for a return furlough. He's probably got as many if not more decorations than any other local boy, 12 Oak Leaf Clusters with the Air Medal.

His mother hadn't expected his arrival so soon . . . and she had made a beauty shop appointment for a permanent so she would be all "prettied up" for the great day . . . but even tho he came earlier than expected it was still wonderful . . . you can always get permanents but it isn't every day your boy comes home.

OCTOBER 12, 1944

We said months before and we say it again, one of the most heart rending assignments a small town editor has nowdays is the handling of war casualty stories. On a city daily you could handle them in a routine way but here each one hurts . . . deep . . . because you either know the family . . . and what the loss means to them . . . or you know the lad himself.

We're getting so that we jump in apprehension every time we see the yellow envelope of a telegram. A mother and father of a boy walked in the other day with one . . . but that was all right, it was the announcement that their son was the proud father of a baby boy. And when Hugo Moeller walked in with a telegram we thought "who now?" But it was only the announcement that the National Housing Agency had given approval for reconversion priorities.

(Since the above lines were written . . . Hugo Moeller has walked into this office carrying a telegram which told that his wife's brother, Sgt. Harold O. Meyer, has been seriously wounded in France.)

But it wasn't so happy when Geo. Hofelmann walked in last Monday and with tears in his eyes shuffled the yellow piece of paper across the counter. "I've got to take this home," he said. And you can see not only was his own heart broken but he knew what his arrival with the message would mean. If ever a youth personified the typical American boy . . . it was Russell Hofelmann, fine clear eyes and clean face . . . a boy who could have been dismissed from the navy because of long and serious illness but who fought to stay in and "see it thru."

And then you talk to Clarence Bly, still stunned by the sudden death of his son, Jean, in a west coast Marine hospital. It snapped shut the door on a world of dreams because Jean was making his post war plans for his own farming career and his hopes for success as a livestock man.

No—it isn't easy for anybody nowdays. And no one knows the price of war, in hours of anguished worry, better than the loved ones back home. It should spur us all on to not let down for a second . . . to do all in our power to hasten the end of the war.

──── ★ ★ ★ ────

A kind hearted California woman sent Mrs. Mike Ormseth of Canby a picture the other day. That doesn't sound like much, but it was the most welcome picture ever received in that home. It showed a group of five American soldiers who are being held prisoners by the Japs and Russell Ormseth (a brother of Norm of Luverne) was one of the group. The California woman's brother was a member of the group and he had sent her the picture and written the names of the boys on the back. So she had copy prints made and mailed one to the parents of each of the boys.

Russell looks very thin, otherwise not "too bad," although those that know him say he looks older . . . but when they stop to think they recall that it's nearly five years since he left home. (The 20th of October.) Russell, a marine, had been in China, then was taken prisoner at Guam shortly after the attack on Pearl Harbor.

──── ★ ★ ★ ────

"Pepper" Martin sends word back to his mother that he was one of the very first units of American troops to enter Paris after its capture.

(We should identify "Pepper" as Pvt. Bernard L. Martin and his mother as Mrs. Frank Martin of Luverne.)

The exuberant youth said, "I'll never forget that experience if I live to be 110 years old.

"Well, Ma," he wrote, "to tell you the truth, you just can't imagine what it was like. We all went in on a few trucks and on account of the people it took us several hours to reach the center of Paris.

"We stayed in Paris all that day, that night and a few of us just 'got lost' for two days after that."

Pepper quarrels with the official population records as regards Paris.

"They say," he wrote, " that there are six million people in Paris, but I don't believe them, because I believe I was kissed at least by five million of the girls—and I mean beautiful girls."

———— ★ ★ ★ ————

Making records for rolling bandages in two World Wars is Mrs. Luella B. Way, daughter of Mr. and Mrs. Mark Swedburg. A clipping from "War Times," the newspaper printed at the Pentagon building, official U. S. army headquarters, which houses 40,000 employes at Washington, tells of Mrs. Way setting a record of 60 dressings an hour.

In the first war, while attending school in New York, the former Luverne girl folded surgical dressings five nights a week and all day Saturday from 10 a.m. to 10 p.m.

"Now," said the army newspaper, "she's folding surgical dressings in this war, three nights a week for two hours and more during 1943 and 1944 while doing a war job at the Pentagon."

Mrs. Way, who is a stenographer for the signal corps in the unit training section, military training branch, hasn't missed a night at the surgical dressings unit in a year and has set a record of 60 dressings an hour.

Her faithfulness puts a lot of the rest of us to shame, doesn't it?

OCTOBER 19, 1944

Poor Martha is taking a terrible teasing about trying to put her husband, Sgt. Howard Haakenson, into a prisoner of war camp. Driving back to Luverne from Texas Martha insisted on being the direction giver. Howard wanted to take one road but Martha insisted the sign post to Roswell, New Mexico, pointed the other way. So like a good husband Howard gave in muttering to himself. Pretty soon they found themselves at a prisoner of war camp. Those who accuse Martha "of doing it deliberately and after being married such a short time" have told her that most women who want to get rid of their husbands "throw them into jail."

"But they can get bailed out of the jail," retorted Martha, which only made matters worse.

OCTOBER 26, 1944

War hasn't perceptibly changed that blithe young spirit of Lt. Bob Haakenson who has just returned after too long an absence. Too long we say because this Haakenson is one of those town characters whose antics are always provocative of news copy or laughs.

Here he goes thru four major invasions as a beachmaster for the navy, unscathed, to come home and sign up for another "major campaign." And we wish him all the happiness in the world.

——— ★ ★ ★ ———

There is one scene that we would have given a lot of money to have witnessed. That was the time that the army was bitterly critical of a practice "dry run" of an invasion maneuver. The army was blaming the navy in damning terms. So they held a conference and Bob, then but an ensign, was sent to represent the navy . . . and who did he have to parley with but about three or four army generals, General Truscott included. And the Luverne boy won his point.

We say war hasn't changed him much . . . well maybe . . . there are moments when that youthful face, and he's still just a kid, turns grimly solemn.

There are some tough times, he admits, but it isn't the writing of letters home to loved ones of men who have paid with their lives for their country's cause.

"The toughest job," says Bob, "is keeping up the morale of the men who have been badly wounded, they've got what they always expected would happen.

"It's tough too when boys get word that loved ones back home are critically ill and they know there's no chance in the world to get back in time and that all they can do is 'sweat it out'. There isn't much you can say at a time like that.

"And a hard job is writing letters home to the families of men who have died. You can't send them until you have received word that official notification has been made. If you wait till then everything has become just a blur . . . so you have to write the letters immediately and then hold them to send later."

Scared? Yes the navy officer says he's been scared plenty but the worst was the time they were sent in for a second run north of Salerno, this time a "flanking end run" of a naval maneuver which all the men knew would be almost a case of suicide.

But he'd rather not talk about the war . . . or the time their "duck" ran over a German land mine with the resultant death of two of the crew and the destruction of the craft . . . he'd just rather talk about what a swell place Rock county is.

NOVEMBER 2, 1944

Some of the boys overseas have pointedly asked for another report on how things seem back home. To anybody here at home there isn't any "news" in what follows . . . it's addressed solely to the men overseas.

Dear Gang:

This is being written on the night of October 31st. You ought to well remember what night that is . . . because it's only been a couple years since you were one of the "big boys" who helped raise particular "Ned" round the county long after the small fry had gone home to bed.

How time flies . . . it hasn't been so long since you were lifting gates, upsetting outbuildings, hoisting startled cows and horses on to unexpected roosting places. Now you're still Hallowe'ening but a different sort . . . now you are tipping over "you know whats" that belong to Adolph and Tojo.

It's a typical Hallowe'en as you would best prefer to remember it. There's the biggest, fattest, yellowest, full moon riding high in the sky that you ever saw and there is a pungent haze hanging low over the town, the smoke that comes from scores of bonfires of burning leaves . . . and there's nothing that reminds you so much of fall as that pungent unforgettable, pleasant smell of burning leaves.

The small fry are out in force in a big way . . . nearly every window on Main street is well soaped by now. About every ten minutes you hear a car horn start to blow incessantly and now and then you can hear the crash of an overturned garbage can. Little tykes, wrapped in "ghost" sheets, and masked and carrying lighted pumpkin faces are running around the streets "scaring" passersby.

The local "gendarmes" are preparing to really earn their money tonight because they aren't being fooled by the harmless antics so far. Even tho they know the action won't be as violent as when you birds were here they still know that the "big guns" will be unlimbered a bit later.

Compared to days gone by there really wasn't much being done here. Hugh Fay, Ray Fritz and Oscar Martenson were standing on the street corner watching the youngsters roaming the town and we thought the three of them were wistfully yearning to be a boy again "just for tonight," Hugh was telling about the time "some of the boys" (wonder who) found a box car on a siding and how a number of horses and cattle were quietly loaded inside. Unknowingly the railroad crew switched the car onto the regular freight train. Some 50 miles away the profane crew discovered their bootleg cargo and had to haul it all the way back again. Lloyd Johnson (some reader of Dick Tracy has already scratched "Snowflake" on the back of his car) recalled the time "somebody" managed to persuade a cow to be led into the bedroom of a neighbor's home.

But it's nothing like that here tonight. The cops answered a call that somebody had stretched a rope across the street and that some startled motorist nearly had the hood of his car ripped off by the impact. The police discovered it wasn't a rope but a garden hose. Some pranksters, and the girls were busier it seemed than boys, were letting the air out of car tires and puffing middle aged men were cussing with every stroke of the tire pump as they inflated the tires again. A number of the slats at the picket fence of Mr. and Mrs. Harold Jordahl were ripped off and the prowlers damaged the picket fence at the J. T. Winter home. Other than that it wasn't "bad." The most excitement in town was at the hospital where two babies arriving five minutes apart furnished all the Hallowe'en commotion the staff ever will want. (It was a son to Mr. and Mrs. Lloyd Rapp and a daughter to Mr. and Mrs. Louie Goettsch, of Hardwick.)

We just wanted you to know that everything "back home" is just like you'd want to remember it.

Only thing unusual is the weather. Only once in a blue moon will you see weather as warm as what we're having, more like

August or September weather instead of what you'd expect as we turn the corner into November.

The corn was unusually high in moisture but this weather is drying it out fast. Some of the farmers who were in a big hurry to pick and crib are finding out to their sorrow that some of their corn is already starting to mold. Speaking of corn . . . there's more of it than you "ever did see." Some of the yields you hear about would make you think that local fishermen were telling some of their tall tales. We've heard some fellows claim up to 125 bushels an acre.

That's a lot of corn in anybody's book . . . but even if we don't run that big a yield we're still having a bumper crop. And there aren't half enough corn pickers or hired men available to do the picking job. Now that picking season is at hand the streets are deserted daytimes in Luverne. But you wait till Saturday night and it will make you think that the county fair was going full blast.

Well—that's just about enough for now . . . this was just a line to tell you that nothing back home has changed . . . nobody is "letting down" for a minute, they're pitching and working and praying to speed the day when you will come home again for good.

Best regards,

ACMc

——— ★ ★ ★ ———

Keen eyed Pfc. Kelmer Remme, down at Ft. Bliss, Tex., spotted a picture page in Parade magazine and clipped it out and sent it to us. There is a story in the magazine of a G.I. Party in China and there is a half page picture of Sergeant Russell W. Blinsmon zestfully jitterbugging with Bernice Yu, a most winsome looking Chinese girl. In charge of the parties for the U. S. Air Force is Dorothy Wilson, a Red Cross worker from Los Angeles, who works closely with Madame Chiang Monlin, head of the local Chinese Women's Volunteer Service.

——— ★ ★ ★ ———

For three long years Phil De Buck of Hardwick has wondered about how his relatives were faring in occupied Europe. Last Friday he received a letter, written June 8th, from his sister which came from Belgium. She told the Hardwick man that their mother had passed away May 26. This, the first news from Belgium, was relayed thru the Red Cross.

———— ★ ★ ★ ————

If you saw a Fortress flying south last Friday about 6 p.m. Cpl. Lloyd Lund was on board but when he was over his home county he was busy at the time, he almost forgot to look around—let alone think of paying a visit to his parents, Mr. and Mrs. John Lund. A gunner on a Fortress Lloyd was making a routine flight from their Casper, Wyo., base but he was so busy he didn't have much chance to look about.

NOVEMBER 9, 1944

"To train in Hollywood for several weeks" is an assignment that wouldn't be hard to take for any "G.I." But that's the good fortune that Frieda Medill reports has befallen her son-in-law, Nels Hedemark, formerly of Luverne. Hedemark, now stationed at Camp Roberts, Cal., has been chosen to go to Hollywood to play a part in the picture which will depict the career of Ernie Pyle, beloved war correspondent.

NOVEMBER 16, 1944

Former members of Battery E will be interested to hear that "The Kodiak Bear" is no longer. The difficulties of printing the publication by long distance (it was printed 300 miles away) became too much trouble. The boys in charge of the Bear said that it was started at first because of the shortage of reading material but now there are plenty magazines and papers. The "Bear," which became just about the most famous of all the army publications in the world, has been succeeded by a small "mimeograph" successor, "The Kodiak Cub."

———— ★ ★ ★ ————

We heard a "chiller" the other day . . . that on Nov. 4th the alarm went up and down the east coast that a huge pack of Nazi submarines had slipped thru our patrols and had been sighted 600 miles out. And every one had a robot bomb launching platform on its deck. Planes roared out . . . what happened nobody knows but the gossip is they all came back with empty bomb racks.

———— ★ ★ ★ ————

What funny weather! Monday night, Nov. 13th, there was lightning like a mild August storm and altho there wasn't a drop in Luverne at the time it was nearly a cloudburst east of Adrian.

NOVEMBER 23, 1944

Remember when your youngster climbed to the highest branch of the tallest tree in your yard and yelled down "look at me now, Ma?"

That's the thing I always think about when a home town boy "buzzes" the town in his plane. It's the grown up version of the little boy who used to say from the tree top, "look at me now, Ma."

I've often thought, too, the thoughts that must be in the mind of the boy that skims the roof tops of his home town. Altho only about 150 feet separate him from the earth he still is as much as 200 to 1,000 miles away from "home" because his base is located that far away. It must be quite a sensation buzzing over the old town and wanting, so desperately, to let everyone know who you are, how you would like to be able to say "goodbye" with a kiss and a hug of loved ones instead of making a farewell salute by dipping the wings of your plane.

There was quite a bit of speculation as to the identity of the bomber that kept circling over Luverne Monday. The grade school youngsters got a real thrill out of it. They were waving to the plane and all the members of the crew were waving back at the ecstatic youngsters. Almost to a man everybody said that's "Jack Smith." But we said, "no, it couldn't be Jack because the plane was flying too slow, if it had been Jack he would have been blasting the town at about 300 miles per hour and standing the plane on its ear."

As usual—we were wrong again. It was Lt. Jack Smith, who is now based at Sioux City getting ready for his hop overseas.

———— ★ ★ ★ ————

The front cover of the November issue of "Northwestern Bell" magazine, which goes to all employes in five midwestern states, has a scene taken on the Carstens Brothers turkey farm north of Luverne. Shown in the picture with a yard full of turkeys is W. J.

Leimbach, telephone company employe who up until just recently lived in Luverne. The story going round is that Eddie Nett, who has been trapping near Lake Wilson lately, trapped 81 mink in ten days time. If you were doing a little mental arithmetic you'd multiply 81 mink by $10 apiece and get $810 and that wouldn't be bad for ten days trapping time. But, if Arnold Halsne is right, Eddie did a lot better than that. He got $14 per pelt for 50 of the smallest mink. All told he sold over $1,200 worth of skins. Arnold says Eddie is the nearest thing to an Indian when it comes to outdoor craftsmanship. "We'll be going along," said Arnold, "and Eddie will say 'go look at what's in that trap' and I can look till I'm blue in the face and I'll be doggoned if I can even find the trap." We can't understand why there was such a "to do" made because somebody sighted a wolf in the northeast part of the county . . . come to town and you'll see dozens of "wolves" on Main street any Saturday night.

———— ★ ★ ★ ————

He "wasn't back yet" but he pays a 55 year old debt.

Diogenes can hang up his lantern and quit his age old search for an "honest man." The "most honest man in the world" was found last week and his name is Fred Day and he lives in Roscoe, Ill.

It was last week that Day paid off a debt that he has owed for 55 years and he paid 5 per cent interest besides, on a debt that even the heirs of the man to whom it was due had completely forgotten.

Last week F. A. Leicher received a letter addressed "To the heirs of Adam Leicher." In a pencil scrawled note Day wrote:

"I owed Mr. Adam Leicher $5 since 1889. It was lunch for my help. I told Mr. Leicher I would pay him the first time I came back. And I wasn't back yet. Herein enclosed is check for $18.75 which covers the $5 and 55 years interest at 5 per cent. I came thru there in Nov. 1889 with 4500 head of sheep."

Mr. Leicher recalls the incident well. It happened at the family home near Loganville, Wisconsin, when a tired, dirty and seedy looking man came to the farm house in the evening asking for lunch for himself and the men who were helping him drive the 4500 sheep.

——— ★ ★ ★ ———

When Elbert Efner left to join the U. S. Marine Corps a few months after Pearl Harbor his dad, W. M. Efner, said "Here son, carry this testament with you . . . it will be your 'ticket' back home."

There was a story behind that little Bible that the boy was given. "Bill" Efner, his father, had carried it all thru World War I while serving in France, and the boy's grandfather had carried the same Bible for four years and four months while serving with the "North" in the Civil War.

The other day "Bill" Efner, now of Sioux Falls but formerly of Luverne showed us a letter from Elbert, written while he was still on Tinian in the Pacific.

"I lost all my personal belongings," he wrote after the campaign, "and the only thing I have left is the Bible. It got a little wet because it laid in the water all night. I had oil cloth on it so it dried out all right."

Truly—after going thru Tinian, Guadalcanal, Saipan and all those other bloody campaigns—it does seem as if he did have a "ticket back home" in that little Book.

——— ★ ★ ★ ———

Seems there is a slight disagreement between certain clergymen and the VFW and American Legion posts as regards to the handling of military funerals. The ministers object to the firing squad volleys as being too hard on the grieving families. The veterans say that it isn't a military funeral without the firing squad and they can't take part unless it is a military funeral in every sense of the word. Personally—we don't think anything is "harder" on the emotions than the blowing of "taps." We noticed in the coffee shop the other morning when "taps" was heard on the Armistice Day radio program from Arlington, that several of the local "toughies" (who like to boast of how hard boiled they are) were furtively wiping away the tears that suddenly sprung to their eyes.

——— ★ ★ ★ ———

There were cigars passed round "for free" at the Rotary luncheon a week ago. This was different from the cigars usually passed out by proud papas—they were German cigars sent back by

L. N. Schoonover's son-in-law, now fighting inside Germany, they were part of the "prizes" captured by the American troops.

———— ★ ★ ★ ————

Probably after the war you won't be reading so many want ads of farmers offering to give away corn cobs. It's estimated that the post war corn crop in itself may develop into a hundred million dollar business. A Chicago firm has developed a dryer and pulverizer which will convert the cob into furfural, a liquid used in the manufacture of synthetic rubber and high octane gas. The cobs may some day be worth $6 per ton.

———— ★ ★ ★ ————

Another Rock county boy who should have been aboard that wrecked Challenger train but luckily missed it was Arnold Sexe. His dad, Leonard Sexe now of Fairmont but formerly of Beaver Creek, had a wire from Arnold saying he just missed the wreck. Was supposed to have been on the second section but missed it. Arnold is now with the Navy on active duty somewhere in the Pacific.

NOVEMBER 30, 1944
REMEMBER "SILO?"

Then think back a few years to the time when Luverne got some national publicity when "Bud" Heck caught himself a nice case of scarlet fever. When Bud, who resembles a silo (and is just as hard to fill up with food) gets sick he gets sick all over, because he stands just a shade under seven feet.

He was a one man walking epidemic with no place to go. If we remember right he slept in the doorway of a building one night, nobody wanted him . . . then they put him in the city jail . . . and the cops were playing waiters, rushing in food to him. (That was one thing Bud . . . sick or well he always did a lot of eating. You could always see him draped over a restaurant counter or having a light snack of say a dozen or two doughnuts.)

Anyway the city finally shipped Bud out to the county poor farm to recuperate . . . where he had a most elegant time sleeping and eating.

You would hardly have known the big fellow the other day . . . only it is 2nd Lt. Merrill Heck of the air force, now based at Denver.

We can't tell you, for reasons of censorship, everything "Bud" is doing. Suffice it to say that he is a first pilot on a B-24 and he is training engineers for big army bombers. Of all the nice assignments he seems to have a dandy. These young flight engineers have a lot of things to learn about fuel consumption and plotting courses, etc., so each day Bud usually picks a different city for his destination. If he feels like flying to Los Angeles . . . then okeh everybody goes to Los Angeles, if he feels like flying to Florida then everybody goes to Florida, "lays over" for the night and then returns the next day. He certainly gets to see a lot of country.

Bud bubbles and sparkles with his love of flying . . . and the young scant that used to have the nickname "Silo" no longer ambles down the street. He's as military as can be and he's just a walking encyclopedia of aviation knowledge.

One thing Bud says . . . "the more you fly the more careful you get . . . when I just graduated I thought I was a pretty "hot rock" but I'm getting over the idea of taking chances . . . I don't go for this 'buzzing' a bit . . . I wouldn't fly lower than a thousand feet over a town unless it was absolutely necessary, like if I was lost and wanted to read the town name on the railroad depot. If you don't go lower than a thousand you've got a half a chance to get out if something goes wrong, otherwise you don't."

DECEMBER 7, 1944

It's a kind of a sickening thud to pick up the latest report from state headquarters. There are 87 counties in Minnesota . . . that you know . . . but did you know that the latest report shows Rock county in 82nd place in percentage of quota raised in this Sixth War Bond Drive?

In other words . . . after everybody has bragged all these years about Rock county being tops of all midwest . . . we see the cold facts showing that only five counties in the state have a more shameful record than we have to date.

You figure out what's the reason. Is it too much unwarranted optimism about early victory . . . have we gotten too "cocky" because we slid over so easily in previous drives . . . have some people who could afford to buy a fat chunk of bonds been content with buying just "a bond" (and not a very big one at that) . . . have some people gone land hungry and started climbing out on the inflation, bankruptcy, limb again. We haven't got the answer . . . you figure it out . . . but something's got to be done . . . and quick . . . because it would be an all time badge of shame for Rock county to wind up in the "cellar" in state war bond sales standings.

That's the reason we don't have much zest for writing Chaff this week.

But mark it down in the book . . . this drive has to go over the quota and we might as well buckle into the job of getting it done.

———— ★ ★ ★ ————

Some time ago Lt. Roy Fodness wrote us from a foxhole . . . this time he writes from the lap of luxury but he is afraid the soft life is getting him down.

"I've located in a friendly French family's home and they gave me a bedroom with a real honest to gosh bed in it, with an inner-spring mattress, feather ticks and clean white sheets. I had a heck of a time getting used to it but after the third night I mastered it. I don't think the change, from sleeping on the ground, was good for me because I caught a terrible cold. In fact I stayed in bed all day today and the people of the house brought me hot soup."

———— ★ ★ ★ ————

One G.I. not worrying about what job he'll take after he gets out of the army is Red Skelton, the comic. He is being offered to radio ad agencies for $1,000 a week during his service with the army just for the privilege of having first "call" on him when he goes back to civilian life.

DECEMBER 14, 1944

Because Nick Stavenger's eyes were a bit misty when he pulled a telegram out of his pocket and handed it to me yesterday morning I couldn't help thinking "bad news." But those weren't tears of sorrow . . . they were tears of joy for he had received the finest Christmas present in the world.

The telegram dated from Bradley Field, Connecticut., read as follows:

"On my way home, will wire arrival time later, love, Johnny."

Second Lt. John Stavenger has been flying a B-24 over Germany from a base in England.

"I don't give a darn if I get anything else for Christmas for this was the greatest Christmas present anyone could have," said Nick.

———— ★ ★ ★ ————

People have the mistaken idea that all business is a pretty hard boiled proposition. Every now and then you hear of something that makes you feel good all over because somebody went out of their way to be kind.

Sarah Van Aalsburg, the manager of the Red Owl store, has been in pretty much of a fret because her fiance is back in this country after 31 months overseas, recovering from his wounds.

Sarah who is conscientious to the nth degree rather timidly asked Wilbur Damson, supervisor of the stores for this area, for a few days off so that she could see her fiance.

She not only got the days she asked for but a couple of weeks in addition. And it's Mrs. Damson, the wife of the supervisor, who will give up her own holiday plans to come here from her home at Springfield, to take over the management of the store while Sarah is gone. A wonderful gesture of friendship we'd call it.

———— ★ ★ ★ ————

Sgt. Kermit Bierkamp, who is stationed at Buckley Field, had one of those lucky travel breaks last week. He was killing time in a Denver hotel waiting for a train home, knowing he had about a day and night's travel time ahead. Just then Lt. Erwin Brown, who is one of the weather men for the Sioux Falls air base, happened to saunter in the hotel. The two Luverne men had a brief reunion. Brown mentioned he was a member of a crew of a transport that had just made a routine flight to Denver. Kermit mentioned he was heading for Luverne. "Come on and ride back with us," said Brown. So they were all back in Sioux Falls in about two hours and a half, saving Kermit about a day's travel time.

———— ★ ★ ★ ————

Mrs. Harry Wieme of Luverne is wondering whether the grim Christmas present her husband sent her came from a "live one or a dead one."

She received a tiny Japanese wrist watch (Citizen make) from her husband in New Guinea. Sgt. Wieme, who has been overseas 15 months, said about 30 members of his platoon captured quite a few Japs recently but didn't say whether or not the watch came from a captive.

DECEMBER 21, 1944

The chap that once said, "you don't have to be crazy to be in the newspaper business but it sure helps" really knew what he was talking about . . . for here we are slowly going crazy (operators note—he isn't as far away as he thinks) trying to write some Christmas Chaff.

The worst thing about writing columns or editorials about coming events is that you have to mentally condition yourself so many hours or days ahead of the physical conditions under which you are actually working at the time you write.

And I ask you how can any one slip into a "jingle bells and Christmas stocking" mood with all the banging and hammering that is coming from the back shop. To say nothing of Irid sitting in one corner of the front office, mooning and moaning Christmas Carols in Norwegian to himself; Georgia in another office corner muttering because Irid busted the handle on the adding machine; and Alice, making as much noise as fifty mice as she wraps packages of finished job work. I repeat—in an atmosphere like this how in the world can any editor bat out anything that halfway makes sense.

And all the time you know that Elmer and Rolly, the linotype operators, are walking around out in the backshop wringing their hands screaming, "how in the world will we ever get this Christmas edition out if that lug doesn't get down to business and write some copy." [. . .]

It's hard, if you didn't know that down the street the stores were jammed with shoppers, to realize that Christmas is at hand. Sitting in the office here you look out and see the brilliant sunshine. Unless you stepped out into the biting cold you wouldn't know it was winter.

Somehow it never seems Christmas without snow. And Max Voelz, who has been huddled in conference with his barometers and other weather gadgets, solemnly announces in discouraging tones, "I don't see any snow for Christmas." But like all good prophets he slips in a hedging note by adding "so far." Mr. Rucker, the foreman, refuses to get drawn into any controversy about the weather but cynically predicts that it will be "hotter than Billy Blazes unless somebody gets busy and writes some copy to fill the Christmas edition."

By the way . . . it's a good thing that Ruck is a sober, law abiding citizen for he'd be the easiest guy in the world to catch. All my detective would have to do to catch up with Ruck would be to follow that trail of cigarets that he leaves. "Par" for Ruck on press day is three cigarets burning at one time, one in his mouth and two in places where he has hastily laid them down for "just a second" and then forgotten about them. If the cigaret shortage gets any worse we don't know what he'll do. Wait till he reads the prediction of the New York newspaperman who wrote that at the rate America is burning up its reserve of cured tobacco there won't be any cigarets by 1947. We'll all be envying Irid who doesn't include smoking as one of his vices. But—we nearly swooned the other day when, ambling down the street, we spied him in front of the Pix theater lighting a cigaret. But he's still "pure"—what he was doing was lighting a cigaret for Santa Claus, who was afraid that his flowing whiskers might catch on fire when he lit a match himself.

We've always felt that Christmas without snow wasn't really Christmas. I don't think there is a more forlorn sight in all the world than that of a youngster with a new sled on Christmas day and only bare, frozen, ground outside. But even if we are minus the snow the Christmas spirit is still around us . . . you can feel it in the air, the laughter of happy people, you can see it in the smiling faces of the pushing crowds.

We never fail to get a thrill out of driving about the streets at night and seeing the gayly lighted Christmas trees of the homes, each tree proclaiming to the world that inside is a happy family, bright with the joy of Christmas.

And the joy of Christmas is here. You can see it in the faces of the little tots. They come to our office window, and we enviously watch them, as they rub their noses against the cold window pane to look at the Santa Claus and his reindeer drawn sleigh that is on display in the window. You can hear them giggle as they look at the Christmas angels (cleverly fashioned from Christmas cards of other years), that are "marching with Santa." You can "see" Christmas in the faces of the children as they hop and skip along down the street, hanging tight to "daddy's hand" enroute to a store to get something for "mama."

There is wistful envy in our hearts as we watch these youngsters and we'll admit it. The line "backward, turn backward, oh time in thy flight, make me a child again just for tonight" keeps running thru our head. We envy the youngsters and their ecstatic expectations of Christmas Eve, hanging up their stockings with care tomorrow night awaiting a visit from Santa. We'd give anything in the world to recapture that childhood thrill of Christmas.

We soberly realize that there is a joy for grownups too at Christmas time. You can see it in the faces of the people on the street, their smiles seem different. The joy of Christmas seems to bring new laughter. We find that Christmas is something in which all of us, regardless of age, can anticipate with happiness and enjoy with deep satisfaction. A world without Christmas would be a sorry place in which to live for that is the one time in the year that people aren't afraid to reveal how soft their hearts really are after all.

——— ★ ★ ★ ———

We come now to the time when each member of the Star-Herald organization wishes to voice its holiday wish to each and every one of you.

Getting out a newspaper each week, in the face of shortages of all kinds, isn't anything but hard work but there is a real satisfaction in getting out a paper when we know that it goes to such a wonderful family of readers, not only in this area but thruout the whole world. You've twitted us about our mistakes and land knows we deserved all the ribbing and more too. Don't think that all of us don't know and apreciate what wonderful folks the Star-Herald readers really are . . . and we want to wish you as sincerely as we can:

A MERRY CHRISTMAS
AND A
HAPPY NEW YEAR
Irid Bjerk
Georgia Molitor
E. E. Rucker
Alice Hamann
Sebe Vail
Rolly Fillbrandt
Elmer Fehrman
Max Voelz
Al McIntosh

DECEMBER 28, 1944

Major J. Russell Wiggins didn't quite play fair with his family and friends when he came home for a brief visit last week wearing "civies." He would have cut such a dashing figure in a resplendent uniform.

But Russ said it was wonderful to get out of uniform and "quite okeh" with the army as he is now on "terminal leave," subject to call again by the government.

The one time owner of the former Rock County Star would really talk about anything else in the world, international policies or politics probably, than his own participation in the war for nearly three years. He leaned over backwards in modesty as to what he had done and would try to make you believe he had never been in any more danger than if he had "been crossing seven street corners."

Attached to the air corps as an intelligence officer, Major Wiggins will soon return to his former post as managing editor of the St. Paul Pioneer Press and Dispatch.

We couldn't help getting a kick out of Russ, and we didn't recognize him at first because he's lost about 25 pounds, as he wandered thru the Star-Herald shop. Occasionally he would lean over and affectionately pat a piece of equipment and say, "that once belonged to me." He asked in particular about the health of the Babcock Optimus "pony" press. It evidently recalled to him the time a printer was careless in a lockup and when the press was started up pieces of metal flew all over the shop, causing a fat repair bill to the press.

The war may have caused Major Wiggins to lose a little weight but it hasn't changed that flashing smile of his or slowed the enthusiastic conversational pace he maintains.

Since his return to St. Paul, Major Wiggins has written a note which concludes: "[. . .] I hope I can spend a few more days [in Luverne] soon. Merry Christmas was not so 'Merry' this year with the war situation as it is; but perhaps we dare to wish each other a New Year that will be really 'Happy' before it comes to an end."

J. R. Wiggins.

——— ★ ★ ★ ———

We're not telling any "tales out of school," because it's more than all right with him, when we tell you what happened to Johnny Wahlert's "stripes."

When John came back from going thru the terrible days of the Italian campaign he was wearing a nice string of campaign ribbons and a neat assortment of sergeant's stripes which he had won the hard way.

But when he was in to say hello last week his arm was nice and clean, unmarred by any rank designation.

"I suppose," said John, flashing that little boy's roguish smile of his as he delicately eased that big frame of his into one of our frailer office chairs, "you're wondering what happened to my stripes."

Not one to bring a painful subject up we intimated that we had been a bit puzzled over the demotion. So John went on to tell the story.

Down at Fort Sill, Okla., there was a "guy from New York" in his outfit. To use John's own words this chap was wearing himself very thin on the nerves of everybody for miles around.

"All day long," said John, "this guy whines how he 'doesn't want to be in the army' and he 'doesn't want to go overseas' until we are all getting very fed up with him indeed.

"I argues with him gently that nobody really wanted, unless he's got a hole in his head, to be in the army in the first place. But as long as we was in we might as well get it over with. But no dice.

He's still unconvinced. Then I gives him a bit stronger talking to, telling him I'd like to have him 'across' pushing him along with a bayonet. But he still don't learn.

"So it goes and he's getting me so jumpy with his chatter that I nearly go nuts."

(For the sake of the record the other fellow was no puny infant but a strapping six footer.)

"One day he keeps right on chattering after I tells him to shut up. Something snapped and I ups and busts him a good one."

John freely admits he made two mistakes: first, because he hit the New Yorker in front of about 200 men who were all very happy about the affair, and second, because his sergeant came around the corner at the very second John was sitting on top of the New Yorker pummeling him for dear life.

"They tells me," said John, " 'that'll cost you your stripes' but to me that was just like the guy who said 'you can't fire me I quit' because I ripped them off right then and there." A couple weeks later the order came thru demoting John.

He's eventually headed back for overseas, hoping it is to the European theater of war, and it's a safe bet that he'll probably have his stripes back again in a couple months.

———— ★ ★ ★ ————

We've always had strong belief in our "hunches" and we always had a hunch that Jarnet Johansen, who had been reported missing in action as of September 27, would sooner or later be reported a prisoner of war in Germany. So it was a double shock when the word came Wednesday morning that the Hardwick boy is now reported as being killed in action, September 27 . . . because it's hard to believe when you've kept in close touch with a boy to realize that you're never going to get any more letters from him.

Jarnet was one of those refreshing correspondents . . . he was always bubbling over the business of living and the joy of living. He had so much fun down south when he was in camp, he was a member of the Glee club at the camp [. . .] It was from [England] that he wrote us many vividly descriptive letters of all that he saw and did. Jarnet was always in a hurry . . . when he came home on furlough, he'd bounce into the office with a bang and it wouldn't be but a few minutes before he'd be dashing out to zoom away in his car.

It's hard to believe that he has passed on . . . we not only lost a good correspondent but a real friend and his parents lost a fine son and his country lost a real fighting man.

Rock County Star-Herald

Continuing The Rock County Herald, Established in 1873

Continuing Rock County's Oldest Business Institution, The Rock County Herald

LUVERNE, MINNESOTA, MONDAY, MAY 7, 1945

ZIS QUIT

Germany Surrenders
The Allies Uncondi...

General Dwight D. Eisenhower, commander in chief of the U. S. and British forces in the European theatre of operations, "saw the European war through" from start to finish. It was in his headquarters in France that the unconditional surrender was signed shortly before 2 a. m. battle time, or about 8 a. m. Luverne time on May 7.

1,441 'Faces' Pictured In This Edition

In this Victory in Europe edition of the Star-Herald you will be able to find the picture of nearly every one of your friends and neighbors, who are in their country's service.

Pictured in the pages of this special issue are to be found 1,441 "faces" of Rock county individuals. Of course there will be numerous duplications. This is unavoidable. Because individuals who appear in pictures of service groups leaving for the service will also be shown in picture.

Even allowing for these duplications the Star-Herald believes that it has run more pictures of men and women in service than any other paper in the midwest, of comparable size.

Despite the critical shortages of film, photographic paper, flash bulbs and photo engraver materials, which at times made it appear that picture possibilities would have to be suspend, the Star-Herald still wants to run the picture of every Rock countian in service. There is one charge. When your "boy" comes home have him drop in at the office so we can get his picture for the paper.

But Thanks Be To God, Which Giveth Us The Victory.—1 Cor. 15:57

The War in Europe is over! That was the good news which broke world around, Monday morning, May 7.

All morning long, Monday, Rock countyside their radios, tense and hushed, listening coming over the air. They first heard the "ender" order issued by Admiral Doenitz...

Then at about 8:37 a. m., they heard shouting "the war is over, the war is low has been officially confirmed."

Our V-E Day Edition

TO THE READERS OF THE ROCK COUNTY S...

We are happy to commemorate the long hoped for Victory in Europe with this special Victory in Europe of the Star-Herald.

This edition not only commemorates the r... achieved in Europe but records the contributions country's men and women are serving everywhere the world.

No one has any illusion that "it's all over" or is but a step farther down the road. Everyone that our struggle ahead will be long and hard and price must still be paid in human lives to bring Victory.

That though has been stressed by the adve... this edition possible, in their messa readers—that this is time for solemn rejoici for dangerous optimism.

A "photographic edition" as possible, on picture is worth 10,000 words" and far more

For many months before the actual the Star-Herald has striven as consistent secure pictures and make newspaper cuts man or woman who appearing in this edition are no longer in service and who failed to o... to take group pictures at the time the sel left for their periodicals. Many of these m they were ready and regret to answer th men have been discharged from the th they should be recognised in this edit part.

In the handling of hundreds of cu some would be damaged or lost. regret because we wanted to make it it was humanly possible.

We appreciate the assistance giv... the past two years in furnishing us men and women.

We also wish to express our th and friends of men and women in furnished information and pictur service. This stars and Bars co many months of war one of the this newspaper.

The V. F. W. post of Rock assisting with the preparation of service.

It is a privilege to present county's part in the realization... our readers.

WORLD WAR II- A CHRONOLOGY

War, which in the 1920's was thought to be outmoded by the Treaty to Versailles, loomed on the International horizon long before the first Jap dive bombers screamed into peaceful Pearl Harbor on the morning of Dec. 7, 1941.

To be sure, war of a world-wide scope seemed remote to many people at least, even on Dec. 6. It seemed even more remote in the years previous, although other nations were already "in". The Japanese situation had passed the smoldering stage long before. It had reached the red hot stage in Manchukuo, where Japanese took the first...

...the minds of thousands of ex-service men who had sons just reaching the prime of life. They hoped that they would be able to "stay out of Britain. Nazi officials warned the it", as it were, but by this time they were also planning a defense so as not to be caught unprepared.

National Guard Converts

One of the first of these defensive movements which was felt in Rock county was the conversion of Luverne national guard unit from an infantry company to a coast artillery anti-aircraft battery. This conversion took place July 1, 1940, and was then called to have been done "to protect the state's iron mines, industrial and transportation centers in case of war."

Also effective July 1 was a new tax levied to off...

Germany) off the coast of Finland, the ship then went through the mined waters off the coast of Great Britain. Nazi officials warned the ship to shift her course to avoid the German mine off the coast of Scotland, but Capt. B. E. Torning stuck the course as outlined by the United States Department of State and slipped his ship through the mine filled waters in a 45-mile-an-hour gale.

Beginning of Selective Service

In the nation's capital, the Burke-Wadsworth bill, which established the Selective Service Act of 1940 was passed, and approved by President Roosevelt on Sept. 16, 1940. It provided for the registration of all men between the ages of 21 and 35 inclusive on Oct. 16, 1940.

About the same time, a number of promotions had come through in the ranks of Rock county's A. A. Anderson...

Ahrendt resigned after a short time, and was replaced by H. L. Fay, who was appointed to succeed him. As soon as the October 16 registration was over, they were at work. About the same time, Dr. to W. Betenkamp the county mining physician for the county and Ivan O. Hansen was appointed government appeal agent.

1,362 Register First Time

Up to Oct. 16, the prospects of Rock countyans' wearing army khaki again had seemed almost impossible as the general public hesitated to believe that war's inevitable. On registration day when 12.5 per cent of Rock county's total population, or 1,362 men to be exact registered for selective service, there was hardly a family which did not feel that the war blood was rolling faster and becoming darker.

On Tuesday, July 29, 1940, Secretary of War Stimson in Washington drew from the great lottery number 158, the first...

1917 And 19...

Contrast; P...

Warfare in World War I More Lightning Like Destructive Than in W...

Those who have lived to s... country involved two wo... Wars are agreed that 25 y... make a lot of difference.

It was spring, April 6, 19... exact, when the U.S. ente... War I.

It was winter, Decembe... when this country declar... Japan, and December... similar declaration... against Germany and It...

Not only was warfar... against Germany on a bigger, m...

1945

*"Then the next day came the report of Mussolini's
quick and sudden end. Most everybody expressed regret
over his death . . . not because the once strutting bully
of the balconies of Rome had met death in a gutter . . .
but because he had been killed so quickly and cleanly.
'It's too bad that he didn't get some of the torture he
caused so many,' seemed to be a common expression."*

—Al McIntosh

JANUARY 4, 1945

This is from a letter written by S/Sgt. Carl Schroer, former Sioux Falls and Plankinton young man, who enlisted at the same time as Lloyd and his brother, Capt. Merle Larson did. He is now in Temple, Texas, where he was sent after he lost his arm in the fighting in France: (written after he heard Lloyd was missing, but before he heard he had been killed in action.)

"Lloyd, Merle and myself left Sioux Falls for the army together, and from that day, Lloyd and I were inseparable. Always went every where together and worked hand in hand. Do not think any one could be closer friends. When we reached France, we both fought our hearts out, and then on August 4, while fighting, I lost my right arm. Lloyd must have been wounded shortly after I was as I just received a letter from him dated October 24 and he told me about everything that was happening.

"You can be very proud of his good work. It is with my deepest sympathy for all that I say, I hope he is safe."

Lloyd's last letter was written on November 13 to his brother, Wayne, an aviation student at Tucson, Ariz. He wrote:

"Yes, I was out of action for a little while. I got a good rest out of it and a Purple Heart so I didn't do so bad. Also a two-hour ride in a C-47 to a hospital. It was rather rough that day and lots of the boys got air sick, but it didn't bother me.

". . . There is no glory in fighting (although) it may sound that way in the papers but it is a different story over here. If you knew where I am writing this letter, you would know that it is no picnic here.

"I saw Stanley (Lloyd's brother) a week ago. Was only with him for about two hours. He is getting along okay, and looking as good as ever. He has been about five miles from where I am for about two weeks, and I just located him about a week ago.

"I was in Paris a couple of weeks ago . . . Am now sweating it out getting to Berlin. I hope it won't be too long before I get there."

Lloyd was twice hospitalized before he met his death. Once he had a narrow escape when his tank upset during training maneuvers in England, and his hand was crushed by the hatch cover. His wound, for which he was awarded the Purple Heart, was sustained when he was shot through the wrist by a German sniper.

———— ★ ★ ★ ————

If you want to know what Col. Roosevelt's latest wife, the former actress Faye Emerson, is like just ask Sgt. Jean Helland. The current bride of the president's son did a show one time at Camp Roberts where Helland was stationed. Jean and a companion escorted Faye part way to her destination after her arrival at the base. Before they had reached the destination a lieutenant, noting how beautiful Faye was, shouldered the non coms aside and "took over" the escorting job.

JANUARY 11, 1945

Case Van Engelenhoven hasn't furnished us any Chaff for a long time—not since the day he got fancy down at the elevator and started using a pinch bar under a freight car's wheels and started a runaway which ended when five cars were derailed.

But he more than made up for his quietness in a news way last Friday. Case and his wife got into the pickup truck to take their son Gerrit, who was leaving that day for the navy, to Sioux Falls where he was to report.

After saying goodbye to their son Case decided he wanted to take a look at the Sioux Falls air base, which he had never seen . . .

"I drove around it," said Case, "and then I followed a street which went into the base." Van Engelenhoven stoutly asserts he saw no stop sign, in indication of "no trespassing" sign and certainly no sentries. He chugged along thru the street at the base and then he saw a big coal pile. Being a connoisseur of coal, himself, he dallied long enough to admire the efficient way the "clam shovel" operator was loading a truck from the coal pile. And at heart Case was fervently wishing Emil Mollberg would buy one of those power shovels so he wouldn't have to do any more hand shoveling to unload coal cars.

Sighing to himself, Case started up the pickup and drove on, seeing what he could see. Just then a jeep loaded and overflowing with Military Police roared up to Van Engelenhoven.

They yelled to Case, very emphatically, that he was very, very lucky indeed not to have been shot for going past the sentry post and to go back at once and report to the gate.

So they took Case to the sentry house at the gate and gave him a good grilling. (In the meantime Mrs. Van Engelenhoven was sitting, shivering in the cold, in the truck. One thoughtful soldier took her to the U. S. O. room.) But moon faced Case was getting no such consideration. From the sentry post they yanked him to the Provost Marshall's office. Then they took him to see a captain. Then to a major's office. Vehemently denying he was a spy or saboteur, that he had only come over to deliver his boy to the Navy authorities Case just about had the Major convinced. The officer said, "maybe we better excuse him" but another officer said, "we never excuse anybody." So then they haul Case down to the Sioux Falls police station, the chief of police pushes a button and detectives swarm in and give Case another going over. By his own admission his "stomach had been turning over a thousand times a minute." Then they released him with a stern warning.

But as always Case had the last word.

"Listen," he said, "there wasn't any stop sign, no sentry in sight, I didn't know I was supposed to see any guard. I belong to the Home Guard at Luverne and when we guard any place, brother, it's guarded." Anyway—Case's "five minute" visit to the base turned into a three hour delay.

———— ★ ★ ★ ————

Dr. David J. Eastburn just about qualified for his "pilot's wings" recently when he was driving north on Highway 75 with his father. His car went out of control on the icy pavement and dived down into the ditch, at the curve near Trosky.

"Don't say a word dad," he said, as he fought the careening car to keep it right side up. They bounced along in the ditch and finally he piloted it up on the pavement again. Although it was a mighty cold day the pastor was sweating plenty.

———— ★ ★ ★ ————

A few years ago we never knew Roy Fodness very well . . . he just seemed another happy go lucky chap without too many serious thoughts, apparently.

But the army changed him . . . and from him, now Lt. L.K. Fodness we have had some of the most serious and thought provoking letters of all the ones that we receive from servicemen.

Not so long ago Lt. Fodness wrote from France in which he worried about the prospects of a soft peace. We used his remarks as the basis of an editorial a month ago. "Why Pay the Price Without Getting the Merchandise." In his letter Roy had said that he knew full well what he was facing, that he was afraid of only one thing, and that wasn't death or injury, but the danger of a "soft peace." "I'm willing to pay the price," he wrote, "but what I worry about is whether or not we'll get the merchandise, a real peace."

Last week came word that Lt. Fodness had paid his part of the price of victory . . . he had been wounded.

———— ★ ★ ★ ————

It used to be in the "good old days" that you could find Don Martin in some coffee shop half a dozen times a day, killing time. But after being away nearly two years in the Pacific you hardly knew he was home, he was downtown so seldom. Don confesses it was fun to do "as you please" and just hang around home . . . and what he liked best was having his folks serve him breakfast in bed every morning at 11.

———— ★ ★ ★ ————

Joe E. Brown in his unforgettable book, Your Kids and Mine (and you can get it at the library here), says that never did he have his picture taken with any G.I. during his travels that a couple hundred letters would come in from parents saying "that was our boy."

It gives you an idea how closely loved ones scan news pictures today in the hope it might be "their boy." Russ Haakenson, now in France, wrote that he had his picture taken in the shot of "General Patton's Choir." His folks here have seen picture of the choir but they can't identify Russ—unless he's the chap who moved when the camera shutter clicked. Anyway—it's all a blur. And Mrs. Ada Knowlton is positive that the picture which appeared in the Sioux City Journal, showing a wounded Yank being carried to a Leyte hospital by seven members of a letter squad, includes her son, Dale, in the group.

Pvt. Darrell Lester, son of Mr. and Mrs. Ray Lester of Magnolia, now in New Guinea thought he recognized a familiar face not so long ago. He went over and took a second look—it was Capt. Herb Cain, also of Magnolia.

———— ★ ★ ★ ————

Remember Lyle Odden that used to play the electric organ here in Luverne? Lyle's been playing at the Rome hotel in Omaha for several years and now the story is that he has a very tempting offer from Hollywood.

———— ★ ★ ★ ————

Production is getting under way on ration free shoes for children made from "pig strip" or BACON RIND to you. Production of nearly 10 million pair a year is expected. Rationing of leather shoes, for grownups, is expected to continue two years after Germany's defeat. Half of all the shoes made now in England have wooden soles.

———— ★ ★ ★ ————

Two of the very top American war correspondents disagree on the blame for the Nazi attack. One says that the Allies have long tried to entice the German armies into break thru tactics such as now are in progress but that the attack "for a few dark hours came close to delivering a blow that might have delayed the outcome of the war from one to two years."

The other, pointing out that it might well be the final death rattle of a dying snake, says "don't be too quick to criticize, wait and see what happens." He believes that the Allies deliberately set up what is known in football as a "mouse-trap play." General Bradley himself contributed to the suspicion that the counter attack was invited by declaring "this may be a blessing in disguise," in getting the Germans to come out from behind the Siegfried line.

———— ★ ★ ★ ————

Veterinary research has developed a new "sex hormone" drug which can make a rooster stop crowing and eventually cause him to develop many characteristics of a capon.

———— ★ ★ ★ ————

One reason pajamas are scarce is that it takes 50 yards of goods to make a dozen. So manufacturers are using their quota for shirts instead because it only takes 30 yards per dozen.

———— ★ ★ ★ ————

Are you an average woman? If so, you spent $2.37 per month on cosmetics.

JANUARY 18, 1945

Coaches of the Eighth district are chuckling with glee, while gloom predominates at Luverne high school, over the fact that Robert "Ace" Canfield leaves for the army tomorrow, the very day that he would become eligible to play basketball with this year's team.

It was "Ace," who probably would have ranked as one of the all time "greats" at Luverne high for truly he is an athletic "natural," that Coach Meyer was counting on to help win the district championship.

"Ace" is one of those "once in a blue moon" type of natural athletes who did everything so smooth it looked easy, whether it was basketball or football. He was accurate as a sniper in basketball, particularily when it came to free throws.

Ace was twice winner of the J. E. Treat trophy for the best free throw record of Luverne players, twice was rated on the all district team and if an all regional had been chosen he would have surely rated a place. [. . .]

Well—Ace is putting on another kind of a uniform tomorrow . . . and it's no exaggeration that this free and easy, happy go lucky, youngster will still be making a name for himself.

For the sake of the record Meyer and Manion say that Billy McCormick was one of the best linemen to ever play on a Luverne team. Two other athletes, Marlin Hudson and Gordon Krantz, entered the service before graduation but later received their diplomas even tho they weren't here for the graduation exercises.

——— ★ ★ ★ ———

You've heard a lot of outraged denials that Nazi prisoners have been "coddled" by American prisoner of war camps. Here's one that makes you wonder:

Lena Horne, the Negro actress and singer, was giving a U. S. O. show at Little Rock, Ark., declares a Negro newspaper. Attending the show were white American soldiers and officers and . . . Nazi prisoners . . . but Negro G.I.'s were barred. To entertain the members of her own race the star scheduled a special early morning show but walked out when she discovered more Nazis present again.

The army "nixed" the play, "A Bell for Adano" as the "command performance" play for the President's Birthday Ball celebration in Washington, Jan. 28. Among other reasons why the army said "no" was because Lt. General Patton, now in high favor with everybody but the enemy, is the general referred to in the book so unflatteringly.

———— ★ ★ ★ ————

Getting out ahead of the German army but losing all his personal belongings in the December battle of "the bulge" was John Conover, we understand.

JANUARY 25, 1945

Will you forgive if we get just a bit more personal than usual? For these are the days that people live with lumps in their throats. You hear some news and then all the rest of the week you feel depressed. And this has been another one of those weeks, ever since we heard that Lt. John Jensen was killed in action.

It's not right to write about only one boy when you don't write about them all because each man's sacrifice is just as great and the import to each family of that yellow telegram's meaning is just as tragic. But not all of the boys did we know personally. And when we write about John we are, in our hearts, symbolizing the loss to the family and this community of each boy who has paid the supreme price for his country.

We said that we didn't know all of the boys. But here was "one that was just a bit different" . . . for if you didn't know John you would have had to have been deaf, dumb and blind. For you could hear or see him coming a block away.

There was a man, every inch of him, one of the three fighting Jensen brothers. Big, any way you looked at it, whether you measure by physical stature or by the "heart."

John might have been a big chap physically—and he was just that—but he didn't take advantage of his bulk, like some birds do, to push anybody round on a bullying way. If there was a fight he wouldn't be the one to start it because he wasn't the sort that "threw his weight around."

Big and beefy and usually red faced from laughing or talking he had hands as big as hams . . . and when he slapped you on the back you felt like you had been felled by a falling tree. He had a fog horn bellow of a voice and a laugh . . . say when that chap laughed everybody else laughed too, just from the infectious quality of that guy's laughter. And when you got thru laughing you wondered to yourself what in the world had been so funny. And when he grinned his face split from ear to ear.

They'll never put up Christmas street decorations in Luverne that we won't think of Johnny Jensen for we remember well the last time he and his pals put up the Christmas decorations in 1940. That was just about the last thing they did in the way of private employment before they left for the military service which eventually led to Kodiak.

There they were, perched high in the air on the precarious elevated platform on a truck, swaying in the wintry breeze while they strung evergreens and all the rest of the decorations on the overhead light wires and the light poles.

They worked like troopers all right but not so hard they didn't have a whale of a good time while they were at it. These "Merry Andrews" bellowed wild "hellos" at all their friends, whistled and yelled at the girls, made a few ribald comments to old friends and all in all it sounded like a three alarm fire in progress.

Somehow we never could have believed that Jensen's "number" would ever "come up." He was one of those chaps so abounding with life that you somehow felt that here was one chap that would live forever.

For Johnny was a "throwback." He was in reality a twentieth century counterpart of his Viking ancestors. He lived hard, he played hard and we'll bet our bottom dollar he fought hard. He did his long stretch in the Aleutians and we'll never forget his first time back on leave . . . he barely averaged a block an hour as he tried to make his way down Main street . . . everywhere he went he was surrounded by people shaking hands and wanting to visit or "throw" a party for him.

John was a big man, we said, in every way . . . and it wasn't just his bulk but he had a great heart in him, generous and tender. He was all man in every way and we'll gamble that he was a doggone good officer . . . one of the kind that said "come on" instead of "go do it" and when he fell he probably still tried to keep crawling . . . forward.

John belongs to that gallant band of men who never will come back . . . home . . . but his memory, like theirs, will live forever.

——— ★ ★ ★ ———

We haven't had a letter from Lt. "Chuck" Davis for a long time but he bundled up a lot of copies of "Stars and Stripes" and English newspapers, which he had evidently picked up in an officer's club, and mailed them to us this week.

And from the far Pacific area comes from Warrant Officer Robert Cavanaugh a copy of the "Yank." (The "Down-Under" section.) So all in all we are acquiring quite a library of service publications.

——— ★ ★ ★ ———

Altho you've read a lot of reports about the "blackmarket scandal" in France which has brought prison terms to many American army men the worst scandal is yet to be revealed, when it comes to food and supply leakages. One high Yank officer said we lose more at Naples "than we do at the front." Even though there have been scores of arrests and courtmartials the army can't halt all the racketeering.

American khaki blankets bring $8 to $10 each from the Italian blackmarket operators. These are then dyed and made into suits, coats, or dresses. A pair of O.D.* pants is worth $6 and two pairs makes a woman's skirt and four will make a man or woman's suit.

G.I. woolen socks bring as much as $1.75 a pair, the women even unravel them and knit them into sweaters. Even G.I. shoes are worth $12 a pair and are made over into men's or women's shoes. An army shirt is worth $7.50, coffee $3 a pound, butter $2 a pound, laundry soap, $1.50 per bar, etc.

——— ★ ★ ★ ———

Much as we feel terribly inadequate every time we sit down to write this column . . . which too many times requires the habit of "fluffing" a normal two line item into a full paragraph, we'll have to continue. But after hearing Wilbur Peterson, the editor of the Marshall Messenger, say that he gained six pounds after he quit

---

* olive drab

writing his column then we know we don't dare quit . . . no matter how bad you think "Chaff" may be. For we're too fat already . . . another six pounds weight and that would qualify us to be turned in to the "waste fats" campaign.

FEBRUARY 1, 1945

Knowing that the annual Red Cross drive was coming up soon we couldn't help taking an eager interest in the fine words of extravagant praise that Lt. Ben DeHaan had to say about the Red Cross. (To freshen your memory—he is married to the former Helen Barrett.) And we only hope that some day soon we can tell all of the thrilling story that the lieutenant is not permitted to reveal now.

"The Red Cross has done a swell job of boosting morale," said the air man. He went on to tell about what the Red Cross had done in the European theater of operations, providing recreation centers, reading rooms, and larger clubs in the big cities. "It may not sound like much but the Red Cross club-mobile and the doughnut wagons really meant a lot to the boys right up front."

There are a lot of Red Cross activities that DeHaan knows about and praises, what the Red Cross does for prisoners of war (really keeps them alive), the Blood Plasma and all the rest of the things that you know about.

But last but not least is what the Red Cross has done in maintaining morale. "They've really helped a lot of boys over the hump," said the lieutenant, "the Red Cross has been swell in every way, they've meant more than I can say."

A good thing to remember when the drive rolls round next month.

And while we're on the subject of the Red Cross we'd like to touch upon a subject that's been in our minds and on our hearts for a long, long, time. It concerns a chap who, if they were handing out home front medals for "Distinguished Service," would certainly deserve to be decorated first. And the funny part of it all is that he's doing his efficient work so quietly that not one in a thousand people have the slightest idea of the magnitude of the work he is so magnificently doing—and all because of his love of humanity.

That chap is Ray Engan.

When Ray levels those piercing eyes at us we begin to squirm. Inwardly we wonder if Ray only tolerates us or whether he secretly doesn't have much use for us. I guess that's his customary poker face expression as a lawyer . . . you can't tell what he's really thinking.

But nobody who ever calls on Ray Engan, the Red Cross Home Service Chairman, has to wonder what he's thinking. They find the man all compassion, helpfulness and tender sincerity. We say he deserves a medal . . . and we repeat it. Time is about the only stock in trade, outside of his books and his brains, that a lawyer has. Yet rotund Ray gives unstintedly, and without charge, of his time. It is no exaggeration that he devotes from three to four hours a day of his time to Red Cross matters. (And without a penny compensation, either . . . how many of us can match that record of unselfish service?) On the basis that you see Ray get down to work, usually about 11 a.m. or later, you might say that he puts in a pretty short day. But check how many nights you see the lights burning in his office and you'll begin to realize what the Red Cross job means to him.

One night last week he was up at 2 a.m. sending wires to Red Cross directors in far away camps arranging for emergency leaves for men so that they could hastily return for the funerals of a loved one. It was the same thing all over again a couple of nights later. Time and again too many times to mention here, Ray has arranged emergency leaves for servicemen whose loved ones were critically ill. And not just a few times the youngster has come home riding a fast army transport. There are just a lot of youngsters who should always gratefully remember that it was Ray who, thru the Red Cross, pulled the strings and cut the red tape that got them home in a hurry in time of sorrow.

Tuesday was a typical day at his office. His first caller was a World War I veteran who wanted to get into the veterans hospital at Fort Snelling, in a hurry. Ray arranged for that, by telephone call to the hospital and then writing the necessary letters. His next caller was the mother of a man killed in action who had to be shown the details that would have to be handled in connection with securing gratuity pay and insurance.

His next caller was another mother . . . of another Rock county boy who had been killed in action. She wanted help in filling out the necessary forms and help in providing necessary information required by the government.

The last person in was the father of a boy, just home after 30 months service overseas. This father wanted to know if a furlough couldn't be arranged for his other son so they could all be together for a reunion, before the second boy was shipped out.

And that's the way it went . . . all day long, every day of the week, and Sunday too. "Nothing spectacular" says Ray, "but you do get a thrill when you can render service and get prompt action on some request."

Ray would be the first person to "bust" out laughing if anybody ever called him "an angel of mercy." (With his "figure" and all.) But in his earthy, human, way he is performing countless deeds of great service, with his only reward being a "thank you" and the satisfaction of doing his job. We don't think there are many who can equal his record of unselfish service . . . and we don't think there's a better Home Service Chairman to be found anywhere.

——— ★ ★ ★ ———

Remember Johnny Wahlert who lost his sergeant's stripes because he smacked a bird that didn't want to be in the army? Well . . . our Rock County Slugger sends word as follows: "tell Al that I'm back up to a corporal again and that the guy I had a fight with is getting ready to be shipped out and doesn't have too much to say now."

——— ★ ★ ★ ———

Now that the government, in order to save electricity and coal, has ordered the "brown out" and no bulbs brighter than a 60 watt we can't help wondering what the 53 REA members who won 100 watt bulbs, as attendance prizes, at the REA meeting last week are going to do.

Speaking of the "brown out" Herman Jochims whose two theater marquees are so lavishly lit up that they look like a Hawaiian sunset clams it's going to make him some money, on the electricity he'll save. But when Herman said it we could see his heart wasn't in it . . . for we think he loves those brilliantly lighted fronts even if they do cost a pretty penny.

———— ★ ★ ★ ————

Mrs. Henry Krogmann was in the other day with what seemed to us a very legitimate criticism.

She was saying that when the selective service contingents leave from Luverne it certainly is doubly hard on the families of the men.

"It seems to me," she said, "that they should open up the armory instead of just that little hallway. People come down early, and if you live in the country you can't wait till the last minute before the bus goes like the town people do, and they either have to wait outside in their cars or pack into that one narrow room.

"Over in Worthington when men leave for the army," she said, "they open up the coliseum and the Red Cross serves coffee and doughnuts."

It doesn't seem right—and it's a good thing she spoke her mind because it was one of those things that nobody had thought about. Hugh Fay, member of the Draft Board, said he thought the entire armory, not just the hallway, had been unlocked all the time. But if somebody had slipped it would be unlocked in the future, he assured us.

Mrs. Nora Campbell, draft board clerk, says that the armory has always been open after 6 a.m. on days when men leave.

———— ★ ★ ★ ————

Rumors aren't news and should be ignored but one rumor has been so persistently spread that it is now accepted as fact and should be "spiked." Regardless of what you hear "Bill" Jessen, son of Mr. and Mrs. Pete Jessen is NOT missing or a prisoner of war. His last letter was written January 13 from Belgium and he was all right at that time.

FEBRUARY 8, 1945

Thanks to Erv Grunklee we learned that Mr. and Mrs. R. W. Chapin of Hardwick had their "next to the biggest thrill in the world" Tuesday night. That afternoon they received a wire from

Radio Station WHO Des Moines, saying that their son, Roger, would be heard in a broadcast direct from the western battlefront.

No words of ours are necessary to describe what a thrill that must have been for them . . . to hear their boy's voice, coming from a battlefront thousands of miles away. We said "next to the biggest thrill"—the "biggest" would be having him home again.

The men were interviewed by War Correspondent Gammack of the Des Moines Register. He was talking to an 11 man 155 howitzer "team" of the 104th artillery. All but Sgt. Chapin were Iowans. Gammack kidded Chapin about being from "way up in Minnesota" but the Hardwick boy reported that his home was not so far from the Iowa line, only 15 miles or so. Asked by Gammack if he had had any close calls Chapin said once . . . when to duck mortar fire he had to run his jeep in a ditch. The broadcast came thru fine and clear from the front. This is the first Rock county boy, to our knowledge, whose voice has been heard at home via overseas broadcast facilities.

FEBRUARY 15, 1945

In these days of frayed nerves and short tempers it is bad business to be over quick in "pointing fingers" or passing judgements. The color of a person's skin or how loud he sings the national anthem is not the measure of loyalty.

What prompted the above paragraph is the fact that we heard a story that made us wince. Even though the woman isn't a local woman one feels like tracing down the soldier involved to apologize because it happened in "our town."

A woman pushed her way onto the crowded north bound bus here Saturday afternoon to say a last goodbye to some relatives who were leaving on the bus.

As she entered she spotted a chap in army uniform sitting in the front seat, across from the driver. By appearance he was obviously not a native of this area and so this woman did what is always dangerous . . . she jumped at conclusions and delivered herself of some unpardonable remarks.

"A Jap," she shrilled, "has no business on this bus. Put him off." And she is supposed to have warned, in loud voice, her friends to "look out for your belongings, there's a Jap on board."

Her remarks were too much for the temper of Ralph Steffens, the driver of the bus.

"Lady," he said, "this man is in American army uniform, that's no way for you to talk." And with that the driver courteously but firmly escorted the woman from the bus to the sidewalk.

Undaunted she made another effort to board the bus but the driver quickly slammed the bus doors and locked them.

It might have interested this woman to know that this man was no Jap. He was an army captain, by the way, and a native Hawaiian who has served his country well. His home was burned to the ground as a result of the Jap bombing of Pearl Harbor. (We heard but have not been able to verify the fact that he is supposed to have been wounded and that both his parents were killed in the Jap attack on December 7, 1941.)

It just goes to show you . . . how brutally unfair some people can be who act on snap judgements.

──── ★ ★ ★ ────

When John Bosch was in Luverne last Friday he happened to stop and count the gold stars on the Honor Roll board and said, "there are now 20 gold stars." He didn't know it then but the 21st star would be that opposite the name of his own son, Pfc. Everett Bosch, who was killed on Luzon. The message telling of his son's death was handed Bosch when he reached his home at Steen that afternoon.

Here is a conicidence Steen residents talked about. Pfc. Everett Bosch and S/Sgt. Jay Aykens entered the army the same day. They were together in training camps during their entire stay in the states but when, after 18 months, it came time to receiving overseas assignments Bosch was sent to the Pacific theatre and Aykens to the European battle zone.

Mr. and Mrs. Bosch received word Friday of their son's death. On that same day, Mr. and Mrs. P. D. Aykens received word that their son, Jay, had been wounded in action for the third time, on the western front.

──── ★ ★ ★ ────

We would like to enter this Ben Padilla in the next endurance eating contest—we think he'd walk off with the championship.

What that chap can eat at one sitting isn't human. One night a couple months ago at Dick Creegers, we watched Ben polish off a Dutch lunch, almost all of a Bermuda onion, about a pound and a half of cold meats, cheese, pickles, bread—in an amount that would have satisfied three husky farmers during threshing. When he got all thru his hostess served him a big slice of chocolate cake. Ben poured cream on it. Then he longingly eyed the tin of sardines (the big ones—about as thick as your thumb and about six inches long) then he placed two of the sardines on top of the cake, sprinkled everything with sugar and ate the whole mess, as his table companions drew back their chairs in alarm fearing that Ben would explode before their very eyes. Then he ate another piece of chocolate cake and two helpings of home made ice cream.

But Dana Danforth sees nothing wrong with such a combination. "Sardines and cake are wonderful," he maintains, "and if you want something delicious, eat sandwiches of spiced herring and doughnuts."

MARCH 1, 1945

Lt. "Chuck" Davis hasn't been heard from, at this office, for quite a spell but we knew he was still in England because he bundled up a bunch of English papers not so long ago and forwarded them to us. But he finally crashed thru with a letter from England.

"I enjoyed reading about Quentin Aanenson," he wrote, "Several months ago I met Quentin one afternoon in a Red Cross club in London. Three days before he had been shot down while on a low altitude strafing mission near the beach head in France. His C. O. had given him five days off to "forget about it" and Quent had crossed the channel and was seeing London for the first time. We spent the afternoon comparing notes, and he had some 'wild times' in his Thunderbolt shooting up German tanks, trains, etc."

Chuck goes on to say "it's too bad that crazy uncle of his isn't sixty years younger, as I think his temperament would be ideally suited for shooting up tanks and ammunition trains—he's so fond of excitement." Then he asks if the uncle has been "to Sioux City lately to see that platinum blonde."

It's a small world . . . Davis writes that several months ago he was wandering thru Piccadilly Circus when he heard someone yell, "Hey Chuck." He looked up to see Lt. Homer Craig crossing the street . . . and they had a brief reunion, and talked over old times in Rock county.

———— ★ ★ ★ ————

Speaking of Quentin Aanenson—he has been promoted to the rank of captain and has now been taken off his low altitude bombing and strafing assignments and has been given a ground job. Here's a quirk—he was grounded a few days before Christmas and on Christmas day both of the planes which he had been flying were shot down by German flak and enemy fighter action.

———— ★ ★ ★ ————

The men overseas, in England and in Europe, are getting their Star-Herald again . . . but it was pretty bad about the time of "the battle of the bulge." Everything but munitions, food and supplies was sidetracked and none of the papers got thru for a while. But Lt. Davis, John Conover, Major Marty Jensen and a dozen others send word that the Star-Heralds are coming thru all right now. Just to show that the army does take good care of soldier mail Pete Jessen brings in a copy of the October 26 issue of the Star-Herald which was returned from Italy to Luverne to his son, Cpl. Albert Jessen. (He left the Italian front Nov. 15.) The paper has been chasing him ever since, and finally arrived back in Luverne.

———— ★ ★ ★ ————

Miss Mildred Suurmeyer, daughter of Mr. and Mrs. Ben Suurmeyer, whose marriage to Clarence De Groot, of Magnolia took place Friday morning, had an unexpected but most welcome guest for the event.

It was none other than her brother, T/5 George Suurmeyer, who dropped in without warning the day before, and who up until the time he stepped on the Suurmeyer porch was thought to be in France.

It happened this way. The soldier son of the Luverne family was serving with a general hospital unit in France when things began to happen. (What it was that happened cannot be told until it has been cleared through proper military channels). Anyway, he was asked by one of his superior officers if he wouldn't just as soon have a furlough back in the states, and it wasn't hard for him to find the right answer to the question.

He wrote his parents an air mail letter telling them of the good news, and after arriving in this country, he sent them a telegram, confirming the fact that he was coming home. But he beat both the telegram and the letter in arriving home before they were delivered. The day after he came, the letter he had written was received by his parents.

He has a 30 day furlough, but after that, he doesn't know what he will be assigned to do. Likely, his parents feel, it will be back to France, but he's hoping that it won't be.

———— ★ ★ ★ ————

If everyone could have had the experience that Lt. Sidney R. Hammer, Jr., had last week end, it wouldn't take long for Rock county to raise its Red Cross quota next Monday and Tuesday.

Lt. Hammer, as you recall, returned to Nashville, Tenn., before the arrival of his new daughter. When he left, he was sure he'd never see the child until after the war, for he was overseas bound. But things took a serious turn for the worse. The young officer's wife required the attention of a specialist, and was rushed by ambulance to a Sioux Falls hospital, and for a while, the outlook was not bright. Here is where the Red Cross stepped in.

Lt. Hammer's father called Ray Engan, Red Cross home service chairman in Rock County, and told him the story. Ray immediately wired the Red Cross at Nashville. This was about 8:30 a.m. Saturday.

At 10 a.m., Lt. Hammer was flying toward Madison, Wis., in a B-25 bomber. He said later he was out of Nashville within 15 minutes after he received his papers, authorizing a 7-day emergency leave. Arriving in Madison, he boarded a Northwest Airlines plane for Minneapolis, and then a Mid-Continent plane from Minneapolis to Sioux Falls.

The story could end there, but there were a few more details to be worked out before the young man reached his wife's bedside in a Sioux Falls hospital, and viewed for the first time his new daughter.

The weather was bad when he reached Sioux Falls, so the big plane couldn't land. After droning over the field for several moments, the plane continued on toward Sioux City. S. R. Hammer, Sr., drove to Sioux City to get him, and it was 7 a.m. Sunday before they got back to Sioux Falls.

By that time, the emergency was over. The baby was born at 4 p.m. Saturday, and both she and the mother were "doing nicely" when the sleepy, but happy and excited first-time father sat down with a sigh of relief in the hospital waiting room.

———— ★ ★ ★ ————

If you didn't happen to listen to Kate Smith's program last Sunday night, from 6 to 7 p.m., you missed the radio find of the year in a comedy way, Cpl. Harvey Stone. He'd never been "on the air" before but after he had finished his 15 minute monologue, which kept the studio and listening audience in convulsions of laughter, that chap doesn't have to worry about his post war future. They've booked him for a repeat performance next Sunday night—better not miss it.

MARCH 8, 1945

We didn't know it till this week but among the overjoyed American prisoners freed in Manilla were two Rock county residents . . . Mr. and Mrs. Arthur H. Riss, formerly of Steen.

Mr. Riss used to be the mail carrier there and still owns property at Steen. For a number of years he had been a school teacher in Manilla.

Like the American radio announcer just freed by the Japs who prefaced his first broadcast after liberation in Manilla by stating, "as I was saying when I was so rudely interrupted" Riss wrote Frank F. Michael in answer to a letter the attorney had written over two and a half years ago.

In his letter he says, in part: "You may be sure we are overjoyed about our most timely release. We were all suffering intensely from slow starvation and many had already succumbed. Mrs. Riss and I are not ill but were MERE WALKING SKELETONS (capital letters are ours—not Riss's) when Gen. MacArthur's boys rescued us on Feb. 3, we could not have stood it much longer. Now after only eight days on good American army food I have already gained 8 lbs. I was down to 108. Many people worse than that. Men 90, 96, and 100 and many women down to 70, 75, 78, 80. It will be a slow climb back to health and strength but most of us will make it now.

"I shall be anxious to get back to good old Minnesota and its invigorating climate.

"Well, Frank, please extend my greetings to all old Rock county friends and you may give the general facts of this letter to the Herald for publication. It will probably be the best way to reach my many friends in that part of the state."

———— ★ ★ ★ ————

Monday morning Louis Haraldson got up early to take his daughter, Lois, down to the train so that she could get over to Sioux Falls. The day before had been the birthday of his son, Berdell, who has been with the navy in the Philippines. Haraldson was wondering where, and how, Berdell had spent his birthday. The train rolled in . . . Haraldson picked up his daughter's grip and carried it down to the coach door. Who should jump off . . . but the son . . . just back from the Philippines. Was that unannounced and unexpected reunion at the depot a happy one? You know it was. Berdell had a ten day leave when his ship docked to the west coast . . . he didn't even wait for his mail . . . he didn't even take the time to wire because he knew every minute counted if he was going to get two or three days home . . . but dashed for the nearest bus terminal. A surprise for him too was the fact that his other brother, Vernon, (who had been with the navy in Iceland) was also home at the same time.

———— ★ ★ ★ ————

Not from anything we've ever been told but by a process of "iffing" we arrive at the conclusion that a well known Luverne boy was "in" on the historic conference at Yalta recently. We know the president went to the Crimean conference by ship, in naval convoy, and not by plane. We know that his top ranking army and navy aides were there. So if Admiral King went to Yalta isn't it reasonable to assume that Lt. Robert Wildung, his supply officer, went along too?

———— ★ ★ ★ ————

Lt. John Greene hasn't changed a bit . . . same roguish twinkle in his eyes . . . same forceful way of talking . . . and asking questions. John is on his way to Stanford university from Princeton, where he has been attending the navy's school of Military Government. He's on his way to Stanford to learn the Japanese language so you can figure out what the navy has slated John for "sometime." The government of occupation forces move into a country right after the first waves of assault troops. John used to be operations officer at one of our big Pacific air bases, on the island of Maui. We asked him what his post war plans are . . . he says that he learned to like the Orient when he visited Japan and China, on a world cruise years ago, and "if there is some money to be made" he may decide to remain there, after the war.

MARCH 15, 1945

You can be sure that one chap that is paying close attention to developments at Remagen, Germany, where the Americans made their surprise crossing of the bridge there is Albert Schmuck. Albert had crossed that bridge many times in World War I, having been stationed near Remagen for four months.

———— ★ ★ ★ ————

No matter what the calendar or the thermometer may say, spring is officially here. Because, the first robin has been officially reported as of Sunday.

We'll have to hedge a bit. We had a report last week from a chap who said he'd seen a robin at Hardwick. But this character is one who is very averse to fresh air and sunlight so we didn't put too much stock in what he said . . . asking him what Soren or John were doing letting birds fly around in their places of business.

But our report Sunday came from a most reliable source, a young, red headed, lad who called us up on the phone. "This is Jerry Malone," he said, "and I just saw a robin. I know it's a robin because I made my daddy go out and look at it and he said it was." So—it's official now.

And another sure sign of spring is the way you can see youngsters in the street "lagging" along with their marbles.

MARCH 22, 1945

Pvt. Howard "Red" Iveland was a quiet sort of a kid when he was in Luverne. He went about his business quietly and never had much to say when there wasn't anything really to talk about. But this soldier is winning himself a reputation for being the "indestructible man." Remember—"Red" was reported missing in action last fall and it wasn't long till he bobbed up again with his outfit to get in the fighting some more. Then he was reported missing again and hopes were gradually being given up. But this week his parents, Mr. and Mrs. Albert Iveland, received a letter from "Red," written from a German prison camp. And they received the letter before they received any official notification from the U. S. War Department that their son was a prisoner of war.

"Dear Folks," he wrote:

"A chance to write for which I am glad. I am fine, healthy, just like before, so you have nothing to worry about. JUST KEEP THE HOME FIRES BURNING. I suppose everything is fine at home and I imagine it is plenty cold about this time, if I know Minnesota. Write to Orville and Boyd and tell them I am all right and say hello to the rest of my friends. My buddy from St. Cloud, Minn., is still with me. We are going to try to stick together as long as possible. We all hope the war is over soon so we can all come home, something we are looking forward to. Will write whenever they let us. Lots of love and hope this reaches you soon." Howard.

Well . . . if a kid in a grim, lonely, "underfed" camp can tell the folks back in Rock county to "keep the home fires burning" none of us have a right to complain have we?

———— ★ ★ ★ ————

Pfc. Maurice DeWolf, Hardwick, is a paratrooper in that 101st Air Borne Division group of heroes which won immortal fame at Bastogne, the first division in all American history to receive the Presidential unit citation for valor.

———— ★ ★ ★ ————

There was rejoicing at the Peter DeBoer home when their son Otto S. DeBoer, S 1/C, arrived home at Ellsworth for a 30-day leave after having been in the South Pacific two years. Otto and another Ellsworth boy, Orville Budgett, left for the service at the same time and were "buddies" for nearly two years. Both were on the U. S. S. Omnibey when it was torpedoed and both were fished out of the water by rescue ship crews and transferred to another ship. Again—their ship was torpedoed. In the excitement of the second sinking, the buddies became separated and both thought the other was lost. Now on his way home Otto spent two days in the city of Oakland, Calif., not knowing that Orville was in a hospital there suffering from nervous shock. It is hoped they can have a reunion before they go out to sea again. Mr. and Mrs. Peter DeBoer have five sons in service, you'll remember.

MARCH 29, 1945

This is one week we (like the grasshopper who danced all summer) dawdled too long in the coffee shops. We came down to the deadline of getting out the Star-Herald and then it dawned on us we didn't have any chaff to speak of. That's why the letter back from Germany of Major Marty Jensen came to us as a lifesaver. Not only interesting is the letter but what's just as important to a procrastinating editor . . . it will fill up a lot of space.

Anyway . . . we're glad Marty writes such long letters so here goes:

"Just listening to the news and hear we have completely taken Cologne, spelled Koln over here," writes Marty. "That makes another large German city on the right side of the ledger and they say Cologne is 95 per cent destroyed by the heavy pounding from the air and artillery. From all reports it was a beautiful city before the war. And I can easily believe it by seeing these cities that have been taken. Some were as large as 250,000 people. Beautiful buildings laying in ruins, some of them hundreds of years old, streets are wide and lined with nice trees. It certainly is a shame to have to destroy them. But it has to be done.

"And these people were so much better off than the other countries I have gone thru.

"Right now our battalion is quartered in four civilian houses, that had all the comforts anyone could ask for. I understand it was a great silk manufacturing center, and I presume these houses were homes of some of the minor officials in the company. We are in the residential section of town and it has not been hit very hard.

"When we come along we just pick out the houses we want and tell the people to get out and we move in. Sometimes they move into the basement if it has a separate entrance. No German family can live in the same house with U. S. troops. And we have to have the houses so they have to move.

"The houses are beautifully furnished, one of them having two pianos, a grand and an upright. And the other furniture is excellent. Clothes still hanging in the closets were good. In my room there are two good suits and lots of other good clothes. Also stored in there were cases of cookies and cases of cocoa for making hot chocolate. There are things we never saw in England, France, Belgium or any other country. Shows that these people were on the right band wagon for a while but they sure are on the wrong one now!

"You would think that rather than have those cities ruined they would know enough to quit. Someone said these people seemed to act like they were liberated, now that they didn't have to worry about the bombing, and also the Gestapo all the time. And it must have been hell for them.

"There is so much worry about what to do about postwar Germany but it looks to me like they'll have to spend the next few generations building up their cities again. After we take a town the people start to trickle back again. Of course some of them go with the German army, but not all of them.

"Those who come back try to get on the 'band wagon' and of course they have to have some form of government. They're all screened by the Military Government and if they are considered okeh are marked with an arm band. There are always a few who are willing to pick out the Nazis and they are taken care of. The rumble of guns sounds like a thunder shower at home. Hope it isn't too long before we won't have to listen to them at all. "And I don't think it will."

—"Marty"

———— ★ ★ ★ ————

A number of the boys in service have mentioned in their letters lately they'd like to know how things are going "back home." So . . . we'll make a brief report on a few items that come to mind.

Dear Gang:

So—you've been wondering how things are going back home. Well, today most of the folks back home have been wondering how things are going "over there." The day started off with a big mistake caused by an over enthusiastic radio broadcaster who got the idea that a "Victory" flash was coming up in a few minutes.

To tell you the truth it didn't cause much of a flurry on Main street. People have had tentative dates for victory before and have seen their hopes dashed before so they've evidently made up their minds to keep their heads down and keep working until there is no doubt of victory any more.

It would be a lie, tho, if we didn't say that the main topic of conversation wasn't how long "it will take." Common attitude is "it might happen tonight but it will probably take another six weeks." And don't get the idea that the folks at home think it's a "grand waltz" into Germany. They know the fighting is brutal and costly . . . and that lots of our best boys have been lost in victory drives before. They are praying and hoping that the struggle, for your sake, will be mercifully short.

Other than that things back home are just the same. When we say it's "spring again" you should be able to shut your eyes, wherever you are, and imagine what everything looks like. The lawns are turning green again, and you see the green in flower beds bordering the homes. The farmers are getting into the fields, ditches in the countryside which, a few weeks ago, were almost bankfull are normal again. Al Hemme insists that he saw some white and yellow flowers over by Magnolia this afternoon and he doesn't want any wise cracks about his eyesight either.

Everywhere you drove in Luverne Tuesday night you could see people starting to work out in the yards. (Seed catalogs are favorite reading right now.) Everybody, papa, mama and the youngsters are out raking lawns. And wherever you go there is the pungent smell of bonfires made from the leaves and dead grass. And, of course, the youngsters are busy poking at the bonfires with sticks. You see a few kites but very, very, few. There is a shortage of string, among other things, so I don't know how the youngsters can do much kite flying. (Speaking of youngsters . . . wouldn't you like to be a child movie star like Margaret O'Brien. On top of her movie earnings she'll make $200,000 this year from lending her name to makers of dolls, dresses, etc.)

This is spring vacation and the youngsters are having a high old time, dawdling around town in their old clothes. Noticed a bunch of girls, suffering evidently from spring fever. They spent most of the afternoon sitting on the Methodist church steps. You don't see many farmers in town any more . . . they're busy getting ready for spring work with a vengeance, short of help and new farm machinery, but they're going to "bull it thru" someway they all say.

We've seen some of our amateur gardeners today doing some light work and right now we can anticipate all the groans we will hear tomorrow and the moaning about sore backs.

Those fellows should be ashamed of themselves (look who's talking) . . . they should take a lesson from William Spease. Now there is what you call a real he man. He's 76. Doesn't have to work. But he finds real honest to goodness pleasure in going down to Rathjen's elevator and unloading a couple carloads of coal and maybe a carload of salt or so. And when he's all thru he walks away as straight as a ramrod.

Should tell one that Mrs. Al Cowan tells on herself. She and her husband were over in Sioux Falls some time ago having a chicken dinner. There was a juke box in the place and so some of the guests were dancing. She and Al took a sedate twirl round the floor. Some G.I. and his girl were doing a very fancy rumba. Mrs. Cowan, wistfully, said, "I wish I could do that." The G.I. overheard her and introduced himself and asked her to dance. So they traded partners and a merry time was had by all, the G.I. teaching Mrs. Cowan to rumba. When they parted for the evening the Sioux Falls soldier said goodbye to Al and said, "bring your daughter over again some time."

Speaking of things being just about the same back home. Well . . . there is one fellow who is never quite sure. Several people have watched him lately. He owns a piece of property on Main street and every morning they notice he walks slowly past, on the other side of the street. He'll walk about ten feet, then turn around and look back as if to see if his building is still there. He does that about 20 times in a block . . . then goes on, evidently satisfied it's not going to vanish in a twinkling of an eye.

Sgt. Vinal Barrett is home . . . with his new bride . . . for a brief furlough. He's with the A. T. C. at Los Angeles. (Wasn't that where the famous "Blaze" incident ended . . . remember the story about the dog sent home from England by one of the president's sons?)

If that caused the administration some embarrassment it was nothing to Elmer Piepgras' confusion one night when an army officer inspected the Home Guard here. The officer stepped up to Elmer and said "what's your name." Friendly as a pup Elmer answered "Elmer Piepgras." "It's Private Elmer Piepgras, SIR," thundered the officer and Elmer is still blushing.

Remember Bill Palm that used to live here? Lives at Windom now and his wife gave birth to a baby boy on PALM SUNDAY. How's that for a coincidence.

A year ago we promised you that we'd not mention Kay Aanenson by name for a full year. Well—that time's up. You know Kay thinks he's the only one that can take a plane trip. Well . . . he saw Art Wood this week and asked where the manufacturer had been.

"London," snapped Art and Kay's jaw dropped open with amazement. "Why, why," he stammered, like he does when he gets to giggling as he sips sugar with his coffee, "I saw you only last week, where did you go from and how long did it take you?"

"Two hours," said Art. Kay wanted to know if he went by rocket plane.

"No," Wood said, "it only took me two hours to fly from Chicago to London, Ontario."

There was a lot of cussing here Tuesday night. The midnight train's engine broke down in Luverne. They had to go wake up Art Huff to get busy on the telegraph to ask Worthington to send over a relief engine. So the train stayed here till 4 a.m. [. . .]

Several of you have written back asking that we publish your complete addresses in the Star-Herald so some of your buddies can write to you. Well . . . we'd like to do it but there is a strict censorship rule, laid down by the army and navy, against publishing complete addresses after a man leaves this country.

Well . . . that's just about all we can think of. It isn't much but it gives you the idea that things here are going along the same old way. Don't ever worry that the folks back home here "don't know there's a war on." They sure do . . . they mask their feelings pretty well . . . but every now and then they let slip how much they are worrying about you . . . and how often they are praying for your speedy return home.

With best regards
ACMc

APRIL 5, 1945

We used to watch George Hedemark take a car round a corner on two wheels and always expected he'd set some kind of a record. And he has. To George, now in Belgium, goes the distinction of being the first Rock county boy to marry an English girl. The son of Mr. and Mrs. P. C. Hedemark, now of San Francisco, George was married March 2nd to Miss Edna Baily of Shropshire, England.

———— ★ ★ ★ ————

Keith Connell got a big thrill recently when he walked into operational headquarters at his base in England, preparatory to making a bomber flight over Germany, and discovered that one of the officers in charge was Lt. "Chuck" Davis. And to make it better yet, Keith wrote, the former Luverne banker had a collection of Star-Heralds that Keith read when he returned from his flight.

———— ★ ★ ★ ————

We were even slower on the "uptake" than usual so the significance of the fact that Major George Fried had on a smart double breasted suit of "civies" the other day didn't "register" with us . . . then we noticed the gold servicemen's emblem in his lapel.

Yes . . . Major Fried is out of the army. And the release came at his own request. George's last assignment was to head the separation center at Fort Snelling. He's had a busy and interesting career in the army the past three years and three months, Camp Haan and then to Kodiak. Then . . . out of the army for a while, just before Pearl Harbor, then hastily summoned back . . . then to an executive assignment at Snelling.

Major Fried was a good friend of a lot of fellows during the past three years . . . and he did many a good turn for many a Rock county boy.

He's not revealing his future plans—yet.

———— ★ ★ ★ ————

Did you notice how many women in Luverne's "Easter Parade" Sunday wore elaborate corsages? Maybe their "ever loving spouses" felt that even if there was a shortage of lilies that flowers were still very much in order. Speaking of lilies . . . we used to import 20,000,000 or more lily blooms each year from the Japanese, paying them 8 to 10 cents a bloom.

Now that the source of supply is a thing of the past some folks are getting rich almost overnight growing lilies in certain parts of the northwest. A big difference in price to the wholesale florists, costs have jumped over 1,000 per cent. Certain sections of the country where volcanic ash predominates in the land, formerly valueless, are now selling during the "lily boom" for as much as $3,000 an acre.

———— ★ ★ ★ ————

Sgt. Donald Shelstad wrote us recently from the Philippines. You hear a lot about shipyard wages, was the gist of his statement, but there is such a thing as "shipboard wages."

"Everybody knows that 'on the way over' the dice games get into pretty high stakes," wrote Shelstad, "but what surprised me was the fact that one chap got paid $20 a night just for holding the flashlight so the players could go on with their game after the ship's lights had been turned out."

———— ★ ★ ★ ————

What won't they think of next for the past war world. Now they're announcing a glass that can be sawed and nailed like lumber, bent and twisted like aluminum; glass that will float and bounce.

One of the wildest rumors yet (but they say Henry Kaiser, the ship builder who only wants to "ride the yellow railroad cars" when he travels, is interested in its possibilities) is the one about a "gasless car." Who ever started the report says that the car will run on a secret fluid, using a quart for every 1,500 miles and has no clutch or gear shift or ignition; just a brake pedal, throttle and reverse.

And if you think that's a wild one . . . then listen to the story of what Dr. Jose Calva, a Mexican scientist who lives in Minneapolis, claims he has perfected . . . a plastic fur coat. He claims he can make an indestructible fur coat of plastic (applying the plastic concoction to a base of shorn sheepskin) in imitation of any fur coat you want, fox, mink, skunk, seal or what have you. He claims his plastic imitation is so perfect that he can fool furriers at ten paces.

Calva's company is busy on war work now, making jackets for fliers, but the scientist claims his next step is to produce plastic carpets. If they get dirty, he claims, all the housewife will have to do is wash them like linoleum.

April 12, 1945

Better late than never even tho nearly 27 years have elapsed.

Back in September, 1918, in a battle area in the hills near Nancy, France, Walt Bonnett was the victim of a German gas attack. "It knocked me clean out," said Bonnett, who now farms near Kenneth, "and I was taken back to an evacuation hospital and then by Red Cross tram to a base hospital." On top of the gas attack Bonnett was hit by a bad attack of pneumonia. He never did get back in the lines again.

This week, nearly 27 years late, he received a letter from the War Department advising him that he was being sent the order of the Purple Heart.

————— ★ ★ ★ —————

Here's a serious warning. Thousands upon thousands of those "walky talkies" will be dumped on the market from the government and manufacturer's surplus pretty soon. Radio executives predict that unscrupulous promoters are going to perpetrate one of the biggest rackets in history by a door to door sales campaign for these short wave radio outfits.

They'll come to the farmers and say "here's an outfit that you could use and your wife could call you and give you a message while you're a mile away plowing." They're going to be pretty foxy about telling you what a hundred uses you can make of these things.

But here's the joker . . . the salesman will say "go ahead and buy one and get your Federal Communications Commission license later." There won't be enough radio wave lengths to go around and 98 per cent of the people who buy these surplus walky talkies may never be allowed to use them. So give the boot to the walky talky peddler if and when he shows up with a glib story.

———— ★ ★ ★ ————

Here's a quirk. M/Sgt. Curtis Sabie, son of Mr. and Mrs. LeRoy Sabie of Pipestone was a veteran flight chief in charge of six planes in the Pacific area. He had more than his share of experiences . . . wounded once and then returned to action again. His next experience was surviving a plane crash in a jungle area and painfully walking, guided by natives for five days to reach help. After all those experiences Sabie was doing his job every day. Finally he received one of those rotation furloughs. Now he's stationed at an Arizona base but the army strictly forbids him to go up in a plane at all. They say he isn't "fit" physically.

———— ★ ★ ★ ————

For some time it hasn't been much of a secret that most of the boys from the old Battery E outfit wound up with General Patton's fast and hard rolling 3rd Army. But when a boy who hasn't seen a home town man in nearly a year meets a lot of his old buddies in Germany . . . then that is news.

In the same mail Monday came letters from Lt. H. G. "Blitz" Craig and Major Ray Frick, both "somewhere in Germany," Ray's letter, far more lengthy, appears elsewhere in the Star-Herald but we thought we'd use "Blitz's" letter.

"It has taken quite a while to get around to answering your letter," he writes, "so I decided to spend the entire afternoon writing letters. It is another beautiful day here and quiet FOR A CHANGE so I should get pretty well caught up. Needless to say I owe everyone a letter. It is warm out today so I am writing this out in an orchard. It is hard to believe that great battles were raging here only a few days ago. The news has been most encouraging the last couple of weeks, and it gives me hope of being home before the year is up.

"I ran into all the men from old "E" Battery a couple of weeks ago. I was able to spend parts of several days with them and we had some good talks of the good old days. It was really a surprise to see Vernie Fremstad walk into my C. P. I had to leave before the rest of them arrived but I came back the next day and spent it with them. Heiden, Ringen and I spent one day at a little town in Luxembourg where I met Frick and Hagemeier. In all I guess I saw about thirty men from Rock county. It was the first time I had seen anybody from Luverne since last June when I saw Chuck Davis and Phil Helland in London. I am hoping for an early reunion back in Luverne with all of them. We are still rolling along at a pretty good pace with Patton and getting closer to Berlin by the day."

"Blitz"

APRIL 19, 1945

"OH NO!"

Those two, simple, words seemed to be the most common expression heard last week when people learned of the sudden passing of President Roosevelt. Those two words summed up the multitude of thoughts set racing by the news of the president's death . . . thoughts combining sorrow over the passing of the man who had shattered so many traditions, regret that he couldn't have seen the actual realization of the victory so near at hand, and worry over the future of the nation.

We just didn't believe the news when we heard it. Just a short time before we had been sitting with Fred Christopherson, the managing editor, in the news room of the Sioux Falls Argus-Leader. When we heard the news down the street later that the president had died we just didn't believe it. But—later when we walked back to the newspaper and into the Associated Press room and read some of the bulletins streaming out of the racing teletypes then we believed.

Outside stood J. D. Coon, the republican leader well known here, staring at the bulletin in the Argus window. His face was drawn and haggard and you could almost see a suggestion of tears in the attorney's eyes. "It's tragic," he said . . . and walked away.

Here in Luverne the news spread swiftly. Rev. A. N. Williams heard the first radio flash and immediately telephoned the Star-Herald office to give the news. From then on nearly everybody stayed close to their radios.

They realized that one of the biggest stories of the year, or even a decade, was being told with dramatic suddenness. The first Argus-Leader extras to reach Luverne were grabbed up, hastily read and then re-read before being put away carefully to be kept as keepsakes.

Norman Johnson, manager of the local telephone exchange, said that beginning at 4:45 and continuing for an hour, the flood of telephone calls through the local exchange was so heavy that six telephone operators were working at full speed to keep up. The rush, which lasted for an hour, was the biggest of any in any recent year, perhaps in history, Mr. Johnson said, and he added, "It gives us some idea what we can expect when V-day arrives."

It was amazing how quickly the mood and tempo of Rock county living slowed to a walk. Contributing to the general air of solemnity was the mournful tone of the radio programs. One of those obnoxious Duz or Dentyne gum singing jingles would have sounded like sacrilege. There wasn't much talk in any restaurant. People sat and speculated as to the possible effect the president's death might have on the international situation and the coming San Francisco conference.

Friday morning one merchant put out his flag at half mast, for a long time the only one visible on Main street. Soon another business man spotted the waving flag and he put his out . . . and then it wasn't but minutes till every flag was up and in place. The flags on the public buildings soon were lowered to half mast.

Saturday brought Mayor Fay's proclamation closing all business institutions from 1 to 3 p.m. The Memorial Services held at the Palace theater drew hundreds and hundreds of Rock countians who sat thru the dignified service in hushed quiet. Outside on Main street it was quieter than any Sunday. No sign of life in any business institution, hardly. Few people to be seen at all on Main Street . . . and everybody talking in hushed tones . . . as tho they were in church.

This isn't anything you didn't know . . . but some of the boys overseas will probably want to know how the county reacted to the news.

We should add that the most chagrined man in the county was the chap who walked into one of the institutions here about noon Saturday.

"What are all the flags doing out," he asked. He nearly fell over when told the news. He explained that he doesn't subscribe to a daily paper, he hasn't been able to get a telephone and has been unable to buy a battery for his radio set, and he had been so busy he hadn't had a chance to visit with his neighbors.

★ ★ ★

One traditional bit of skylarking following weddings—is the custom of giving the newlyweds a noisy ride thru the streets of Luverne. Car horns blowing wildly and the jangling clatter of tin cans are the inevitable penalty the blushing newlyweds must pay.

But when Alice Iveland married Pvt. Robert Mann last Friday there was a startling innovation in the customary "parade."

You might have noticed the heavily bearded chap driving an aluminum colored truck with an Alaska license plate on the car. That was Carl Hammond of Fairbanks, Alaska, and with the truck he had his sled (mounted on wheels) and a number of huskie dogs. He makes appearances at fairs, schools, etc. Always with an eye to advertising and promotion Hammond, when he spotted the newlyweds, quickly offered to give them a ride.

So he hitched the dogs to the sled and gave Alice and Bob a ride thru the streets. When Bob offered to pay him for his trouble Hammond graciously declined. "But," he added quickly, "I'll settle for a kiss." And with all that "brush" on his face he grabbed the bride and planted a healthy smack on her cheek.

"Oooh, it tickles," was Alice's startled comment.

★ ★ ★

Proud possessor of two trophies . . . the kind that she wouldn't ever want to publicly display . . . is Mrs. John Kooiman (formerly Elizabeth Perkins) who has two Nazi flags sent by her husband. One of the blood red banners with the hated Swastika emblem is huge, measuring at least four by ten feet. Corp. J. A. Kooiman, who is with the First Army, also sent his wife the insignia from the uniform of an S. S. officer. "A very tough guy," added Kooiman.

APRIL 26, 1945

A lot of us are chronic complainers . . . but I learned my lesson last week.

Sitting in the depot waiting room in Milwaukee waiting for the Hiawatha I saw an M. P. walk over quickly to a soldier standing at a ticket window. A big pillar obstructed my view but a careless glance gave me the idea that maybe the M. P. was "frisking" the soldier for liquor or something. But the M. P. walked away quickly, tight lipped and grim faced. I was puzzled . . . till the soldier turned away from the window and walked past me. He was a "kid" about 22, chin up with a big smile on his face and his chest covered with service ribbons. And then I knew what that M. P. had been doing at the window . . . he had been putting the soldier's ticket and change in his blouse pocket . . . For the boy had no hands, you see, just two steel hooks instead.

And I said to myself, then, "McIntosh . . . if you ever complain again about having your 'hands full' when that kid can grin without any hands, then you ought to be kicked."

— ★ ★ ★ —

You never know when a "local boy" is going to pop out in print, in the movies . . . or on the air. You wouldn't have seen him anyway but in that movie at the Pix the first of this week one of the big bombers in the picture, "Sunday Dinner for a Soldier" was being flown by Lt. Vince Prahl. Most of the flying scenes were shot at Drew Field, Fla.

And if you heard the Washington Concert Band playing over the Mutual network this week one of the musicians was Roy Paulson, 1st Musician, U. S. Navy. The band, now playing at Washington, D. C., is said to be the World War II equivalent of Sousa's famous band. Formerly stationed at Bainbridge, Md., Paulson was assigned to the navy's music school in Washington, D. C. and after an audition was assigned to play the French horn in the band. One of the broadcasts was beamed to U. S. troops in the Orient and the other to troops in the Occident.

———— ★ ★ ★ ————

Cost to the radio industry as the result of revenue lost by canceling programs for coverage of President Roosevelt's death totalled $7,000,000. If VE Day comes by May 10th the 7th War Loan drive will be called the First Victory Loan in honor of FDR.

MAY 3, 1945
"YOU CAN'T BEAT A G.I.'S INGENUITY"

Bouncing round this county is a car. To be accurate we should label it what it really is . . . just a jalopy. But that car has the most elegant set of tires you'll see in many a month nowdays. If you looked real close you'd see that the tires are stamped "Made in England." It seems that some very enterprising G.I. had the old car for sale but the tires weren't fit to drive round the block. This young man being in a particular branch of the service whereby he makes frequent flights between this country and England is permitted to bring back a piece of baggage each trip. You guessed it—in four trips he managed to lug back four tires he had purchased and this enabled him to sell the otherwise unsalable car.

———— ★ ★ ★ ————

Mrs. Tony Suurmeyer says that Mrs. Arthur Ahrendt, who lives near Luverne, has three Gloxinia plants which are 31 years old. All are in bloom now and one plant has 34 buds of flowers. One plant is white and the others are pink. These plants were started by Mrs. Ahrendt's mother, Mrs. Giedeman.

Don Kolbert was in the other day to exhibit a four legged baby chick, which at last reports was still living.

———— ★ ★ ★ ————

Pfc. Howard "Red" Iveland has been referred to before in this column as the "indestructible man." Reported missing in action last winter he bobbed up again with his outfit . . . then he was lost again . . . then he was reported a German prisoner. Now he's safe again. (Elsewhere on this page appears a letter from "Red".)

Here's a quirk about the whole affair. When "Red" was liberated by the Yanks in Germany from the prison camp his brother, Sgt. Boyd Iveland, who he hasn't seen in four years was only two miles away. But the two still haven't had a reunion.

Red writes: "When I was on the ambulance going back I told another fellow on the truck that I had a brother (Boyd) in the 76th. He asked me what his name was and I told him and he knew him. Boyd was in Sietz, Germany, the same day, April 14, I was. This fellow said Boyd was on the outskirts of the town with his men, waiting to be called up. This was only two miles from where I was held prisoner. This fellow, who said he had been together with Boyd in Alaska, said he was as happy as ever."

———— ★ ★ ★ ————

Arthur H. Riss was three years late in registering with his local draft board, but then, he had a good reason. This week, the local board received a registration card from a San Francisco Board for the former Steen man who was held a prisoner in the Philippines from January 6, 1942, until his liberation a few months ago. Under the selective service act, he was to have registered on April 27, 1942, the fourth registration.

———— ★ ★ ★ ————

What a hectic week this has been.

It isn't often that one sees so many world rocking events take place in such a short span of time.

When the first flash came Saturday night of that false "surrender" report it was as tho somebody had placed a quieting hand on everybody's shoulder. There was no shouting . . . no excitement . . . people stood on the streets . . . quiet and tense . . . not saying much. There was no laughing . . . and neither were there tears . . . because people have learned to be cautious after having had hopes raised so high so many times.

Then the flash at 8:40 from the radio saying that President Truman said the report was without any confirmation. Then the next day came the report of Mussolini's quick and sudden end. Most everybody expressed regret over his death . . . not because the once strutting bully of the balconies of Rome had met death in a gutter . . . but because he had been killed so quickly and cleanly.

"It's too bad that he didn't get some of the torture he caused so many," seemed to be a common expression.

Then, Tuesday to have the report come in of Hitler's death was almost anti climax.

Everybody agreed it would be good news if true but there was a cynical air of doubt concerning the report because of memories of other cruel hoaxes perpetrated by the Nazis.

To have the two men, who set the world aflame and led their nations back into the dark ages with their unbelievable barbarism, die a few days apart would be great news indeed.

History was being made so fast with the news bulletins crowding each other on the teletypes and over the air, that one's mind could hardly grasp the pace at which the war in Europe is drawing to a close. President Truman says he has reason to believe Hitler is dead . . . the long and costly bloody Italian campaign has ended in complete victory with Nazi surrender . . . a new German government is being formed . . . General Von Runstedt is reported captured . . . whole chapters of history have been written within a single week. Cause for sober rejoicing? Yes . . . but not for wild celebration . . . to do that would be to break faith with the men in the Pacific who see long, bloody, months of fighting ahead. This is no time for rowdy rejoicing . . . instead it requires sober courage to muster strength for what yet has to be accomplished.

May 7, 1945

Well . . . it's . . . half . . . over. Before we throw any hats in the air and give vent to any wild rejoicing we should take time out for the sobering thought that we are a long ways from total victory.

We will be breaking faith with the men in the Pacific, and the men in Europe who know they have to go to the Pacific, if we should be fools as to adopt an "it's all over" attitude.

There is real occasion for solemn rejoicing over our hard and costly won triumph in Europe over an ugly foe . . . but we must not take time out for a minute to relax until the Jap empire has also been smashed. We have to work even harder and sacrifice more . . . because there will be many more of those tragic yellow telegrams delivered to Rock county homes before final victory comes.

It seems a long time since war began . . . and it has been over three years of the longest time that thousands in this county will ever put in . . . not only the countless hours of anxious worry of parents . . . but over three years of the best period of life of hundreds of Rock county men have been devoted to war . . . instead of the furtherance of their careers and happiness.

Nearly everybody saw war ahead since that fatal night when the news came that the Nazis had rolled their armies into Poland. Yet all of us, hoping against hope, had clung to the tiny straw of hope that maybe some way war would be avoided. We waded into war gradually, the steps forward were so faltering and short that we failed to realize just how far along the road to war we had gone . . . until that fateful Sunday of December 7, 1941. Then came the brutal impact of the news from Pearl Harbor . . . and we knew then . . . all of us . . . that "this is it" . . . we can't sidetrack the inevitable any longer.

We will never forget the first selective service contingent . . . the leaving of Battery E . . . long before the outbreak of war . . . remember how those first selective service men had said goodbye with "I'll be back in a year." But after Dec. 7, 1941, we knew then it would be long over a year.

This country and this county did everything possible to win the war the first few months. We responded to the aluminum drive with a whoop and a holler . . . housewives threw brand new utensils into the aluminum drive depots . . . which months later remained as monuments of ills.

We said that "we did everything possible" and yet that is far from the truth. There was not much that we could actually do for the whole nation was desperately, with time running out against our feeble forces in the Pacific, marking time as we started to build and equip a great army and navy.

It seems but a short time ago, tho the months and years have been cruelly long, since those first few days. Speed and tire restrictions and rationing were still a long ways "around the corner." False hopes of quick and easy victory were speedily crushed. The nation realized suddenly that it had a long and costly war to fight and that the end would take years . . . and that many of Rock county's best young men would pay the supreme price with their lives.

Day by day, week by week and month by month the war has gone on. More and more young men slipped away to enter their country's service, usually returning for a brief furlough or leave before being "shipped out." The tearful goodbyes of loved ones said at bus or railroad depots were so personal and so touching that one felt it profane to eavesdrop on the grief of others.

There will be many more "goodbyes" said here in Rock county and there will be more of those tragic, yellow, telegrams bringing sad news to more homes.

There is cause for solemn exultation that the forces of the Nazis have been smashed and that a great and notable victory has been won.

But—talk to any veteran home from the Pacific area and he will shake his head and soberly say he hasn't any idea how much longer it will take to smash Japan too—so that we may have hope of peace again in this world and in our time. Talk to those veterans and you won't find any premature optimism.

We've got a long row yet to hoe . . . we can't afford to let down or get cocky and think we can "coast on in." We can't. The Jap is a savage, cruel, beastly foe. To date we haven't come to grips with his main armies . . . we have only defeated his outposts. If we let down then the lot of the men who have yet to go all the way to Japan will be doubly hard.

Again we say . . . let's have our day of rejoicing . . . let's ask for strength and courage to go the rest of the way. The war is a long ways yet from being over. Let's do everything possible that we can to speed complete victory.

This Victory in Europe edition has been somewhat like "off again, on again, gone again Finnegan." It was last summer when the country, gripped with premature optimism, caused by Patton's race thru Normandy, believed that the end of the war might be in sight within a few weeks or months. That feeling, dangerous as it proved, was not actively discouraged from Washington. A note of strong optimism characterized all official announcements. [. . .]

It was long before the "Battle of the Bulge" that we realized that Victory in Europe was still a long way from realization. Already some of the top sections in each bundle were beginning to show that faint yellowish tinge that aging paper acquires. So the shop crew took and wrapped bundles of the sections and stored them away . . . for use when the big day finally came.

There is a saying in the printing business that there is always at least one error of some kind in everything that is printed. Errors are elusive and hard to find even under the best of circumstances. But in an edition such as this where work on it has been carried on, piece meal, over a period of months we have that fearful realization that there are probably scores of errors. There will be names omitted, there will be pictures that are missing, there will be men unmentioned for honors who should have been given special credit. Let us say that whatever errors have been made were of the unintentional, not deliberate, variety. We want to be told of these errors so that they can be righted in a subsequent issue.

One thing we regret. Last week we took six or seven pictures of returned servicemen. Those should have been in this edition but at the time we slapped this paper together to put on the press those cuts hadn't been returned from the engravers.

Probably no paper of its size anywhere in the midwest has any larger collection of newspaper cuts and pictures of the service men of its county than does the Star-Herald. We have conscientiously tried to get the picture of every man in the county, some way or the other. We may not have pictures of every man in uniform and there have been many men who slipped away, to quietly enlist in branches of the service that we have missed.

(We still want pictures of every man from Rock county that is in service. If you have a good picture, of the type that we can use in a layout, we want to make a cut of it so that the picture can appear in the paper.)

That's the way the Victory Edition was handled . . . page forms have been made up the past few days in type and held open . . . ready for last minute corrections and news so they could be placed on the press and released as soon as the Big Day came.

May 10, 1945

We believe the men overseas would have been mighty proud if they could have seen the way the folks "back home" reacted to the news of Victory in Europe.

From time to time shallow minded observers from other sections of the country, utterly unable to comprehend the stoic calmness of the agricultural midwest, observed that out here "they don't know there's a war on." They can't understand that the patriotism of midwesterners like still water, runs deep and isn't manifested by orgies of emotional exhibitionism.

Unlike New Yorkers who whooped, hollered, tore up tons of paper to throw in the streets the news here was greeted with quiet dignity and reverent restraint.

The decision to close the stores Monday was a natural one after the word had been received that stores in Sioux Falls had been closed. Nobody knew then that there was a battle between rival news services raging because the Associated Press had scooped the world on one of the biggest news stories of all time. For hours the pulling and hauling and controversy as to whether or not the news was official would continue. Early Monday morning and for several hours it looked as if the VE Day proclamation would come at any minute and that belief was justified inasmuch as President Truman and Prime Minister Churchill were ready to go on the air with the official announcement.

One by one the flags blossomed out on Main street and store by store the employes quietly filed out and the business places were locked up for the day. There was no shouting, no hilarious display of any kind. Most everybody went home. There was quiet exultation over the fact that a great victory had been achieved but that rejoicing was tempered by the sobering knowledge that there was another great war yet to be won.

A number of the churches did not wait for the official VE Day proclamation, which was probably just as well as it is hard to believe that people could sustain that high pitch of emotion for long, and held their special services.

Those churches Monday, and again for those who held their services Tuesday night, were crowded with reverent worshippers who came to give thanks to Almighty God for victory and prayers for strength for the days and months to come.

Yes—the men overseas would have been proud if they could have seen for themselves the dignified and reverent way their home folks celebrated Victory in Europe.

The announcement did result in the lifting of some government bans which can be noticed on Main street. The theatre marquees were lighted again, and so were the neon signs and store windows, the first time since the "brown out" went into effect. The curfew, which has meant midnight closing for restaurants, night clubs, theatres, and other places of entertainment has now been lifted by order of War Mobilizer Vinson.

———— ★ ★ ★ ————

If you have hopes that VE day meant more films for you there's disappointment ahead. This is the story as we get it, and it came fairly straight from one of the biggest men in the photographic industry. He claims that the army is building a huge photo finishing plant in England and two more are scheduled for the continent. G.I.'s are going to be furnished plenty of films to use while they are awaiting re-shipment home or to the Pacific. The army plans to do all the finishing in these laboratories of all the pictures taken by the servicemen in their sightseeing. And don't look for the cigaret shortage to ease—a representative of a tobacco firm told us the other day there was little hope for more cigarets for nearly another year.

———— ★ ★ ★ ————

A PERSONAL NOTE OF THANKS

To the scores of kind people who stopped in, wrote or telephoned to voice their praise of the VE edition of the Star-Herald we want to express our appreciation. It was a long, hard, job of preparation but when people are so wonderful that they go a long ways out of their way to express their enthusiastic approval it makes everything seem worthwhile and worth the effort.

MAY 17, 1945

One of our favorite magazines is the New Yorker . . . not only because it contains some of the best writing and humor to be found today but we like to read the ads. Beguiling advertisements featuring watches for $778, fur coats for $12,000, chocolates at $10.50 per pound, ear ring clips at $150 per pair and bow knot pins for $550 and brooches for $1,600, make for good reading. We're definitely not prospects but it's always interesting to see how the "other half" of the world lives, or spends.

In a recent issue was a fascinating report of life aboard an evacuation ship returning from Italy and the account of the reaction of the returning veterans to their trip "home."

We were surprised to find the name of an Ellsworth man pop up in the story. Here in part is what the article said:

"The Thirty Fourth Division, one of the senior American outfits in point of European service was naturally well represented in the furlough group aboard the transport. One of its men was Sergeant Lambert Witt, a tall, tired, blue-eyed farm boy from Ellsworth, Minnesota. He had been shipped abroad three years before. Witt was a combat engineer, a fair amount of whose time had been taken up with finding German mines, one of the Army's trickiest assignments.

'After a while', Witt told me 'that and everything else gets to be a deal. Even the country I've seen, which they tell me is beautiful, and I suppose it is, became a deal. At Hill 609 in Africa, the poppies were blooming and the crops were ripening, but the S mines and the tellers seemed to be blooming, too. In Italy the country was greener and the trip wires harder to find. The pretty mountains never helped us any. Finding a crater hole in a narrow mountain road is a tough job.

'The rivers were also nice, but the heavy rains swelled them and our pontoon bridges would be washed away. We saw more poppy fields in Italy, but that meant tank country. A gully is a place where the infantry tries to take cover when they're moving up. I'm a hell of a tourist . . .'

Going home, Witt figured, was probably a good deal, but you couldn't be sure. 'Maybe here won't be any fighting while I'm gone, and when I get back all hell will break loose. But if there is fighting, then I ought to be there. You tell me'. One thing about his return, however, he knew for certain was a good deal. 'I'm going to be able to drag my feet,' he said. 'Wherever I've been I've always had to step just right. My family has a few acres out in Minnesota. Big cornfield at one end of the property. When I get home, I'm going to put on my overalls and take a walk toward it. Nice level country there and you can see for miles around. Honest-to-goodness trees—cottonwoods, no sawed-off olive ones. I'll keep moving out toward the cornfield, dragging my feet and not worrying about trip wires, even when there's six-inch alfalfa covering the ground. My dog will be along and I'll have a gun with me again, but it'll be a 22 and I'll use it for polishing off any gophers we see along the way. I'll stop off and ask some neighbors how the crops were. After that, I'll lie down for a while under a cottonwood and look up at the sky and expect to see no planes that would strafe me.' He seemed more cheerful. 'That's my kind of country,' he said. "That's a good deal.'"

May 24, 1945

The old rule in police work of "Cherchez La Femme" still holds good and this will explain to you why Officer Schneekloth made that mad dash into the hotel at noon Saturday.

All morning the Sioux Falls air base Provost Marshall had kept wires to Luverne hot. They were after a Madison, Minn., soldier who had been A.W.O.L. since April 22 and they had strong reason to believe he would meet his wife here.

As urged by the Sioux Falls authorities Harry met the 8:30 a.m. bus from Sioux Falls but no soldier was on board but a blonde woman got off, obviously looking around for someone she expected to see. Harry trailed her to the hotel and then kept close watch on the hotel and the police "red light."

About noon he saw a soldier saunter into the hotel and Harry followed and was forced to interrupt the reunion the man was having with his wife. The fellow refused for a while to show his "dog tag" but finally yielded. It was the chap Sioux Falls was hunting. He had been on "permanent party" detail at Sioux Falls but was transferred to Madison, Wis., and then went AWOL. Evidently the M. P.'s had kept a close watch on the wife, who had been working in Sioux Falls, perhaps they had even tapped telephone wires, who knows. Anyway . . . the provost marshall sent Harry a $15 reward.

———— ★ ★ ★ ————

Have you ever given a thought to the anxiety that is in the hearts, constantly, of those parents who still haven't received word of their sons who were German prisoners?

1945

The war with Germany is over. Yet for weeks reports have been received of other boys that have been liberated. But, still no word of their boy. It must be cruel torture what these parents are going thru, and all of them so bravely silent.

One woman that we know about can stand the worry just so long. Then she leaves the house and goes out in the garden to work in an effort to try to occupy her mind.

A person hates to keep asking these parents so that they will have to reply slowly, "no word yet." If they had received word you could read it in their faces, anyway.

But for one home Tuesday there was joy reigning triumphant. That was at the George Nelson home when word came that their son, Lt. Darwin Nelson, had been liberated. If you could have heard Mrs. Nelson's voice over the telephone, that deep note of thanks and happiness for Darwin's liberation would have made you feel good all over.

Nobody will ever forget the way Darwin rattled the roofs of Luverne when he bid a lasting farewell with his Flying Fortress as he flew over, enroute for the overseas hop.

There are a lot of good boys still unreported.

All Rock county will join in rejoicing with the Nelson family . . . and all the county expresses hope that all the other boys are reported soon.

And then more good news came Wednesday when Mrs. H. O. Hansen came in to say that their son, Lt. Lloyd Hansen, was a free man again. She was just bubbling over with happiness. The long ordeal of listening to every broadcast, scanning every list of liberated prisoners, is over.

MAY 31, 1945

No use getting in a fret about it . . . you've got a far better chance of being hit by lightning than you ever have of seeing a Jap balloon.

Probably one of the most ridiculous of one of the "hush hush" home front war secrets is the Jap balloon situation. Every newspaperman has known about them for months. But, strict censorship orders have prevented anybody from writing a single line about them.

Byron Price, director of censorship, boiled over with anger last week, tho. He was wrathy because press and radio couldn't so much as mention the balloons but FBI and War Department representatives were addressing groups of school children and civic organizations about them. So Price finally forced the war department to let loose of the "secret."

There's still a lot that can't be said about the balloons. Because, the Japs are desperate for information as to where and when they are landing. They are being floated in by prevailing winds from the Jap mainland and probably take about 80 hours to reach this country. They've caused very little damage. Only once have any casualties resulted . . . and that was to a group of children.

The only thing to remember is—if you ever should see a suspicious object that resembles what you might think to be a balloon bomb . . . don't touch it. Call Sheriff Roberts. He'll investigate. If by a million to one chance, there might be "anything to it" he'll get in touch with the proper authorities.

JUNE 7, 1945
STREET SCENE

If any of the boys who are away have a bit of trouble remembering just how life goes on in the "home town" we'll refresh their memory with a few candid jottings taken on Main street Tuesday. Dear Gang:

It's another "bad day." The rain is slanting down. Farmers, disgusted with the bad weather breaks and their inability to work in the fields, are starting to drift into town. Pretty soon every doorway, every implement and garage office is filled with farmers talking together.

On an afternoon like this it seems that about all anybody does is drink coffee and talk about the weather. Max Zack, however, stands in the drizzle, to watch the excavating progress at his property which he purchased from the Green estate. (The former Spease Tire Shop location.) Understand the Co-Op Oil has leased it from Max.

Never saw anybody work steadier than George Pitts . . . there isn't a lost motion as he digs. He knows the underground "layout"

of the city's steam, water and sewer lines better than most housewives know their own kitchen. Ray Fritz parked in his coupe . . .
evidently trying to think which of the hurry up calls he better
answer first. Bill Goodale taking a leisurely stroll back to the
hotel before it's time to go back to the lumber yard. Sid Boden
parks his car so carefully at the curb (if everybody parked as
exactly the cops wouldn't have any tickets to hand out) and says "a
little more rain."

"Pete" the hawk eyed highway patrolman slides to the curb and
motions to Harry Schneekloth . . . either they're going to have
coffee or else "something's up." C. B. Soutar stares out of the
window of his Club Cafe . . . bet he's dreaming of some "big ones"
that he thinks are biting way up north. Must be a headache for the
banks and the postoffice trying to keep Club Cafe Charles B.
Soutar and Clerk of Court Charles W. Soutar "straight." But C. B.
says it's really no bother at all . . . except mostly on Christmas cards.

Sheriff Roberts, sauntering into his "down town office"
(Gimm & Byrne's) to take his favorite chair in the back room. He
must be having a chill . . . because he's wearing a vest. Neil looks
relaxed . . . now that they solved the robbery of Leo Connell's car.

John Jensen hustling along . . . he's probably the fastest walking
farmer in the county. Little John Piepgras escorted by his dad
comes out of Doc Dale's dental office. "I won 20 cents from dad,"
pipes up John. Elmer, his father, is no fool . . . he bet John 20 cents
that he'd cry when his tooth was pulled. John got so interested in
winning his bet he forgot to think of whether or not the tooth
pulling hurt. Incidentally—young John has a couple envelopes that
will be stamp collectors prizes some day. His uncle, Elroy, had two
letters mailed to him at the inauguration of Northwest Airline's
first "Northwest Passage" flight, one envelope from the starting
point, New York, the other from the finish, Seattle."

If Mrs. Charles McClure makes up her mind she's coming
down town nothing is going to stop her, weather or not. She just
puts a white scarf over her head and bustles along. "Frank's on a
new ship and has a promotion," she says in passing. Two big
trucks pull away with the last of the equipment from the Red Owl
Store, officially marking "finis" to the store here. Mrs. Ed Leicher

seeks shelter from the rain, with an armful of groceries, at Dave's Market. George Edmonds walks along with head down as if he was trying to duck the rain drops. But, with hatching season just winding up, he has a cheerful grin of relaxation on his face. What a relief, he says. Ivan Hansen walking slowly down the street headed for the mid day coffee, crumb of cookie and the cross word puzzle book. Still looks a bit peaked from the operation.

Bert Rozeboom, talking to a couple of friends and propping up the Luverne National Bank building with both shoulders for about an hour. "Just couldn't move it an inch," he explained afterwards.

Lt. Ed Hudson, walking so fast he almost runs, trying to get a lot of things done in the brief time home. Why is it real estate men don't stick to their offices more than they have to? Bill Merrick spends a lot of his time in front of the bank and Bill Larkin still likes to transact his deals while sitting in his parked car.

Bill Preston's taking no chances on weather changes, he won't discard that red plaid mackinaw. Chris Remme of Kenneth telling friends that the high wind last week really hit his garage and machine shed. His neatly arranged tools were scattered, literally, over ten acres. Bill McDermott is never seen without that trusty, underslung, pipe of his. Rev. J. O. Mundahl saunters along leisurely, hat snapped down and coat collar turned up, carrying a bundle of groceries. As if to explain he says, "can't eat breakfast without half a good grapefruit."

John Reimer, the track star, slowed down from a gallop to limping along on crutches. Tom Borgum, hands in pockets, stops whistling long enough to mutter "rain, rain." Did anybody ever see Delmar Mitchell walk that he didn't have both hands jammed deep in his jacket pocket. Hugo Moeller and Elmer Thon make a dash in the rain to the coffee shop. Al Christensen, the blushing bridegroom to be, chews a toothpick . . . maybe to calm his nerves.

Wilbur Rienstra hustles along . . . no raincoat and his white, bakers trousers are getting soaked. That reminds us . . . there seems to be a shortage of bread, of all things. Pete Glaser had a terrible time trying to round up enough bread and rolls to run the "Eighty" over the weekend.

Ernest Ulrich cutting slowly across the street from the bank to see how things are going at "The Little Casino." Vic Bowman— never says "hello" that he doesn't wave. Gerritt Smith . . . never saw him yet that he didn't have a big smile. Charlie Ehlers, not a bit concerned by the dismal weather. He had an umbrella but didn't bother to use it, except as a cane. Doc Haggard with that ever present cigar in his mouth. That isn't an army car in town . . . it must be one that was sold at one of those "Surplus" sales . . . anyway it seems to belong to Alfred Rogness of Hills.

Jess Searles has joined the parade "to town." Slipped a suit coat over his overalls and hurried in . . . doesn't seem too down-hearted about the weather. Understand Phil Ordung had to drop out of that fancy airplane trip to Oklahoma because he might have to replant a bit. Hans T. Christian Kvaas holds up two fingers to signify that he now has two tail-less lambs. He hasn't given up hope of developing that characteristic.

Nels Haakenson takes time out for coffee . . . the cigaret shortage isn't going to worry him so long as he can find plenty of pipe tobacco. Mark Swedburg plods along deliberately . . . he has an umbrella too, (only the women seem to put them up for protection against the rain) but has it neatly rolled up . . . carrying it belligerently like a sword.

Bud Rasche stands in front of Rober's . . . cocky as ever and grinning at the world . . . enjoying life to the full . . . a big contrast to some of the horror he has endured. Fern Soderholm, the 4-H club leader who you never see without that big, beaming, smile on her face . . . and she has just about as much blarney as if she were Irish. [. . .]

Oscar Martinson saunters along . . . looking ten years younger now that his son is home. And—if you were paying attention to the newsreel at the Palace you would have seen Marlyn in that group of Eighth Air Force crewmen who flew from England to LaGuardia field. Earl Walker, hands stuffed in his pockets, and puffing away at his pipe makes for the bank. He's pretty proud of that Japanese cavalry saddle his son sent him from the Pacific. [. . .]

Well . . . that's about the way things go on, day in and day out, "back home." You can tell life hasn't changed much . . . people don't seem to hurry yet they are getting a lot done, even though they're short handed. They're just marking time until you fellows get back. . . they've got you on their minds all the time. . . thinking of you . . . praying for you.

With best regard always,
ACMc.

JUNE 14, 1945

Rock countians who have been so wonderfully generous should get a thrill of pleasure from Pvt. Wahlert's comment about the Red Cross.

The Rock county boy has gained back nearly all of the 35 pounds he lost as a German prisoner.

Here's what he had to say:

"IF IT HADN'T BEEN FOR THE AMERICAN RED CROSS THERE WOULD HAVE BEEN A LOT OF US GUYS YOU NEVER WOULD HAVE SEEN BACK HOME AGAIN."

Wahlert said the Americans acted like youngsters do on Christmas Eve whenever the American Red Cross parcels arrived. They meant the difference between starving and living . . . and the cigarets and candy made life just a bit brighter. Makes you feel good to hear it doesn't it?

Wahlert said that they were liberated by the 13th Armored and he heard a chap yelling, "anybody from Minnesota."

The youngster, from the 13th Armored, who was doing the yelling was S/Sgt. Jacob Foss, son of Mr. and Mrs. Elmer J. Foss of Jasper. Foss didn't know Arlo Wahlert but he knew some of his brothers . . . and so—before the army moved ahead the two Rock countians had a brief but momentous visit.

★ ★ ★

And if you think Wahlert was laying it on a bit thick then listen to what Lt. Lloyd Hansen had to say, Wednesday.

"If it hadn't been for the American Red Cross there wouldn't have been any of us (that is fellows who had been prisoners over 6 or 8 months) who would have come back alive.

"That's a big plug for the Red Cross but they've got it coming.

I'll have a donation waiting for them when they come round for the next drive."

About the first place Lloyd headed for after he got home was for the barber shop. "I haven't had a decent haircut for years it seems," he said.

"Those were 21 long months in prison," he said, "there was mighty little food or anything that made life worth living. The Germans gave us one fuel briquet . . . and that had to keep four men 'warm' for four days. We slept with our clothes on because the camp was lousy, dirty and wet. About the main 'medicine' they ever handed out was aspirin."

Lloyd has gained back most of the 40 pounds he lost. "I've been eating like a little pig," he said, "they started us out on a baby's diet for quite a while because we couldn't handle other food."

———— ★ ★ ★ ————

So long as this is "returning prisoner of war week" we should mention what a joyous homecoming there was over at the J. G. Klutman home at Valley Springs last week.

Unannounced Pvt. Walter Klutman, just liberated after being a German prisoner of war for 27 months, walked in when the family were seated at the breakfast table.

"Nobody could eat, we were so happy," said Mrs. Klutman.

Walter's first comment was "dad—you've gotten awfully grey."

Ask Klutman where he'd be if there had not been Red Cross parcels arriving at the prison camp about once a week and he shakes his head. "I just would not be here," he said.

"All they ate over there were potatoes turnips and sauerkraut."

Strangely enough . . . Mrs. Klutman served sauerkraut the other night . . . and Walter said even after 27 months of the stuff, that he actually liked it.

"I always did and guess I always will," he said.

———— ★ ★ ★ ————

Capt. Phil Helland knew the army was full of surprises but he didn't expect to be surprised like he was when he arrived at Fort Snelling a couple of weeks ago after 14 months overseas.

The former Luverne young man served as lead navigator on 29 missions over enemy Europe and was awarded the air medal with three oak leaf clusters, the distinguished flying cross and four bronze stars to his ETO campaign ribbon.

Given orders to return to the states, Capt. Helland expected a 30 day leave "like the rest of the boys" and then another assignment. Officers weren't getting any consideration under the point rating system any way, he figured, so the thought that he'd ever be granted a release never entered his mind.

Going through the routine at Fort Snelling, he was asked out of the clear blue sky, "Captain, would you care to get a discharge?"

"My eyes were as big as saucers," said Helland. "I thought he was kidding me, but he shoved a piece of paper over to me that he had just received from General Marshall, which explained that an air force officer with eight months of duty overseas and five decorations was eligible for a release, subject to call later if necessity demanded it.

"I was stumped; after you've been in the service a while, and have a proposition like that tossed in your lap, you just don't know what to do."

"Tell you what," Helland told the officer. "Give me a 30 day leave, and I'll let you know when I get back."

But Helland's proposition was frowned upon by the man in charge. "Oh no," he replied, "we can't do that. You've got to decide what you want to do now. If you want a release, go over to that desk over there and sign up." With that statement he pointed to a desk across the room.

"I guess that was the thing I'd been waiting for ever since I entered the service, although I just didn't realize it. I signed my name, and they gave me my discharge button, and discharge papers."

Always interested in traveling and sight seeing, Capt. Helland says that his tour of duty overseas gave him an opportunity to see a lot of the world which he never would have had the opportunity to see had it not been for the war. Not that he would not have rather have lived these last four years in peace rather than war, but he felt that as long as he had to be "in it" anyway, he might just as well make the most of it.

He took hundreds of snapshots and visited various places in the British Isles, traveling through the country on a bicycle. He visited Loch Lomond, in Scotland, and went for a boat ride on the famous lake.

Only once during the time he spent overseas did he ever see some Rock county man, and that was for just a few minutes. He was standing on a street corner in London, when he recognized a face as being familiar, but he wasn't quite sure who it was until he heard the man talk. "The minute I heard his voice, I knew it was Homer Craig," he said, "so I went over and slapped him on the back. He was waiting for a cab so I only had a few minutes to talk to him, but it really was a thrill to see someone from home."

For the present, Capt. Helland is visiting with his parents, Rev. and Mrs. M. E. Helland, at Sacred Heart. He plans to enroll at the University of Minnesota later on, and work towards a master's degree in education.

He and his parents are expected to arrive today to visit with friends in the Luverne community.

JUNE 21, 1945

It was a lot quieter homecoming for Lt. Darwin Nelson Tuesday night than the going away blasting he gave the town. (Remember—a couple years ago how he blasted the town with that Flying Fortress, rattling the roofs and grazing the flagpoles?)

Darwin came home on the late bus from Fort Snelling and it was a great thrill to dive into his own bed at his farm home . . . when you remember that he was a German prisoner over 17 months.

We'll have a complete story next week about this smiling, personable, young airman but we should mention just a few things. First of all . . . you may not recognize him at first glance because he's still 30 pounds underweight.

His prison camp was liberated officially by a lone, Russian, advance scout. The main body of troops came along three days later. "And the Russians really treated us wonderful," said Darwin, "we told their commander we hadn't ever had any fresh meat for a long time. Almost by magic it seemed, they drove in a hundred head of beef."

As to the German espionage system here's how accurate they were: The Nazis confronted Darwin, during questioning, with more information about his group than he knew himself. They knew of his squadron commanding officer's promotion of but two days before, they knew the identity of all the crews, when men were flying out of position, whether certain crews came to England by ship or by plane. They had maps of every airport in England and of all dispersal strips. They confronted Nelson with a thick book which had every last detail, it seemed to him, of every air base and training facility in the entire United States.

JUNE 28, 1945

Every time we stick our neck out by making a positive statement everybody jumps on us with both feet to impress us with our ignorance. But we'll try again . . . isn't Corp. Warren Herreid the first enlisted man, who left originally with Battery E to receive his discharge papers?

Here's a funny thing . . . he's been in camps all over this country . . . he's been in the Aleutians and fought all thru France and Germany . . . but the first time he'd ever been in Minneapolis in his life was when he was sent to Snelling to get his discharge.

Warren had been waiting four years and five months to take off "that uniform" and get back into civies . . . but when the time finally came he just couldn't do it. "Hard to explain," he said, "but you become attached to that uniform and it's hard to make the break. I'll wear them another day or so . . . but it's going to seem funny not to be wearing khaki any more."

———— ★ ★ ★ ————

Judging by the trophies round town you can't beat a Yank for being the all time souvenir collecting champ.

Here's the reason W/O Bert "Dinny" Wiggins has that frustrated look. It isn't because he has lost 35 pounds after the war was over but he's still glooming because the army has such doggone unreasonable regulations about what you can ship back from abroad. Why—all Bert and his buddies tried to send back intact was one of Hitler's private automobiles. But the army for some reason or other put its foot down, so to speak.

Dinny and a colonel and a general (what company you do keep Wiggins) went down to Wisensee, Hitler's railroad station near Berchtesgaden. There they learned of his garage which was located back in the woods several miles. They decided on a look-see and hiked down the winding trail into the forest. They found the spot and there they found 28 cars, all of them damaged in some way or other.

"There was a big cream colored job," Wiggins said. "The only one like it in the bunch. It may have been Hitler's private car, I don't know, but it really had been a beauty before it had been smashed up.

"I found one that I was able to get to run, and it was otherwise in pretty fair shape except that the top was ruined. I found another like it with a good top, so just traded tops. It was a Mercedes-Benz, a straight eight, seven passenger open car, with four speeds ahead and overdrive. I had it up to 136 miles an hour one time. We got it a short time after the war ended, and had it until we got to Le Harve and started home. We wanted to take it back as an organizational trophy, but we didn't get the permission. The general of our outfit called another general to have a driver come and get it when we reached Le Harve.

"It was really some car. It had more gadgets on the instrument panel than I'd ever seen. I still don't know what they were all for."

JULY 12, 1945

Everybody's counting points nowdays—whether it's red points, blue points or points for a discharge from the army.

1st Sgt. John Goeske counted up his the other day and found he had 134. But he refused a discharge from the army and re-enlisted for the duration.

———— ★ ★ ★ ————

And did you notice the picture of S/Sgt. Stanley Eberlein taken on Okinawa which appeared last week in the Sunday Minneapolis Tribune. The caption read that altho Eberlein, being over 40, was eligible for discharge he had turned it down and said he wanted to see the whole thing thru.

———— ★ ★ ★ ————

Lt. (s. g.) Lawrence Marsden tells about the night they were evacuating wounded from Iwo Jima, at the base of Mt. Suribachi.

"We had an L. S. T. loaded with wounded," said Lawrence.

"I was up on deck and near me was a fellow who had been shot in the hand and in the back. He was feeling pretty bad and it was so rough that he was just about ready to get seasick.

"Just to get his mind off his pain I asked him 'where do you come from?' and the kid says from Iowa, right near the Minnesota line'.

"Not near Luverne by any chance?" asked Marsden.

"You bet," said the wounded Marine. Lawrence can't remember, now, whether it was Ellsworth or Kanaranzi or where but he thinks the boy's name was Joe Smith and he knows he is a relative of Truman Smith.

All the way back on the rough trip Marsden and the young Marine talked about Luverne and Rock county and the conversation took the boy's mind off his painful wounds.

"Later," said Marsden, "when we got back to the base the boy came over to my room. He found the Star-Herald there and sat down and read every line of every issue. Five days later he volunteered to go back to Iwo Jima. He didn't have to, and he shouldn't have, but anyway he went. That's the spirit that is winning the war out there and that chap deserves a lot of credit."

———— ★ ★ ★ ————

Joyous news was that Ben Padilla received this week. His brother, Pvt. Jake Padilla has been unheard from ever since the fall of Corregidor to the Japs and was given up for dead. But word came this week that he is alive and in the Jap prison camp at Osaka.

JULY 19, 1945

We received a letter the other day from Sgt. George Bannick who is a gunner on a B-29. And after we read the letter we could not help thinking of an editorial we wrote for the Fourth of July last year. It was entitled "Remember the Kid Next Door?" In it we recalled how Fourths in other years were made hideous with noise by the "kids next door" in every town who fired off explosives long into the night. We said, "The kid isn't celebrating with firecrackers this year. Altho he may not be 21 he's a man now and doing a man's job. He'll be busy this 4th, but it won't be with cap pistols but the real thing. He won't be celebrating.

George's letter tells how he spent the Fourth in 1945—and for thousands of other boys like him it wasn't like any other Fourth in their lives.

"Dear Al," wrote George:

"Today is the Fourth of July again. Only this one is a lot different from any I have ever spent. There wasn't any noise of firecrackers or kids running around. Nor could you go to the corner, for any of the refreshments we used to get. In fact, Al, it doesn't even sound, look or feel like the 4th here at the base. That's because all of us are tired and sleeping.

"You see, we did have a bit of a celebration though, very much our own and all of us enjoyed it. Because our Fourth started over the Empire of Japan.

"It was shortly after midnight when our ship hit the coast of Japan. We proceeded on in to our target and dropped the load of incendiaries we were carrying just for them. It was a beautiful sight to see all those 500-pounders going into the target. It was good, because I knew I was getting back at them for some of the buddies of mine who haven't come back from previous raids.

"We had our Fourth alright, fireworks and all; one I'll never forget it either. All of us had a certain feeling of satisfaction as our ship turned and headed her nose for home. We were scared but happy, because this was a new way of starting our national holiday.

"It was important to our crew for another reason, too. Now we are on the downward grade. That put us over the half-way mark. It was No. 18 for us, Al. Eighteen of them down, and seventeen to go. It feels good to know that you are over most of it.

"I got your special on V-E day. It was the best edition I have ever gotten. All of the boys in the Quonset complimented it."

Your friend,
George H. Bannick.

JULY 26, 1945

We met a big strapping fellow the other day . . . he's John Wagner now . . . but it used to be Sgt. John Wagner. He's tickled to death to be out of the army after 50 months. He's all settled down to start farming, which he dreamed about during the 26 months he was overseas. He's rented the Raymond Cross farm across the line in Nobles county. (We suppose the sticklers for exactness would want it to be listed as the NW 1/4 Sec. 19-101-431, West Side township.)

Life would be "heaven" save there's one fly in the ointment. John hasn't been able to get his "Heaven" to the U. S. On Feb. 16, 1944, in England he married Miss Amanda Heaven. So far he hasn't been able to cut the red tape that will permit his wife and young son to join him here. He's all set with the papers for his wife but he hasn't been able to get a passport for his youngster.

———— ★ ★ ★ ————

Your record changers and phonograph albums may be obsolete sooner than you think. Dr. V. L. DiGhilini of Los Angeles has invented a new type slow playing phonograph. On his type of phonograh a 12 inch record has enough space for two hours and 11 minutes steady playing without flipping over. A voice recording can be "cut" on a 16 inch record to play for 5 hours and 28 minutes. It's far ahead of the wire recording system we've heard so much about lately. It takes two miles of wire on a spool to record or play for one hour and then the spool requires ten minutes re-winding time.

AUGUST 2, 1945

Lawrence Marsden has had one of those burning desires to write . . . the kind of a secret "yen" for which there is no cure or antidote. Where he picked up that desire we don't know . . . maybe in some College Curse in Journalism. (No operator—that's spelled the way I mean—just follow copy.) Why he'd want to dedicate his life to punching away at a typewriter when there are so many other nice businesses like safe cracking or coal mining we'll never know. We've tried to warn him . . .sort of "repent ye sinner" stuff but it won't work.

Lawrence has been frustrated for years . . . his secret sorrow resulting from the blizzard of rejection slips that always greeted his manuscripts when he sent his "brain children" efforts away to magazine editors.

While he was out in the Pacific the young naval lieutenant, while on an LST, started to force himself to write a book about the things going on about him. If I'm not mistaken he wrote about life, too, on an attack transport.

He talked it over with us when he was home recently. He was in a dither . . . he thought he had a possibility of an acceptance and then the big hurdle was how to get it censored by the navy.

Because he had a lot of brutal stuff in the book. He was working against time, too, because he only had a few days left of his leave.

But I understand he made it and that the University Press has agreed to publish his book.

———— ★ ★ ★ ————

It's great to have your husband home after nearly two years overseas but when he brings you real silk hose from Brazil then life is really "wunnerful."

"To think," sighed Mrs. H. S. Barnard, "that after wearing baggy rayons after all these months that now I've got some real honest to goodness silk hose."

Barnard is visiting here at the William Schwartz home for part of his 30 day furlough, after 22 months in England and France as a Red Cross field director.

Barnard plans to stay in this country with the Red Cross for the duration but will not go overseas again.

"Three wars is just about enough," he said. He saw action in the Mexican uprising, 19 months during World War I with the Rainbow Division and World War II with the Red Cross.

He served the first Allied Airborne Army which, incidentally, was the army in which Major Dick Ross, Lt. Clifford Ford, and Lt. Thomas Campbell served.

At one time, his office served some 20,000 troops. He had three offices in operation at that time, with three full time secretaries, but even at that, he said, he was doing a poor job of service at that time.

In April and May of this year, 2,500 repatriated American airmen were "cleared" at the bases which Barnard served. Every time a plane would land with these former prisoners, the Red Cross girls would be out to meet them with coffee and doughnuts. "Then I'd start handing out the cigarets, chewing gum, and razor blades," he said. "And funny thing to me was that those fellows had a greater craving for chewing gum than they had for cigarets or any other comfort articles we handed out. I don't know how to explain it."

The period just before D-Day, on D-Day and immediately afterward were the most tense of any he experienced. "All the boys were fatalists," he said. "None of them expected they'd live to come back, so they sent all their money home. As it was, just the opposite was true. To top it off, they all got a seven day furlough or leave so they could relieve the mental strain which had developed during the preceding days, and only a few of them had any money with which to go any where. During that time, my office lent service men 2,587 pounds, more than $10,000 so they could have themselves a time. Sometimes there would be as man as 20 men lined up to apply for an emergency loan."

AUGUST 16, 1945

We tried to write something for this column Tuesday night in the "lull before the storm" but we finally gave it up as a bad job. And it still seems like a hopeless task to sit down at the typewriter and calmly put down on paper what's in one's heart.

The torrential flood of great news had left everyone emotionally exhausted, like a damp dishtowel. Even with the radio bulletins and the screaming of the siren here to signal that Victory was a reality it was still hard to believe.

Lt. Fred Dubbe came into the office . . . he was sort of wondering what the "boys on Enewitok were doing" for a V-J celebration. But Fred said that he couldn't think of any place in the world he'd rather be Tuesday night than in Rock county.

F 1/C Willie Oltmans drove up in front of the office. "Remember," he said, "that I told you that the boys out there were talking that the war would be over by August 15. Well . . . I only missed it one day."

People took it quietly for a while . . . and then the younger generation took over. It was a combination of New Year's Eve, Fourth of July, Homecoming and Saturday night all rolled into one.

G.I.'s from Sioux Falls took over, snake dancing and yoo-hooing thru the streets, cars started racing thru the town with horns blowing wildly. The older generation came down to double park, or stand on street corners, to watch the milling crowds. A bunch of high school youngsters piled into a truck and serenaded the town with band music. It was a good idea for a while but an impromptu parade or horn blowing cars soon drowned out the loudest efforts of the musicians. Youngsters found bales of paper, which had been piled awaiting a salvage truck, in the rear of the Star-Herald, and scattered that from roof tops and around the streets. Every girl, pretty or not, was complimented by shrieking whistles of approval from every G.I. And that was the way it went Tuesday night.

Wednesday morning people were just beginning to relax in the joyous consciousness that the war was finally over. Quiet grins and happy greetings were the order of the day . . . and in the smiles of parents and loved ones of men in the service you could read the abounding joy that was in their hearts . . . that the long conflict was finally over.

Four long years of war are over . . . years that dragged so slowly to heavy hearted loved ones while their men were making history all round the world. We just happened to look at the files for December, 1941, to see what was going on in the county about Dec. 7.

Steen was taking steps toward incorporation and they were rehearsing the Christmas operetta. Up in Luverne M. W. Chunn was announcing he was not a candidate for municipal judge and Dan Main was receiving the appointment. Arrangements were being made to show movies of Kodiak on Dec. 16. Pipestone county was keeping its prisoners, temporarily, in the Rock county jail. The dinner in honor of All American Dick Wildung was being planned. The Luverne Cardinals were swinging into action for the basketball season. In the line up that week were: Keith Connell, Ace Canfield, Marlin Martinson, Hugo Goehle, Sandy Myhre, David Butler, Don Toms, Orvie Jordahl, Bill Brooks. It seems a long time ago.

———— ★ ★ ★ ————

So many people have asked, "will the Star-Herald have a V-J edition like the V-E edition?" No . . . for two reasons . . . first, the sudden ending of the war caught us "flat footed"—second, we couldn't have done it anyway because of the shortage of newsprint which will still be rationed for a long time.

———— ★ ★ ★ ————

We should mention, too, that the full page appeal for the War Chest in this issue marks the final Victory Message page in a series which has been running for over two years. The patriotic minded individuals and firms who sponsored these pages deserve public commendation because much of the success of all the war effort drives in Rock county is due to the fine publicity they made possible. Rock county's system of handling war effort campaign publicity received national attention and publicity and many other communities in Iowa, South Dakota and Minnesota adopted the Victory Message page system as sponsored here. War Bond drives, tin can salvage campaigns, waste paper collection, War Chest, Red Cross, WAC recruiting and many other similar efforts received a big boost toward success in the county by the publicity made possible by the sponsors of the Victory Messages.

—— ★ ★ ★ ——

When Francis "Fritz" Hand used to be band instructor at Luverne high school he was known as a "gabby little guy." Who would have ever thought that he would some day be entrusted with the job of keeping the biggest secret in the world—the atomic bomb.

But that's what happened. He was given full charge of "all security of information in connection with preparations of the new atomic bomb," according to the Worthington Globe.

Release of the first atomic bomb meant a tremendous load off the shoulders of the former Worthington man.

In other words, the "war's best kept secret" remained just that because of the integrity and nimble mind of one of the sons of a small Minnesota prairie city. Here's the way he described it in a letter to relatives at Worthington:

"I suppose you'll think I'm kidding when I suggest that a place was finally found where my 'promoting' and blarney paid off—but the news concerning this being the war's 'best kept secret' was partly the result of my guff."

From that point Hand goes on to relate how he has been director of security for what he describes as all CEW areas. It was also his job to direct and assist the security staffs for security education in each company at the great base where manufacture was carried on "plus keeping TPA and other neighboring groups aware of our desire for 'no gossip'."

This meant something like four editorials or feature stories a week, making up several wall and bus posters a month, and a copy for a few dozen billboards, besides providing movie trailers on security every week for the six theaters in the area.

"Keeping 75,000 Americans convinced that they shouldn't talk or write anything about our 'silent city' was quite a job," Hand admits, "but it appears to have been well done.

"Really, of course," he continued, "it was possible because every American here—famous scientists, 'pipe artists', carpenters, electricians, operators, chemists, etc., all have been willing to place duty to our country ahead of their desire for self-attention."

However, Hand's job for the war department seems likely to go on for a while. Now it must be made clear, he points out, that persons having unpublished project information must keep it under wraps until the proper time.

Some faint idea of what men like the former Luverne band instructor have been up against was given last week in a news dispatch from Washington which quoted the federal bureau of investigation as relating how five German spies, sent to the United States after 1939 to ferret out the secrets of the atomic bomb were induced to double cross the nazis and work as counter-espionage agents. As a result, the FBI said, no sabotage was committed in an atomic plant. The FBI spokesman said the German agents carried specific instructions from the German high command to get information on the atomic bomb experimental program.

Mr. Hand taught school here about six years ago, following which he enrolled in the Harvard law school, where he received his degree.

———— ★ ★ ★ ————

What they won't think of next. Post war news, in the cosmetic business is that lipstick is going to be featured in several flavors . . . including wintergreen, cocoanut and absinthe. Some day, too, you'll go to your grocery store and buy pre cooked dinners which have been frozen in a "dinner foundry." That's the invention of William L. Maxson. He's no chump. He has invented such things as a multiple machine gun mount, an aerial navigation instrument too complicated for description and various fire control mechanisms. A housewife would have to have a "defrosting oven" (costing about $25) in order to serve the frozen meals. Such an arrangement of frozen meals is already being served on Naval Air Transport Service planes.

The following week, August 23, 1945, the Star-Herald *ran a story under the headline,*

JASPER YOUNG MAN ON ILL-FATED SHIP

Lyle Hind, S 2/C, 18-year-old son of Mr. and Mrs. Eugene Hind of Jasper, was one of the survivors of the ill-fated heavy cruiser Indianapolis which was sunk in the Philippine Sea on July 30 with loss of 833 of her personnel of 1,196 men aboard.

A week ago Monday, his parents received word that he had been wounded in action on that date.

He entered the navy February 18, and left for overseas duty on June 15.

The Indianapolis carried the first atomic bomb to the Philippines, and was sunk after it had left the islands, unescorted. . . .

World War II was "officially" over, but Al McIntosh and the Star-Herald *continued its coverage until every one of its young men was accounted for or back home, safe and sound.*

— Obituary —

Alan C. McIntosh, editorial journalist

By Irid Bjerk

The "Tired American" is dead at 73.

Alan C. McIntosh, who owned and published the *Star-Herald* from 1940 until 1968 and became nationally famous after writing an editorial entitled "A Tired American Gets Angry" in 1964, died in his sleep Monday morning [July 23, 1979] at the Luverne Community Hospital.

He had been in failing health for over a year. For the past several weeks he had been living at the Tuff Memorial Home in Hills.

While McIntosh liked to refer to himself as a "country editor," he distinguished himself through his writings in the *Star-Herald*, and leadership in American community journalism. His ability as a public speaker brought him additional recognition.

His acquaintanceship ranged from United States presidents, ambassadors, at foreign embassies, supreme court justices, and royalty, to the man, woman, or child on Main Street in Luverne.

When he bought the *Rock County Star* from E.S. Townsend in July, 1940, and moved to Luverne from Lincoln, Nebraska, there were many in this community who guessed that the dapper city dude wouldn't last long in the hometown newspaper field.

He'd been too close, they concluded, to the rough and tumble news of a big city and state capital to be content with the comings and goings of the folks from Kenneth, Kanaranzi, Beaver Creek and the rest—the kind of news that then dominated the inside pages of the *Star*.

And besides, Mabe Moreaux's *Rock County Herald*, "Luverne's oldest business institution, founded in 1873," was considered just a bit more prestigious than the *Star*.

They guessed wrong, however.

It didn't take long before the *Star*'s readership began to show an increase.

One of the first moves McIntosh made after buying the business was to have a carpenter and a plumber come in and build a photo dark room.

With him from the *Nebraska State Journal*, where he had served as an editorial aide from 1931 to 1940, he brought his trusty 4 x 5 Speed Graphic press camera. A camera he had used to photograph the Queen of England, the crown prince and princess of Denmark, Amelia Earhart, and the Lincoln bank robbery.

He had worked photo assignments for *Life* and *Time* magazines, and in his opinion, if news pictures could sell magazines for *Life* and the *Journal*, then certainly, they could help the *Star*'s subscription list to grow as well.

He was right.

In Lincoln, one of his closest friends was Joe Carroll the chief of police. In fact, McIntosh himself carried a Lincoln police badge many years which gave him an "in" to all the major crime news not only in Lincoln but throughout the state of Nebraska. Among the first acquaintances he made in Luverne were Sheriff Neil Roberts and County Attorney Mort Skewes. He had the same working relationship with them as he did with Chief Carroll.

He became a confidante, a reporter they could trust, one who was demanding when it came to getting the details for a story, but one who wouldn't release a word of it until the time was right.

Reporting, however, was only one of his journalistic capabilities.

He had worked as an ad writer for the *Lincoln Star* during his college days at the University of Nebraska. Luverne business men liked the way he handled their advertising, and the results they were getting as the *Star*'s readership grew.

It was his editorials, however, that brought him the greatest recognition from his peers in the newspaper field.

Weeklies in the Tri-State area would reprint his ideas in their "With Other Editors" columns. The *Sioux Falls Argus-Leader* and *Sioux City Journal* spotted them and reprinted them.

Even the Minneapolis papers—which otherwise gave no indication that they were aware of Minnesota's outstate press—would run one of the editorials now and then.

Writing editorials and his weekly column, "Chaff," provided him with some of his most enjoyable moments as a weekly editor.

He'd sit down to his typewriter, insert a double thickness of copy paper, light a cigarette, take a puff or two, and then begin to hammer the keys.

His employees could detect what the tone of the piece he was writing would be by watching his face. If his lower jaw protruded just a bit, they knew somebody was "catching it."

McIntosh often said that to be a good journalist one must forego having friends, because the writer has the obligation to be totally honest, to tell the story like it is, even to the point of jeopardizing a friendship. To do otherwise would be to break faith with the readers who look to the newspaper for undistorted facts.

If his lower jaw did not protrude as he typed, but his face wore the hint of a smile instead, it was a good guess that he was writing an editorial complimenting someone on an achievement, or an editorial lauding the beauty of summer in Rock County or the glories of being an American citizen.

His face was grim the day he wrote "A Tired American Gets Angry." He'd been downtown for his afternoon coffee. The coffee conversation had touched on how love for these United States and its freedoms was being replaced with cynicism.

He lit his cigarette.

He firmed his lower jaw.

The typewriter clattered the first sentence:

"I am a 'tired American.' "

The typewriter sounded like a muted machine gun for 15 or 20 minutes as he went on for 27 paragraphs, detailing how he deplored what some who claimed American citizenship, and others in foreign lands, were saying about his country.

He concluded it this way:

"I am a 'tired American' who thanks a merciful Lord that he was so lucky to be born an American citizen . . . a nation . . . under God . . . with truly mercy and justice . . . for all."

One of the big dailies called him one day and asked for permission to reprint the editorial. The response was phenomenal. McIntosh started getting letters, most of them applauding, but some of them decrying the editorial.

Other daily newspapers—even one in Paris—reprinted "A Tired American." Weekly papers the country over called or wrote for permission to use it. It appeared in magazines; it was read over the air waves.

The strange thing about the editorial was the length of time that it maintained popularity. Calls and letters for permission to print it continued to come to the *Star-Herald* even after McIntosh sold the paper to Bob and Jim Vance, in 1968. There are still requests today.

One New York newspaper stated that "A Tired American" was the most widely reprinted editorial ever written with perhaps one exception, that being "Yes, Virginia, there is a Santa Claus."

In 1966, Freedoms Foundation at Valley Forge recognized the editorial by awarding McIntosh the George Washington Gold Medal, the highest of its editorial awards.

Future editorials also were recognized by Freedoms Foundation in 1968. McIntosh received the George Washington Medal of Honor for "Just a Rag." He received similar awards for editorials entitled, "Pushers of Worse Than Pot," and "The Year of The Wet Pileau" in 1970 and 1971.

Fellow editors and publishers honored him in many ways.

He was elected president of the Minnesota Newspaper Association. Later, he became the president of the association's national counterpart, the National Editorial Association.

During his year as president of the national association he was successful in obtaining President Dwight Eisenhower as the main speaker for the national convention. It was the first time a president of the United States had addressed the national assembly of community newspaper editors and publishers.

Other journalistic offices included president of the American Newspaper Representatives, president of Interstate Press Association, director of Associated Press Managing Editors Association.

In addition to the awards from Freedoms Foundation at Valley Forge, McIntosh received the National Newspaper Association's Distinguished Service Award and Amos Award. The Minnesota VFW presented him with their Americanism award.

Minnesota Newspaper Association honored him with the Herman Roe Memorial Award for excellence in editorial writing. His "Chaff" column was selected by Minnesota Newspaper Association as the "best column" in one of the annual better newspaper contests.

The *Minneapolis Star and Tribune* selected McIntosh for its "Leadership in Minnesota" award, the University of Nebraska honored him with a Distinguished Service award. He also received a distinguished service award from the Minnesota Safety Council.

McIntosh was interested in politics at the local, state and national level. With tongue in cheek, he would maintain he was an "independent" but those who knew him and read his writing recognized him as a stalwart, conservative Republican. He showed no mercy to any Democratic politician who dared voice a liberal view.

He maintained a close personal friendship with the late Hubert H. Humphrey, but they were as far apart politically as the two poles. One of McIntosh's prized photographs of famous people was one of Humphrey who had autographed it; "To Alan McIntosh—If only his pen and editorials were as warm as his heart."

He was never at loss for something to write about because he was a voracious reader who remembered virtually everything he read. At one time, he subscribed to seven daily newspapers, and twice that many magazines. There was seldom a time that he didn't have a current book ready to be picked up from the reading table beside his chair when he sat down for an evening of relaxation.

He enjoyed travel, and made several trips abroad. Together with his wife, Georgia, and daughter, Jean, he made a trip around the world in 1963, not a pleasure trip but, as he wrote in a foreword to a book made up of a compilation of articles written about it, "as a family study mission—to better inform ourselves, as newspaper people, about this changing world."

During his boyhood and youth, McIntosh developed a love for traveling by train, and for watching trains speeding through the country side, or merely switching in a switchyard. He was aboard the Burlington Zephyr, the first streamline diesel passenger train, on its maiden trip. Even after coming to Luverne, he was often on hand to watch the passenger trains as they came and went at the Omaha depot.

Alan Cunningham McIntosh was born Oct. 7, 1905, at Park River, North Dakota, the son of the Rev. and Mrs. Donald M. McIntosh, both of Scotch ancestry. He was proud of his roots, visited Scotland a number of times and liked to refer to himself as the "Scotchman."

He moved with his parents to Grand Forks when he was five, and from there to Sioux City, in 1918, where his father was pastor of Knox Presbyterian Church.

He was graduated from Sioux City Central High School in 1922, and attended Morningside College, Sioux City, for three years before enrolling at the University of Nebraska where he received his degree in 1928.

Getting his start in journalism as editor of "Nebraska Agwan," a university humor magazine, and as part time employee at the *Lincoln Star*, he moved over to the *Journal* after graduation. He established himself there as a writer as well as business man, and soon decided he wanted to have a newspaper of his own. When the *Rock County Star* was offered for sale, he bought it, assuming ownership July 1, 1940.

Two years later, the editor and publisher of the *Rock County Herald*, A.O. Moreaux, was killed in an auto accident. The estate offered The Herald to McIntosh, and he bought it, consolidating the two publications and changing the name to the *Rock County Star-Herald*.

Georgia Molitor was the *Star*'s society editor and bookkeeper when McIntosh bought the paper. Some eight years later, on April 7, 1948, they were married at Park Rapids, Iowa. They were the parents of one daughter, Jean, now Mrs. Douglas Vickstrom, Bettendorf, Iowa.

McIntosh was a member and former elder of the First Presbyterian Church. He was a long time member and past president of the Luverne Rotary Club.

He also served on the Minnesota "Little Hoover" Commission, on Governor LeVander's Advisory Commission for Economic Development. He belonged to the Masonic Lodge, Knights Templar, the Shrine, and the Shrine Jesters.

He served on the national committee which formulated, presented and secured passage of legislation leading to the formation of the Interstate Highway system. He also served as a vice president of Morningside College.

He used his influence to secure the placement in Luverne of a state highway patrolman, and to obtain blinker signals for the railroad crossing on south U.S. 75 in Luverne and at the Great Northern crossing on Highway 75, just east of Valley Springs.

McIntosh is survived by his wife and daughter.

Funeral services will be held at 10 a.m. Thursday [July 26, 1979] at the First Presbyterian Church. The Rev. Solomon Gruneich will officiate with a former pastor of the church and a close friend, the Rev. Orrin H. Moore, assisting.

Holm Funeral Home is in charge of arrangements.

Pallbearers will be D.M. Lippi, Mort Skewes, Irid Bjerk, Paul Smith, Warren Schoon and Harold Norman.

Index

INDEX

Smook, Harm, 47, 109, 146
Smook, Jake, 47; Joe, 47; John, 47; Lee, 47
Smook, Otto, 47
Soderholm, Fern, 247
Solem, Gene, 29
Soutar, Charles B., 245; Charles W., 129, 245; Paul, 153
Sovereign, Donald. 162
Spease, William, 223
Staeffler, Irvin, 70
Stassen, Harold, 108
Stavenger, John, 32, 169, 188; Nick, 187
Steffens, Ralph, 212
Steine, Mr. and Mrs. Normas, 82; Snoose, 103, 145
Steinfeldt, Bill, 18
Stelling, Vernon, 140
Stephen, Clyde, 36
Stone, Harvey, 216
Storaker, Don, 105; Ed, 60, 95
Strassburg, Floyd, 118–120; Mr. and Mrs. Julius, 118
Stubbe, Clarence, 140
Studsdahl, Herman, 141
Sullivan brothers, 92
Suurmeyer, Mr. and Mrs. Ben, 214; George, 214; Mildred, 214; Mr. and Mrs. Tony, 117, 233
Swedburg, Mr. and Mrs. Mark, 176, 247
Swenson, Ed, 102

Taige, Jim, 32
Tangemann, Arthur, 60
Tatge, Gerald, 140
Thompson, Orville, 141; Mrs. Severt, 99
Thon, Elmer, 246
Thu, Sigurd, 141
Tobiason, Gordon, 29
Tobin, Daniel J., 164
Tomlinson, Bill, 122
Toms, Don, 259
Torrison, Richard, 171
Treat, Jay, 96
Truman, Harry, 234, 235, 239
Truscott, Lucian, 177
Tunstall, Earl, 18, 130; Marbert, 60, 130; Marmon, 60, 130; Maxine, 130

Ulrich, Ernest, 247
Urbach, H. H., 50

Vail, Sebe, 192
Van Aalsburg, Sarah, 188
Van Engelenhoven, Case, 171, 199, 200; Van Engelenhoven, Mrs. Case, 199, 200; Engelenhoven, Gerrit, 199
Van Voorst, Mr. and Mrs. Gerrit, 41; Jake "Bud," 41
Visker, Jullo, 66
Voelz, Max, 80, 122, 189, 192
Von Papen, Franz, 165
Wagner, John, 255, 256

Wahlert, Alfred, 48; Arlo, 48, 248; John, 48, 137, 193, 194, 209; Mrs. Jake, 48
Walker, Earl, 247
Ward, Mrs. Edward, 80
Way, Mrs. Luella B., 176
Weldon, Bertrum "Sandy," 100–102; Mrs. Lois Kroeger, 100
Wendt, Bill, 54
Weston, Mrs. Ray, 90
Wiek, J. O., 77
Wieme, Harry, 188, 189
Wiese, Carl, 160; Mr. and Mrs. Fred, 18; Herman Sr., 134; Sidney, 42
Wiese, William, 79
Wiggins, Bert "Dinny," 252, 253; Bill, 100; Mrs. Gerald, 129; J. Russell, 192, 193; Mrs. Mike, 111; Pete, 95; Russ, 100; Mrs. Russ, 100
Wilder, Russell, 143, 171
Wildung, Dick, 27, 102, 259; Robert, 62, 76, 217
Willers, Frank, 150
Williams, A. N., 230
Wilroth, Nick, 34
Wilson, Dorothy, 180
Winkler, Wes, 78
Winter, J. T., 179
Witt, Lambert, 241
Wood, Art, 224
Wright, C. O., 167
Wuertz, Henry, 143

Youngsma, Lyle, 141
Yu, Bernice, 180

Zack, Mr. and Mrs. Max, 112, 244
Zwart, Floyd, 140

Index of Places
Adrian, Minnesota, 182
Africa, 123, 164, 241
Argonne, 47
Attu, 137
Australia, 42, 111, 131, 164

Bastogne, France, 219, 237
Bataan, 38, 46
Beaver Creek, Minnesota, 73, 87, 120, 157, 185
Belgium, 225
British Isles, 250
Buckley Field, 188

Camp Butner, North Carolina, 109
Camp Callan, California, 137
Camp Croft, South Carolina, 44
Camp Davis, North Carolina, 94
Camp Farragut, Idaho, 109
Camp Haan, California, 130, 225
Camp Polk, Louisiana, 25, 33
Camp Roberts, California, 181, 199
Camp Robinson, Arkansas, 25, 29
Camp Wolters, Texas, 44